SHOCKING BRAZIL

SIX GAMES THAT SHOOK THE WORLD CUP

SHOCKING BRAZIL

SIX GAMES THAT SHOOK
THE WORLD CUP

FERNANDO DUARTE

First published in Great Britain in 2014 by
ARENA SPORT
An imprint of Birlinn Limited
West Newington House
10 Newington Road
Edinburgh
EH9 1QS

www.arenasportbooks.co.uk

ISBN: 978-1-909715-16-5
eBook ISBN: 978-0-85790-802-5

Every effort has been made to trace copyright holders and obtain their
permission for the use of copyright material. The publisher apologises for any
errors or omissions and would be grateful if notified of any corrections that
should be incorporated in future reprints or editions of this book.

British Library Cataloguing-in-Publication Data
A catalogue record for this book is available on request from the
British Library.

Desig[...] Publishing, [...]rgh

Printed by Bell and Bain, Glasgow

CONTENTS

DEDICATORY

To Barbosa, wherever this might find him.

ACKNOWLEDGEMENTS

After almost 20 years of being involved with Brazilian football in a professional capacity, it is a privilege to have an opportunity to pay tribute to the game and to my country in this book. The list of people who helped make this work possible is huge but I'd like to thank specifically Peter Burns and Neville Moir at Arena Sports and my agent David Riding for their courage in taking this leap of faith with me. This work would not be possible without the collaboration of some of the great names in Brazilian football history and once again I'd like to thank former and current players for the time they gave to my questions, especially when they mostly related to some painful memories. I am especially grateful to Zico and Falcão, who made the life of a Brazilian boy back in the 80s something a little less ordinary.

A special hug goes to my father, Marcos Duarte, whose attitude of loving the game while not closing his eyes to its shortcomings has been an inspiration as strong as the afternoons we faced traffic and scorching heat to watch games at the Maracanã. To my mom, Yane, an acknowledgement that she wasn't THAT wrong when telling me I should focus on writing about football rather than trying to play it for a living.

Finally, I'd like to thank profusely friends, family and colleagues who have put up with my mood swings and antisocial work hours over the last months, in particular my beloved wife Fleur and the little joys of my life, Cecilia and Sebastian. You are my guiding lights.

FOREWORD

Ask any Brazilian footballer and they will undoubtedly say that playing for our national team – the Seleção, as we call it – is the highest professional and personal honour he can aspire too. In over 15 years as a professional player, I have been blessed with the opportunity to play 93 matches for my country and represent Brazil in three World Cups. While being part of the 2002 winning side was unquestionably the pinnacle of my career, the two tournaments where we returned home early have never faded from my memory. Those were hurtful experiences, I can tell you, but they also taught me a great deal about life and the game. They showed, above all, how winning a competition like the World Cup is an outcome that relies upon so much more than simply having good players.

Brazil are the team that everybody wants to beat thanks to their outstanding record in the World Cup. But at the same time, I feel this record also poses a grave a threat to Brazilian football, for it serves as a perfect excuse for sticking to the status quo. Even when there are clear and troubling signs that the game in Brazil needs an overhaul, many people both abroad and at home are unaware of the serious organisational problems at the heart of Brazilian football that need to be addressed for the benefit of all stakeholders, from fans to the clubs, if we are to remain as a superpower in the world game.

In this book, Fernando Duarte is not being pessimistic when he focuses on the sad chapters in Brazilian football history. Throughout his tour of World Cup defeats he points out mistakes and lessons learned both on and off the pitch. He also addresses the need for some soul searching as the rest of the world catches up with the Seleção. Like me, Fernando has spent a great deal of his career abroad and from this perspective he has been able to observe that Brazil can sometimes be accused of hiding behind its past successes instead of looking to build upon them.

In late 2013, a group of Brazilian players returned home to help found a player movement that demanding reforms in the way the game is organised, played and run in my country. We called it FC Common Sense. More than simply hailing the good practices we had experienced abroad, we wanted to show the need for collective engagement in improving the standards of the whole football experience in Brazil. A crucial part of our agenda is to show the world that Brazilian football should not be guided by stereotypes and myths and that our problems need to be explained, analysed and understood.

Shocking Brazil aims to do exactly that. Impressive as Brazil's record is, we have to be humble enough to accept we can't be the best in the world all the time. Humble enough to accept our mistakes. And humble enough to learn from them. There is no shame in that.

Gilberto Silva

2002 World Cup Winner
and a member of the Arsenal 2003/4 'Invincibles'

INTRODUCTION

PELÉ. THE 1970 World Cup team. The Beautiful Game. Brazilian football has become synonymous with sporting excellence. Supporters and admirers from every part of the globe are able to recount, recall or refer to joyful tales about Brazil's unmatched achievements, especially the ones relating to World Cup glory. Little attention has been paid, however, to the occasions where Brazil failed spectacularly at the sport's blue riband event. Many followers of the sport will be aware of the 'Maracanazo of 1950', in which Brazil were painfully defeated in the World Cup final by neighbours Uruguay in front of a reported crowd of 200,000 in Rio de Janeiro, or the beautifully-flawed team of 1982, whose flamboyant style of play fell short of winning the trophy but still managed to enchant fans and media. There have been many books about Brazil's golden moments and some interesting accounts of how football achieved a much more intense status in Brazilian society than in many other countries traditionally linked to the game. However, previous narratives generally overlook the crucial transformations undergone by Brazilian football and Brazil itself as a result of the Seleção (the most famous nickname for the national team) failures.

The following pages journey through the defeats that changed the face of Brazilian football. Choosing them was far from an easy task, even if an emblematic game such as the 1950 final obviously picked itself. Even as the most successful footballing nation in the world, Brazil have obviously lost games. The idea here was to choose occasions where circumstances not simply restricted to the pitch had an impact upon results and the consequences thereafter. Given the cultural and financial importance that the World Cup holds as football's premier tournament, it has been around this competition that the most significant defeats – and the changes that came in their wake – have occurred. *Shocking Brazil* revisits six World Cup defeats that led to mutations in Brazilian football, for better or for worse, and the fallout from which spread well beyond the sporting sphere. The 1950 World Cup final once again rears its head as the classic example: that defeat had such a deep impact on the national psyche that it led to the Seleção ditching the colours of their kit in an attempt to exorcise the awful spectre of that match from the nation's conscience. But that game also resulted in one the most regrettable chapters in Brazil's struggles against racism, as shall be discussed.

Considered by many the finest XI ever to have graced a football pitch, the Brazilian 1970 World Cup team has earned a reputation of iconic proportions, especially in the United Kingdom. What few people know is that Pelé, Jairzinho and Carlos Alberto played that entire tournament under immense pressure from the public and a media who feared a repeat of Brazil's humiliating first round exit in England four years earlier, when even Pelé could not avert disaster for his team. While the defeat by Italy in Barcelona in 1982 became almost more famous than the final, Brazil's failure to win it 'beautifully' sparked a crisis of identity in Brazilian football at a time of hardship for most of the country's population.

The losing stories are a significant source of untapped information on the development of the game in the nation that the football world has learned to both admire and fear. Through a focus on Brazil's biggest World Cup defeats, this book will help explain Brazilian football in a wider perspective. The practitioners of the 'Beautiful Game' are still owed an account that demolishes certain long-established myths and addresses events that have never been fully explored.

These games hide narratives of racism, corruption, authoritarianism and corporate power still oblivious to many observers of Brazilian football. Through anecdotes, data and observation, this book intends to show Brazilian football in a different light. It is an account aimed squarely at football fans willing to go beyond the cyclical information about Brazilian football regularly fed to them by mainstream media. And I really hope you'll enjoy the ride as much as I did.

Fernando Duarte

1950

ONE

1950
THE BIG SILENCE

PARIS' STADE DE FRANCE was packed to the rafters on the night of 20 May 2004. To celebrate the 100th anniversary of the founding of FIFA, football's governing body had organised a friendly between world champions Brazil and European champions France. It was a gala affair which a record 79,344 crowd had come to witness.

To make the most of the 'retro' spirit of the fixture, both teams would play the first half wearing replicas of their original uniforms. The French, led by Zinedine Zidane, entered the pitch wearing blue shirts with white collars and long cream shorts with red socks – the outfit they had worn for their first international outing in 1904. Brazil, with Ronaldo, Roberto Carlos and Cafu, donned what for many people looked like a surprising combination of white shirts and shorts with blue socks. Only people with a strong interest in the history of Brazilian football would know that the team that became famous in bright yellow had actually originally worn white when, in 1914, the newly formed Seleção Brasileira (Brazilian Selection) played Exeter City on 20 August in Rio de Janeiro. Thirty-six years later that white shirt would become so tarnished by events at the 1950 World Cup that it became a symbol that would haunt the national psyche in Brazil. Unthinkable elsewhere, with the exception perhaps of Germany, where Nazi revisionism and the partition of the country for almost 40 years led to changes in the Mannschaft uniform, Brazil's ditching of white was a reaction to what renowned anthropologist Roberto da Matta described as the biggest modern tragedy in a country plagued by natural disasters and the great conflicts of the 20th century. Even if they hadn't been born by 1950, there is no Brazilian football fan who feels untouched by the ghosts of the 'Maracanazo'.

On the morning of 16 July 1950, Obdulio Jacinto Varela, like many of his Uruguay team-mates, was trying to steady his nerves while time seemed to drag on and on at Paysandu Hotel, the five-storied art deco building located in Rio de Janeiro's noble Flamengo neighbourhood.

Having checked in two days before, the team were doing their best to steer clear of the carnival atmosphere that had taken over the then Brazilian capital. With its brand new Maracanã stadium, Rio was host to the final of the fourth FIFA World Cup, in which the highly unfancied Uruguayans would lock horns with hosts Brazil – an occasion that had raised patriotic fervour to manic levels around the country. With newspapers desperate to cash in on the deluge of interest in the tournament, the Seleção were front-page news on a daily basis.

For all the expectation being placed on the shoulders of the home team, Uruguay remained dangerous opposition. Not only had they lifted the first World Cup in 1930, they had also won the gold medal in both the Paris and Amsterdam Olympics of 1924 and 1928 at a time when the Games was the only international football tournament. Those feats had led to Uruguay being nicknamed the 'Olympic Celestials', in a reference to their blue shirts. Their status as Olympic champions was instrumental in securing the hosting rights for the first-ever World Cup, which coincided with the 100th anniversary of the country's first constitution – hence the name 'Centenário' given to the new ground they built for the tournament. Uruguay beat rival bids from Italy, Sweden, Holland and Spain and the decision to take the tournament to South America did not please some of FIFA's European core. As a consequence, several countries from the continent refused to take part in the tournament, many citing travel costs as the primary obstacle to their involvement. In fact, by February 1930 no European team had actually confirmed their attendance. FIFA's president, Jules Rimet, then cut a deal whereby the Uruguayan government would help pay expenses for interested teams and that action convinced Belgium, France, Romania and Yugoslavia to cross the Atlantic. In total, 13 teams played in the tournament; seven were from South America, including Brazil. The final was a local derby: Uruguay came from 2-1 down to beat Argentina 4-2. Despite the European boycott, it is interesting to note that the same two teams had played the gold medal match in the 1928 Olympics – bronze winners Italy were the tournament's most noticeable absence.

Incensed at the European snub, Uruguay called for a South American boycott in 1934, when Italy hosted the tournament, but both Brazil and Argentina defied this suggestion and attended. Four years later, FIFA's decision to award the tournament to France would result in another Uruguayan absence, as they argued that a South American country should have been selected. This time, only Brazil did not adhere to the South American boycott.

So it was that, absent from the international arena for all these years, Uruguay were something of a forgotten power by 1950. Between 1929 and 1949, they had won only two out of ten South American championships. Still, for a country whose population was a mere 2.2 million in 1950, and whose territory only measures 177,000 km2, Uruguay had punched remarkably above its weight throughout its footballing history. Obdulio Jacinto Varela and his team-mates, however, were aware that his country's heroics were not restricted to football pitches.

Geopolitical instability in Europe at the beginning of the 19th century had seen breakaway movements in the colonies in South America. In 1811 the region known as Eastern Bank, in the River Plate basin, revolted against Spanish colonial rule, and later formed a confederacy with the neighbouring provinces of Santa Fé and Entre Rios. The Portuguese crown, which feared that the revolutionary winds could reach Rio de Grande do Sul, the most southern province in Brazil, which at the time was considered Portugal's most important colony, ordered the invasion of the Eastern Bank in 1816. Four years later the region became an annexe to Brazil and was renamed the Cisplatine Province, establishing a foothold for Portugal into the River Plate's main port, Montevideo, which was a key trading channel.

Just two years later, in 1822, Brazil itself broke free from Portugal in very peculiar terms – it became an empire headed by Pedro I, King John VI of Portugal's son – and Cisplatine was subsumed into Brazilian territory. The province sent representatives to Brazil's first constitutional assembly in 1823, and was rewarded with a considerable degree of autonomy in the 1824 Brazilian Constitution. Historically, there had been affinities between those in the Cisplatine Province and the Southern Brazilians, such as the importance played by cattle-raising for their respective economies and the gaucho (cowboy) folklore. Practically, however, there were significant differences, starting with the fact that Brazil was the only Portuguese-speaking country in a region dominated by Spanish. It didn't, therefore, take long for an uprising to occur.

In 1825, Cisplatine declared independence from Brazil, backed by the United Provinces of River Plate – the embryonic Argentina. War broke out and Brazil tried to make use of its naval power to suffocate the rebellion but it lacked a strong enough army to make a concerted territorial push overland. Both sides failed to achieve major gains and by 1828 a stalemate forced a compromise. Faced with unrest in Brazil due to the financial costs of the war (at a time when the country was still consolidating its independence process), Pedro I accepted the Cisplatine independence and signed the British-intermediated Montevideo Treaty. In 1830, the Oriental Republic of Uruguay, a name inspired by the indigenous-named South American river, was formally born.

Independence in the newly formed Uruguay was quickly followed by a wave of European immigration helping to build a nation whose population at the time was estimated at only 75,000 people. That influx included British subjects, and although far from a majority group, their arrival had a major bearing on the development of sport – and in particular football – among the nation-builders. In

1901, a friendly match between Uruguay and Argentina became the first international ever to be played outside the United Kingdom. Different to the style developed (and developing) in neighbours Brazil and Argentina, Uruguayan football was marked by diversity thanks to a melting pot of influences that included the arrival of Italian coaches looking for work, and in 1916 the country fielded two black players for the first time at the South American championship decider, when the Uruguayans hammered Chile 4-0. The Chileans would later protest about the inclusion of 'slave' descendants in the team, much to Uruguayan dismay.

In the 1924 Olympics, midfielder Leandro Andrade, who was indeed the son of a slave originally brought from West Africa to Southern Brazil, became Uruguayan football's first hero, leading the side to golden glory. At the time Obdulio Varela was only six years old, but was certainly aware of his country's achievement. Also of African ancestry – as well as Spanish and Greek lineage – Varela, born in Montevideo, had joined first division Montevideo Wanderers in 1938, a year before he was first called up by Uruguay. His international debut took place at the 1939 Copa America, when he came on as a substitute in a victory over Chile. Uruguay lost the title to hosts Peru but in Varela they had found a leader who would later be known as 'El Jefe Negro' (the Black Chief). In 1943, Varela joined Peñarol, Uruguay's most famous club, where he would win three national titles in the 1940s. There, he would also play alongside eight other players who would be selected for the 1950 World Cup squad.

It was hardly surprising that their own feelings of nationalistic fervour and pride were swirling strongly around the hearts and minds of the Uruguayan players at the Paysandu Hotel on 16 July. They originated from a country historically proud of its underdog struggles and its victories against the odds. In the 1950 World Cup, Uruguay, for the first time in 20 years, were locking horns at the highest level and they had once again made it to the final, defying all the odds. While the football world seemed to have moved on since Uruguay's golden days of the 1920s and 1930s, and there had been a fear among the media and fans back home that the team would struggle to be competitive, the players had rallied against all expectations.

'We grew up with the tradition that we would have to always turn into lions while wearing the Uruguay shirt,' recalled winger Alcydes Gighhia, a name that would become intrinsically linked to that competition. 'We would have to fight with our hearts. It always seemed to fire us up when everything was against us, especially the crowds.'

So it was that Manuel Caballero, Uruguayan honorary consul in Rio de Janeiro, knew precisely what he was doing when he arrived at the Paysandu with 20 copies of newspaper *O Mundo*. On the cover was a picture of the Brazilian XI. The use of that image was nothing unusual given the frenzy that the tournament had been causing in the country and the way the newspapers had been exploiting the interest in the team, but the picture was placed under the headline: 'Here Are The World Champions'.

'My commiserations to you, gentlemen,' said Caballero as he put the newspapers on the table in front of Varela, the captain. 'It seems you are already beaten.'

Varela read the headline in silence and then stood. He picked up the stack of newspapers and stalked across the restaurant to the men's room. A few minutes later he emerged empty-handed.

'Go,' he instructed his watching team-mates, with a nod of his head towards the men's room.

As the players filed in they found that Varela had decorated the urinals with the front page of *O Mundo*. Scrawled in chalk on the mirrors, Varela had written a message: '*Pisen y orinen en el diário*'. The captain was ordering his troops to step up and show exactly what they thought of the newspaper's crowing pronouncement.

But for all the bravado of *O Mundo*'s headline, the surge of confidence that was washing through the country could hardly be simplified as arrogance. On the contrary. In 1950, Brazil was no place for an optimist. It was a country still stuck in second gear: half of its 51.7 million population could neither read nor write and life expectancy stood at just 46 years. The Brazilian economy was still largely dependent upon agriculture and its industry was severely hampered by infrastructural challenges, such as the absence of any major highways. While the economy grew an average of 7 per cent between 1946 and 1950, inflation was rife.

Politically, Brazil was a volatile country; in 1945 a military coup had deposed dictator Getúlio Vargas and called for free elections, but the regime change had failed to foster any national unity as the political landscape had simply switched from one dictatorship to another, the main change being that the Communist Party, ferociously pursued under Vargas, was no longer outlawed. It was in this scenario that elected president Eurico Gaspar Dutra was presented with the idea of a Brazilian bid for the 1950 World Cup. The Brazilian interest in the competition wasn't new – the country had presented a proposal to FIFA in 1938 during the World Cup in France in the hope that they would be awarded the 1942 event. Germany, Brazil and Argentina had contacted FIFA, and although the German proposition looked better prepared, the South Americans argued it was time the competition crossed the Atlantic again after it had been held in Europe twice in a row.

Germany's invasion of Poland in 1939 suspended the discussions and the Second World War led to the cancellation of both the 1942 and 1946 tournaments. By the time FIFA reconvened in July 1946, the tables had turned significantly. No European country could possibly organise the competition in the middle of post-war reconstruction, which reinforced the Brazilian case. FIFA were also worried that failure to resume the World Cup could dent interest in the event. So Brazil were awarded the tournament and the Dutra government saw an opportunity not only to score popularity points domestically at a time when his party's defeat in the 1950 elections was deemed a certainty, but also a chance to showcase Brazil's push for modernity to the international community. Besides, football had increasingly grown in importance to Brazilians since the first World Cup and the country's relationship with the sport had evolved from a puzzled interest to a fundamental expression of the way Brazilians perceived themselves. To understand why, it is necessary to look back to the 19th century.

It is common to define 1894 as Year Zero in Brazilian football. On 18 February, among the passengers disembarking at the port of Santos was Charles Miller. Miller was the Brazilian-born son of a Scotsman who had emigrated to Brazil to work in the booming railway construction business. When he was aged ten, Miller had been sent by his parents to Britain for his secondary studies. Now 19, he had returned to Brazil to start work for São Paulo Railway. Bannister Court School, in Southampton, was hardly an academic star in the British educational system but it was there that young Charles had been sent – and, most crucially, it was there that he had been introduced to football. When he boarded the ship to Brazil in 1894 he had packed two footballs, a pairs of boots, a couple of used kits and a pump among his belongings.

A year later, under Miller's guidance, a game between workers from the Gas Company of São Paulo and São Paulo Railway took place on a common in the Bras neighbourhood; São Paulo Railway won 4-2. Historians have often referred to this match as the first to take place in Brazil under the organised rules of the Football Association. There are documents referring to football games in Brazil as early as 1864, 30 years before Miller's arrival, usually kickabouts organised by off-duty British sailors in the vicinities of Brazilian ports – there is also evidence that it was used a recreational tool in religious schools around the country. In Rio's Gloria neighbourhood, a piece of land opposite the residence of Princess Isabel (Brazil was a monarchy until 1889) is described as a place for local games for workers from British companies. All those initiatives, however, had in common the absence of local participation. It was under Charles Miller's guidance that São Paulo Athletic Club

(SPAC), founded by cricket-mad British expats, assembled one of the first football squads in Brazil. Miller was also behind the organisation of the first tournament in Brazil, in 1899, which led to the creation of the São Paulo Football League, two years later.

Another priceless contribution from Miller was his preference for dribbling. His footballing skills had been nurtured in the south of England, where a quicker game was played in comparison to the more laboured passing game popular in the north, and this had a major influence on the construction of the Brazilian style. Miller would play for SPAC until 1910 when he retired having helped the side win back-to-back titles from 1902 to 1904; he was the top scorer in both 1902 and 1904. Much more skilled than many of his fellow athletes, Miller even managed to create a dribble – a deft flick of the ball with the heel – that would become known as a 'Chaleira' in tribute to him. He was also instrumental in promoting Brazil as a destination for touring English teams and after a visit from London side Corinthian Football Club he suggested that a group of railway workers set up the Sport Club Corinthians Paulista, which would become one of the powerhouses of Brazilian football in years to come. Rio de Janeiro would soon have its own league in 1905, but unlike the proliferation of working-class clubs in England, Brazilian football was dominated by the white and rich elite.

One of the last countries in the world to formally abolish slavery, in 1888, Brazil entered the 20th century with a huge mass of freed slaves that increasingly headed from the countryside to urban centres in search of work. It was natural that the working classes would come into contact with football sooner rather than later, but the leading clubs would turn down non-white players and working-class teams were actually banned from playing in the Rio and São Paulo leagues. In a country that was rife with poverty and racial discrimination, football was claimed by the white elite as 'their' game. To tip the balance still further in favour of the wealthy, football equipment in early 20th-century Brazil was expensive. It did not prevent workers' teams from improvising, playing barefoot, with old balls or even improvised ones made from alternative materials in the absence of the real thing. But the rules of staunch amateurism also kept the game 'free' from the poor. It is a curious fact that the racial resistance that so subsumed the fabric of Brazilian football should be broken by the success of Brazil's mixed-race talent.

Arthur Friedenreich was born in 1892, the son of a white German businessman who immigrated to Brazil and fell in love with a black Brazilian washerwoman who was the daughter of free slaves. The genetic combination resulted in a tall boy with brown skin, curly hair and green eyes. Although technically vulnerable to the widespread prejudice in Brazilian society, Friedenreich had a world of opportunities in front of him thanks to his father's elevated position. One of these was football. His father, Oscar Friedenreich, was a member of SC Germania, a club founded in São Paulo in 1899 by German immigrants and one of the earliest adopters of football in the country. In 1909, at the age of 17, Arthur was selected for the Germania squad and became the first non-white to join a league in Brazil. He played for a succession of São Paulo club sides before joining Paulistano in 1916 and was one of the first mixed-race players to represent the national team – which he did with some style, becoming the undisputed star of the 1919 South American championship.

The importance of this tournament in Brazilian football cannot be overstated. Only five years after putting together a team to play against Exeter City, Brazil were hosting their first international competition. With only Brazil, Argentina, Uruguay and Chile taking part, the round-robin tournament was played exclusively at Fluminense Football Club's Laranjeiras Stadium which, although only built in 1905, had been renovated for the tournament, with the capacity expanded from 5,000 to 19,000. In May 1919, the game between Brazil and Chile kicked off the tournament and the first goal was scored by Friedenreich. Fluminense had historically been one of the bastions against racial diversity in football and even their first black star, Carlos Alberto, signed from America FC in 1914, resorted to 'whiting up' with rice powder before taking to the pitch, fearing a racist backlash from the club's supporters. Friedenreich scored a hat-trick in Brazil's 6-0 demolition of the Chileans.

Uruguay, who had won the first two editions of the tournament (1916 and 1917), began their 1919 campaign with a 3-2 win over Argentina on 13 May. They went on to beat Chile 2-0 while Brazil overcame Argentina 3-1. Argentina and Chile played a consolation match in the final round, while Brazil and Uruguay competed for the title on the 26th. A 2-2 draw meant a play-off was necessary and three days later they returned to the Laranjeiras. A goalless draw required extra-time and after a series of quiet displays following the Chile game, Friedenreich scored the goal that gave Brazil their first-ever title. It was Brazil's maiden victory over Uruguay, having previously been defeated 2-1 and 4-0.

Friedenreich became an idol in Brazil and won plaudits from opponents – he became known in Uruguay and Argentina as 'the Tiger' thanks to his powerful stride and rapid movements. Still, as rare pictures of him show, Friedenreich 'disguised' his non-whiteness by patiently using a combination of paste and hotel towels to flatten his curly hair. Nine times top scorer in the São Paulo league, Friedenreich retired at 39, having struck 554 goals in 591 games, averaging 0.94 of a goal per game, better than Pelé's 0.93.

Even by the 1920s, when professionalism had crept into the game, Brazilian football clubs still created entry barriers for the lower classes by demanding, for example, that players be in full employment to be eligible to play. In Rio, being able to read and write was another demand, tested by making players sign official match reports – clubs quickly started funding private tuition for poorer athletes in order to circumvent the law. 'Football in Brazil became popular almost by sheer force from the lower classes,' explains Brazilian historian and writer Marcos Guterman. 'It was a symbolic victory over the elite. Most of the revolutions in Brazilian history, including the Republican uprising of 1899, had been top-down, with the people pretty much observing rather than participating. With football, a game that was much simpler and easier to play than cricket and rugby, the Brazilians realised they could challenge the hierarchy.'

Friedenreich, however, would become an early case of a wondrous player who would never grace a World Cup. By the time of Uruguay 1930 he was still an active player, having been the top scorer in the São Paulo league for the previous three seasons, but the tug-of-war between the footballing authorities in Rio and São Paulo for the control of the national team resulted in a 'Paulista' boycott of the Seleção. Friedenreich and other players from São Paulo clubs were forbidden to join the team and Brazil travelled to Uruguay with a depleted squad. Having been drawn alongside Yugoslavia and Bolivia, the Seleção lost 2-1 to the Europeans and although they beat Bolivia 4-0, it was Yugoslavia who progressed from the group after also winning 4-0 against Bolivia. The bickering between Rio and São Paulo was so strong that newspapers reported scenes of jubilation in the streets of São Paulo when Brazil's elimination was announced.

Four years later, in Italy, another split: this time it was a discussion on amateurism. The Brazilian Sports Confederation (CBD) faced opposition from the Brazilian Football Federation, a governing body created to defend professionalism and which had amassed the support of most of the top Brazilian clubs. An exception was Botafogo, and the Rio club ended up providing no fewer than nine players to the Seleção. For the first time before a World Cup, teams would have to play a qualifying tournament after a total of 32 nations had shown an interest in taking part in the tournament. Brazil were spared the trouble of qualification after opponents Peru withdrew from the play-off. This easy qualification was nevertheless followed by some pretty complicated logistics.

The CBD only managed to put the players on a ship two weeks before the competition, which meant that after an 11-day journey across the Atlantic the team had a meagre 72 hours to prepare for their first round game against Spain. The World Cup would be played in a play-off format from the start, which meant that every game was sudden-death. Although technical staff tried their best to keep the players fit while aboard the ship, their conditioning and focus had been severely hampered by the time they disembarked in Genoa and there was only time for one proper training session before they played one of the best teams in the world.

Spain were leading 3-0 after 30 minutes, although Brazil did miss a penalty and Leonidas da Silva pulled a goal back in the second half. Predictable as it was in retrospect, the defeat came unexpectedly for the CBD directors, who had arranged a string of friendlies for the Seleção against Spanish and Portuguese clubs after the tournament. A hastily arranged game against Yugoslavia to fill the time in between ended in a humiliating 8-4 defeat.

Football was the last stand of the old elite in Brazil; for the first third of the 20th century, agrarian oligarchs from the states of São Paulo and Minas Gerais had dominated the republic's politics, with their outgoing governors alternating themselves in the presidency. It all started to change in October 1930, when a state coup led by Rio Grande do Sul politician Getúlio Vargas – a defeated candidate in the presidential elections months before – deposed the still-serving president, Washington Luis. Vargas was sworn in to the presidency in that same month to oversee a transition. His 'provisional government', however, would last 15 years. Under his centralised command, Vargas immediately sought to attract support from the working class in order to establish a power base from which he could confront the aristocratic influence.

Vargas did not have a clear plan for Brazil, but he was a charismatic man. The messianic tones he used to address the masses irked his opponents but seemed to address the concerns of the common people. It didn't take long for the new president to notice that sport could be used as an easy channel for dialogue with the masses. It was under Vargas that football was formally professionalised in Brazil and recognised as a formal profession in a new set of general labour laws. In his association with sport, Vargas was hardly doing anything new: the 1930s were marked by the utilisation of football for political gain around the world, with Mussolini's propagandistic use of the 1934 World Cup and Italy's victory in the tournament the most prominent example. Vargas understood that in a country still torn by strong political and social division like Brazil, football could be one of the few unifying experiences. That football stadiums such as São Januário, in Rio de Janeiro, would host presidential ceremonies where Vargas would make long and impassioned speeches, was not a coincidence.

But the more formal 'annexation' of football to the political agenda would take place after 1937, the year that Vargas commanded another coup which essentially turned Brazil into a dictatorial regime. Claiming that his government had unveiled a communist plot to overthrow him, Vargas installed emergency law, conveniently just before the 1938 presidential elections. Every sphere of Brazilian sport came under state control and specific legislation was created to limit what the government saw as 'foreign influence' in sporting clubs. Vargas also benefited from the fact that football had experienced a leap in popularity in Brazil throughout the 1930s, fuelled by media interest, in particular the growth of radio as a mass medium. Football through the airwaves became a shared experience and a primary source of entertainment throughout the country. 'Radio was crucial to the growth in popularity of football in Brazil,' explains Marcos Guterman. 'The match commentary was always epic and tales of heroic feats by individuals, who were more and more representative of the socially deprived in Brazil, helped create and reinforce a fantasy around the game.'

Even before the radicalisation of his regime, Vargas had not wasted time associating himself with football: in 1932, when Brazil defeated Uruguay away for the first time and won the Rio Branco Cup (a challenge trophy the two teams contested from 1931 to 1976), the president hosted the team at the presidential Palace in Catete. The notion that the Seleção 'was' Brazil became stronger and even defeats were drenched in patriotism. The team defeated by Argentina in the pitch battle that decided the 1937 South American championships were received like war heroes back home – a marching band played the national anthem twice and even a cannon salvo greeted the players. This was also the period that first saw discussions on style become more frequent. Since the days of Miller, Brazilians had shown an inclination towards dribbling and trickery and players went into overdrive when it became clear crowds were appreciating the show. Commentators and even academics raved about 'ginga', the dance-like movements that they claimed only a country with a mixed population like Brazil could provide. Thanks to state control that had finally freed the Seleção from the internecine bickering that had sabotaged previous campaigns, Brazil put together their best team for the 1938 World Cup, which featured the star of the moment: Leônidas da Silva.

Born in 1913 in Rio de Janeiro, Leônidas was very different to Friedenreich, even though he was also from a mixed-race background – a white Portuguese sailor for a father and black Brazilian cook for a mother. After a humble childhood where kicking a football in the streets was his only source of fun, Leônidas was spotted at 17 by São Cristóvão, his neighbourhood club and where decades later a shy kid with an overbite, Ronaldo, would also start his career. In just two years Leônidas was a Brazil regular and it was his goal that gave Brazil the aforementioned maiden away victory against the Uruguayans. Nicknamed 'the Black Diamond' by the media, he was a common user of the scissor kick, although his claim to have invented the move cannot be verified.

Having sunk with Brazil in Italy '34, Leônidas became the Seleção's main star for the France '38 campaign. But much as recent results had enthused the Brazilians, the Seleção had so far played 270 minutes and two World Cups without yet managing to clear the first hurdle. There would also be another long sail across the Atlantic, with some players arriving in France with 'extra luggage' around their waistlines. Expectations were lower for this tournament and, just as in 1934, every fixture saw the loser eliminated. But a much improved Seleção overcame Poland 6-5 in Strasbourg in extra-time after a 4-4 draw in the regular 90 minutes. Leônidas hit a hat-trick that was broadcast across the ocean to Brazilian audiences and tales of a goal scored with his bare foot after he lost a boot in the muddy pitch delighted fans back home.

A week later, the Seleção faced the Czechs and after neither side could break a 1-1 stalemate, a second match was played 48 hours later and Brazil advanced to the semi-finals with a 2-1 win, Leônidas scoring twice. The replay, however, had left the players exhausted and Leônidas injured and the Seleção had to face world champions Italy without their talismanic player. Brazil fought hard but fell behind to a Gino Colaussi goal after 50 minutes. Italy put the match beyond the Seleção's reach on the hour, with Giuseppe Meazza converting a controversial penalty for a foul committed by Brazilian defender Domingos da Guia on Italian striker Silvio Piola: irritated by something Piola had said, the Brazilian took down his opponent, but the incident had taken place outside the box. Nevertheless, the penalty was awarded and the Seleção lost the game 2-1. Three days later, however, they managed to come back home with a 4-2 win over Sweden in the third-place play-off – Leônidas was back in the side and scored a brace, finishing the tournament as the top scorer.

Back in Brazil, the Seleção's games had been followed by fans who would gather en masse around outdoor speakers specially installed by public authorities. Several companies and public sector organisations also gave workers a free day on the date of the Italy game, which created a national collective experience around the Seleção.

In France, the local media reacted enthusiastically to the exploits of Leônidas and co, who had arrived for the World Cup as an exotic attraction but had left behind evidence that something exciting was happening to football south of the Ecuador line. While they had not won the tournament, the team's performances immediately boosted the country's confidence in their prowess in the sport to the point where arguments that Brazil was 'the land of football' began to spread wildly. It's understandable when one thinks of the combination involving Brazil's huge territorial extension, the populist regime in power and the relative isolationism in relation to Europe.

Hosting the next tournament then became a pet project of the Vargas government. By the time Brazil finally had the green light from FIFA to host the 1950 World Cup, another president was in charge. Unlike the latter part of Vargas' tenure, there was opposition in place and its voice was made clear by the attempts to block the release of funds for the construction of the Maracaná Stadium. Arguments that the money spent on the concrete colossus would be better applied to health projects, alongside proposals for alternative sites, were only defeated thanks to the influence of Ary Barroso, a broadcaster and composer who had used his fame to get voted onto the city council – he was a very popular figure even though he never really hid his passionate support for Rio club Flamengo, often refusing to properly narrate attacks against the team in his match broadcasts. Construction work started in August 1948 and although the stadium would be delivered in time for the tournament, work still went on until 1965.

Alongside the Rio arena, another stadium, the Independência, was built in Belo Horizonte – for English fans, it would become an emblematic venue. The Pacaembu in São Paulo and the Eucaliptos, in Porto Alegre, were rebuilt with public money, while the Ilha do Retiro, in the north-eastern coastal town of Recife, got ready for the tournament thanks to building work done by the 'socios' of Sport Club do Recife. Finally, another southern stadium, the Durival de Britto, in Curitiba, had been built in 1947 and managed to squeeze on to the list of World Cup venues. So Brazil had the arenas, but now they needed the teams to play in the tournament.

While Europe was still recovering from the aftermath of the Second World War, one of their traditional football powerhouses, Italy, had also been hit by the tragic 1949 Superga air disaster that killed 31 people, including ten Torino players who were also Azzurri internationals. While Portugal, Scotland and Turkey all withdrew from the tournament, the defending champions were persuaded by FIFA to attend and they were joined by debutants England, Spain,

Sweden and Yugoslavia. Withdrawals also took place in South America, most notably Argentina, Peru and Ecuador, which meant Bolivia, Uruguay and Paraguay qualified automatically.

Three months before the start of the tournament, there were only 15 teams, which created a curious arrangement, with three groups of four teams and one of three – which featured Uruguay, France and Bolivia. Contrary to the previous two World Cups, the hosts wanted some return from the money invested in infrastructure so insisted on there being more games, which explained the round-robin format adopted for the final round. When the French cancelled their participation, incensed by the fact they would have to travel thousands of miles within Brazil for their group games, a farcical situation ensued: Uruguay and Bolivia would decide a spot in the final four in a single game. India also withdrew and left Sweden, Italy and Paraguay fighting for another spot.

These problems did not dampen the spirits in Brazil, though. Just a year before, the Seleção had broken a 27-year continental drought by winning the Copa America, which they had also hosted. Although they suffered an unexpected defeat to Paraguay in the final round-robin game, Brazil's goal difference over the six previous matches had put the title beyond doubt: 39 scored and only seven conceded. Ecuador were beaten 9-1, Bolivia 10-1 and even Uruguay had been mercilessly despatched, 5-1. While the likes of Leônidas were no longer around, the Seleção boasted talents such as playmakers Zizinho and Jair da Rosa Pinto (who would later become an Inter Milan legend) alongside striker Ademir.

Most players in the squad were from Rio side Vasco da Gama. At a time when there wasn't a national championship in Brazil, they had become legendary when they won a South American club competition in 1948 by beating the feared River Plate from Argentina to the title – River at the time were still graced with the presence of a certain Alfredo di Stefano. Vasco had conceded only three goals in six matches and the performance enhanced the credentials of goalkeeper Moacir Barbosa. He was a natural choice for the Seleção number one shirt. At a time of reduced exchanges of information with European football, Barbosa differed from other Brazilian goalies through his own hard work and innovation. Hardly a tall keeper (he was 5ft 9in), Barbosa had to compensate by learning to anticipate crosses and long passes. Unlike many of his Brazilian colleagues, Barbosa didn't plant his feet on the goal line or restrict himself to the six-yard box; he roved and roamed, closing down space for strikers with carefully timed advances and the clever use of angles. He also resorted to taking his own goal kicks instead of leaving them to defenders. Promoted to the Seleção number one shirt in 1948, he became an uncontested regular in the team managed by Flávio Costa.

Interestingly, Costa was also the Vasco manager. He had been appointed to the Seleção in 1944 after winning four Rio League titles in six years at Flamengo. In 1947 he was offered the Vasco position and was allowed to combine the job with his Seleção role. A staunch disciplinarian, Costa was a keen observer of the game, having worked alongside Hungarian strategist Izidor 'Dori' Kurschner, a manager who had spent the last four years of his life in Brazil (1937–41) and who had contributed significantly to the development of the game in the country by introducing the 'W-M' tactical system to Brazilians. Although the W-M formation had been devised by Arsenal manager Herbert Chapman in the 1920s, it was still alien to Brazilians in the late 30s – until the arrival of Kurschner. The W-M system utilised both a deep-lying centre-half and a centre-half high up the field, creating a 3-2-2-3 shape.

Unlike his predecessors, Costa made sure that, as the Seleção manager, he would watch foreign teams playing in order to try to keep himself as up-to-date as possible with new tactical trends and with the dangers posed by potential World Cup rivals. The manager, however, was far from modern when it came to team preparations: the Brazilian players spent almost three of the first six months of 1950 at training camps in the spa cities of Araxa and Poços de Caldas. In Araxa, there were 45 days of total isolation and no contact with relatives, spouses or assorted companions. Even letters players tried to send to their loved ones were confiscated by the technical staff.

In March, Costa called up 37 players – ten of them from Vasco – but a month later this contingent had already been reduced to 22. In May, Brazil played three matches against Uruguay, losing the first 4-3 but winning the others 3-2 and 1-0. In hindsight, it was ironic that Costa seemed, according to reports quoting some of his players, obsessed with the English, who would for the first time take part in a World Cup. He had seen England and Spain matches during a study tour to Europe and was particularly impressed with Walter Winterbottom's team. Costa kept telling the players they would need to neutralise England if they wanted to win the tournament.

But there were more pressing matters for the Seleção. The Brazilians were drawn alongside Mexico, Switzerland and Yugoslavia, a group that was fraught with danger. On 24 June, they opened their campaign against Mexico in front of 150,000 people at the Maracanã. On a sunny Saturday afternoon, the Seleção won 4-0, with an Ademir brace and goals from Jair and Baltazar.

They then travelled to São Paulo to lock horns with Switzerland. Far from pushovers, the European side had reached the quarter-finals in the last two World Cups and their feared 'bolt defence' had caused its fair share of problems for previous opposition. Costa, however, gave more attention to the appeasement of the São Paulo crowds than to tactical intuition. Although the hostilities that had divided the Seleção in the 1930s were much milder by 1950, Costa was still accused of favouring Rio-based players at the expense of those from São Paulo. The manager's answer was to play to the gallery: on 28 June, Brazil came on to the Pacaembu pitch with a whole midfield line-up of 'Paulista' players – but it was an XI that had never actually played together, even in training. The PR attempt backfired horrendously, as Brazil could only manage a 2-2 draw and the team were booed from the pitch.

Having beaten the Swiss 3-0 and the Mexicans 4-1, Yugoslavia led the group and would qualify for the final round at the expense of the host nation with a simple draw in the last game. Yugoslavia were a formidable side that had finished with the silver medal in the London Olympics two years before. So, on 1 July, 142,000 people were biting their nails at the Maracanã and the players, as if the situation wasn't tense enough, were forced to listen to a speech by Rio mayor, Mendes de Morais, in which he piled on the pressure: 'The battle for the world championship has two parts. By constructing the stadium, Rio de Janeiro did theirs. Now you have to do yours.'

The Seleção were at least able to welcome the returning Jair, who had missed the Switzerland match through injury, and Zizinho, who had hurt his left knee just before the tournament and had sat out the first two games. Ademir, played out of position in the previous match, was back to the centre of the attack. But the biggest smile from Lady Luck to the Seleção had actually come before kick-off: as the teams crossed the tunnel to enter the pitch, Yugoslav striker Rajko Mitić hit his head on a metal rim, part of the unfinished Maracanã works. Bleeding profusely, Mitić missed the first 20 minutes of the match while receiving medical attention – and with these being the days before substitutions were allowed, Yugoslavia were forced to play with ten men while he was stitched and bandaged up. With a one-man advantage, Brazil launched forward and it took just three minutes for Ademir to fire them ahead.

Zizinho, who could barely walk before the game, seemed to have forgotten the pain as the match went on and looked to have settled matters for Brazil with a strike just after half-time only for Welsh referee Benjamin Griffiths to disallow it for offside. On the 69th minute, however, 'Master Ziza' capped a great run on the right side with a thunderous shot past the keeper. The moment was so cathartic that even Brazilian reporters watching the match on the sidelines invaded the pitch to celebrate. Brazil had survived and the dream of their maiden world title was still alive.

In the other groups, Spain had cruised through with three victories in three games, including a 1-0 defeat of an England team still shell-shocked by their surprise defeat to an amateur USA side – although it must be noted the Spaniards left fair play aside and after they had taken the lead spent much of the rest of the match booting balls into the three-metre-deep moat that separated the stands from the Maracaná pitch. Sweden qualified with a 3-2 win over Italy and a 2-2 draw against Paraguay. Uruguay, after basically training and watching the World Cup for the first week, qualified with an 8-0 demolition of Bolivia, the only game they needed to play to secure a place in the final four.

The schedule was paused for a week to allow the surviving four teams to attend a series of commemorative events and dinners and another draw was made to decide the order of the games. Brazil would face Sweden, Spain and Uruguay in that order and thanks to much lobbying from the CBD with the organising committee, it was decided that all Seleção games would take place at the Maracaná – the boos in São Paulo still haunted Costa and the players.

On 9 July, a massive operation was put in place to allow supporters to arrive swiftly at the Maracaná for Brazil v Sweden, which included a special tram service. A crowd of 138,886 witnessed the finest display of the Seleção in the tournament so far. Brazil went 3-0 up after 39 minutes, with an Ademir brace and a Chico goal. Ademir completed his hat-trick in the 50th minute and five minutes later he became the first and only Brazilian to score four goals in a World Cup game. Maneca scored the sixth on 85 minutes, even though he had hurt his thigh at the beginning of the second half, and then Chico made it seven. A penalty by Andersson gave the Swedes a consolation goal. The 7-1 score still stands as Brazil's biggest win in a World Cup match.

On that same day in São Paulo, under torrential rain, Spain and Uruguay had a very different game. The South Americans drew first blood in the 29th minute, with Ghiggia beating the legendary Spain and Barcelona goalkeeper Antoni Ramallets by squeezing the ball round the near post after a dashing run on the right. Basora, however, scored a brace in two minutes and Spain led 2-1 at half-time. After 71 minutes, Obdulio Varela, in a rare forward foray, equalised for the Uruguayans. The result could not have been better for Brazil.

Four days later, the Seleção hosted the Spaniards at the Maracanã and what happened on that afternoon became an unforgettable chapter in Brazilian football. In front of 153,000 spectators, Brazil humbled the Spaniards with an astonishing display of flair and attacking football. After opening the scoring in the 15th minute thanks to a Parra own goal, the Seleção went 6-0 up with Jair, Chico (2), Ademir and Zizinho netting before Igoa pulled one back. The crowd, though, had been celebrating since the third goal, waving white handkerchiefs, setting off fireworks and singing their hearts out.

During the second half, the 'ole' chants led to an impromptu singalong of 'Bullfighting in Madrid', a cheeky carnival song recorded in 1937 and whose composer, Braguinha, was at the stadium – legend is that he started weeping with joy. After the final whistle, supporters partied on the streets of Rio as if Brazil had already won the tournament.

Technically, they had reasons to be cheerful: in São Paulo, Sweden were leading Uruguay 2-1 and even an equaliser by Miguez in the 77th minute meant Brazil would enter the final game against their South American counterparts as virtual world champions given their immense goal difference. With five minutes left, however, Miguez scored a winner that gave Uruguay something to fight for on 16 July, although they would take to the Maracanã pitch knowing that only a victory would suffice.

The Seleção's headquarters throughout the tournament was a mansion on the Joa hills, a place that to this day remains reasonably detached from the madness in Rio but that in 1950 was as secluded as a Tibetan monastery. Costa had intentionally looked to isolate his players from the madness and hype that would surround them in the city. So removed were they from the effervescence downtown, players would often lose track of time. 'We would only snap out of it on match days, where we just wanted to play a good game and then come back to chill, sometimes even with a glass of wine,' said Barbosa in a TV interview in the 1990s. It would all change radically in the first hours of 14 July.

The players were woken up with orders to pack up and hop on the team bus, for they were moving base. The peaceful Joa would give way to lodgings at São Januário, the Vasco stadium, much more conveniently located for the festival of visitors, dignitaries and celebrities who were desperate to see the Seleção. Not only were the players now reachable, they would also struggle with noise and the noxious fumes of a nearby paint factory. 'At five in the morning we would listen to the whistle calling up workers to their shifts,' recalled defender Bigode.

Costa, however, argued that the training logistics were improved thanks to the location of a training pitch adjacent to the players' rooms, which they did not have at Joa. Trouble, however, was brewing among the players.

The Seleção's blistering campaign had attracted the interest of a series of benefactors who began to offer gifts to the players. The treats ranged in diversity from a suit to a piece of land, but it soon became apparent that the playmakers and strikers were receiving more attention than their team-mates.

Media access was suddenly as invasive as it could get and national magazine O Cruzeiro had even approached the players to arrange exclusive deals for articles on the day after the Uruguay match, in order to 'show how a world champion lived'.

Striker Ademir was taken to a hospital in order to 'bless' a boy who would undergo surgery the day before the final. The player would later confess the whole experience had left him shaken. The boy's father had simply wandered into the Brazil camp before convincing the manager to release Ademir for the bizarre trip. Ademir reportedly arrived at the operating room and the 14-year-old simply gave the striker a kiss before telling the surgeon to start the procedure. 'After I got back to the hotel I couldn't sleep,' Ademir would later admit. 'I spent the night thinking of what happened and why that boy was treating me like a saint.'

Things would get even more hectic when politicians invaded

the team headquarters looking for photo opportunities with the celebrated players. It was a year of general elections and the parade of candidates was overlooked by manager Costa, himself aiming to get voted onto the Rio City Council after the World Cup.

The players posed endlessly for pictures, including one for a brand of beer, in which they wore celebratory ribbons – the same that would make the front page of *O Mundo*. 'I had never seen so many people in a team's camp before an important game,' said Barbosa. 'Every five minutes there would be cars, lorries and buses stopping and spilling out people who wanted to talk to us and "congratulate the world champions". We had to talk to everybody, sign every autograph. My right arm actually went numb after a while. It was a party atmosphere instead of a place for us to rest and focus.'

At 10 pm on 15 July, Costa finally gave orders for the players to go to sleep. Unfortunately, not everybody obeyed. A group of players too wired to go to bed ended up playing cards for another couple of hours, while midfielder Juvenal went further and spent the night drinking and partying in Central Rio, returning to São Januário only on the morning of the game, apparently reeking of booze.

While Costa had mellowed significantly since the beginning of the campaign and allowed 'conjugal visits' to married players during the week before the final game, and actually allowed Juvenal a couple of hours out, he was furious to see the midfielder break the curfew and arrive with a hangover that was so bad he vomited in front of the team. Juvenal then threatened to leave the team hotel when addressed by an incensed Costa, which resulted in a diplomatic effort to avoid even more drama.

The players were then rounded up and taken to Rio's famous Capuchinhos Church for a Mass celebrating the launch of a radio station. At the church the players were mobbed by fans looking for autographs and handshakes. And it would still get even more surreal: at 11 am, when the players were getting ready for lunch, the entourage of presidential candidate Cristiano Machado dropped in at São Januário and interrupted procedures so that he could make a speech hailing their heroics. Then came fellow candidate and governor of São Paulo, Adhemar de Barros, who also spoke and promised grants and assorted treats to the Seleção.

Zizinho finally snapped. 'So the game is over already?' he asked sarcastically, only to be reprimanded on the spot by the manager.

Curiously, Getúlio Vargas, also running for president – he would in fact win the election by a landslide – stayed clear from São Januário, in a change of approach from the men who had previously tried so intensely to use football for their causes.

But eventually, even Costa grew tired of the bazaar atmosphere and decided to have the team travel early to the Maracanã. The Seleção arrived at the stadium around midday, which suggests the politicians' appearances simply didn't give enough time for the team to eat properly. Or take a nap after the meal. Instead, they helped themselves to ham and cheese sandwiches and lay down on mattresses in the dressing room (which still smelt of new concrete), and tried to sleep while the crowds arrived for the 3 pm kick-off.

The whole country seemed to be descending on the biggest stadium in the world. By the time the Seleção had arrived, there were already reports of overcrowding, with people falling into the moat around the pitch. Officially, a world record crowd of 173,850 paying spectators attended the game, but it is still argued in Brazil that 200,000 people witnessed proceedings.

While it is extremely important to take these reports with a pinch of salt – a running joke in Brazil is that a second stadium would have been necessary to accommodate everybody who claimed to have been at the Maracanã on 16 July 1950, a bit like the tales in Liverpool about everybody who claimed to have seen the Beatles at the Cavern Club or attended the same schools – the official numbers already represented the fact that almost ten per cent of the Rio de Janeiro population in 1950 was inside the stadium that afternoon. Among them was a young lawyer named Jean-Marie Faustin Goedefroid de Havelange, the man who two decades later would help turn football into a billionaire business, and an 18-year-old soldier named Mário

Jorge Lobo Zagallo, later only one of two men who won the World Cup as a player and a manager.

Already present in the sport's administration circles in Brazil and also working for a major Brazilian bus travel company, it hadn't been difficult for Havelange to get hold of tickets for the match. Zagallo, who had joined other military colleagues on security duty at games, wasn't on duty that day but had blagged his way past ticket control. Others wouldn't be that lucky and tempers were hot outside the Maracanã – rumours that extra tickets would be put on sale caused stampedes outside the stadium and official reports show 169 people were injured trying to get in. In times when ticket operations were rudimentary, the organising committee had chosen to use the ticketing booths of two famous Rio theatres, the Municipal and the Carlos Gomes (named after Brazil's most renowned classical composer). People slept in the queues overnight in their quests for tickets.

While his players tried to relax with the daunting booms of a crowd, whose size they and nobody else in a sporting event had ever experienced before, echoing around the stadium, manager Costa still had to fend off last-ditch attempts to exploit his squad. A representative of Rio mayor Mendes de Morais turned up at the dressing room looking to discuss details of a victory parade the following morning.

After Costa finally persuaded the man to leave the conversation for later, he addressed the players. Like a lot of information concerning Brazil's final preparations for the game, what happened at Costa's talk has differed from version to version told by the players and the manager. What they all seem to have agreed upon in interviews and assorted statements over the years, however, was Costa's concern that his players keep their discipline in the maelstrom. In their five games so far in the World Cup, Brazil had not experienced any disciplinary problems and the manager wanted things to remain that way – although red and yellow cards would only be introduced 16 years later, referees could still send players off. He was also wary of possible attempts from the Uruguayans to wind up his players – it wasn't uncommon for games between South American teams to descend into sledging matches, and as early as 1925 there had been an on-field fight between Brazilian and Argentine players.

Striker Ademir would later say that Costa had specifically asked defender Bigode and midfielder Juvenal to be careful. 'That piece of advice made them nervous,' said Ademir. 'Both Bigode and Juvenal were guys who always had more stamina than skill and to be told to temper their style like that put them on edge.'

Juvenal himself remembered similar reasoning: 'Mr Costa asked Bigode not to kick anybody and that unsettled him.' The manager systematically denied having asked his two 'choppers' to take things easy. 'I knew that Bigode was a hard man, a guy to mark opponents out of the game so I would never ask him to change that exactly for the final game. But the Brazilian authorities wanted a disciplined and civilised tournament [on and off the pitch].'

It is difficult to say how confident the Brazilian players were. After scoring 13 goals over two games in the final stage there was obvious enthusiasm, but accounts collected from players in several works all highlight how careful the team was approaching the real action; they were certainly not buying into the hype the newspapers were building that the result was a foregone conclusion. Captain Augusto reportedly warned his team-mates just before entering the pitch that Uruguay would present a harder challenge than Spain and Sweden. 'Nobody was thinking we would just walk over them,' said Ademir. 'We knew the Uruguayans too well to have any such thought.'

The Seleção had played the Uruguayans 30 times since 1914, winning 13 games and losing 11. Although they had put five goals past Uruguay in their last competitive game, in 1949, the more recent encounters before the World Cup had been closer affairs and included a 4-3 away defeat. There is another substantial difference between the 'two Uruguays' Brazil faced in the space of a year: they were actually two Uruguays. From October 1948 to April 1949, football in the former Brazilian province was shaken by industrial action from top players, including Varela. Their demands included better wages alongside 'respect from the media', which hardly endeared the players to the public and the newspapers. Varela was a particular target and his irritation became so severe that he often refused to pose for match pictures.

However, the three games Uruguay played against Brazil leading up to the tournament meant the two teams knew each other quite well – and until that match, Brazil's element of surprise had been important in their campaign. Apart from World Cup games, Brazil had barely played away from South America, which made any analysis of their play or their players nigh on impossible for their European opponents; although this was also true for Brazil's analysis of their opposition, the Seleção were the ones playing at home and with a roaring mass supporting them. 'We played the Brazilians three times in 1950 before the World Cup,' Uruguay goalkeeper Roque Máspoli recalled. 'Those games were an opportunity to study them. We knew they would not walk over us.'

But not everybody in the visitors' camp was that confident. At the Paysandu Hotel, Obdulio Varela and his team-mates were addressed by one of the Uruguayan FA's directors, Juan Jacobo, who emphasised the importance of preserving the reputation of the 'Celeste Olimpica'. 'We were told that we needed to avoid humiliation at all costs,' said Varela. 'Jacobo told us clearly "not to let those guys hammer us 6-0". We heard that playing the final was already a great feat.' It looked as if pessimism and resignation were already setting the tone among the Uruguayan media and public. But for the players themselves, the mood was quite different – and all the more so after Varela had decorated the urinals with the front page of *O Mundo* and left his instructions to the team scrawled on the mirrors. The underdogs' hackles were raised.

At 2.30 pm, both teams entered the Maracaná pitch for a game few people doubted would end with Brazil becoming the second South American nation to win the World Cup. As the players stood for the national anthems it is possible even now, through the fuzzy archive footage, to see the fundamental differences in body language. While the Uruguayans were clearly fired up, with some players drying tears, the Brazilians stood erect and wooden like soldiers on parade, the tension clear on every face. They had been asked to kiss the national flag by a CBD director before entering the pitch before mayor Morais piled still more pressure on the home players' shoulders by declaring in his long pre-match speech that 'in a matter of hours they will be acclaimed as world champions' and warning the players 'not to frustrate the hopes of 52 million Brazilians'.

English referee George Reader took the toss and the result would later become one of those details latched on to by the superstitious: Uruguay won and chose the side of the pitch Brazil had picked in their games against Sweden and Spain, and in which the opponents had kicked off.

It wouldn't be the only 'fatalism'. The sum of 13 goals scored before the Uruguay game would also be mentioned as well as the soft collision the team bus had on the way to the stadium, in which Augusto was left with a small cut on his head. Barbosa would later also say that he saw the soldiers responsible for the national flags at the anthem ceremony almost raising the Brazilian flag upside down, which left him spooked. For once Brazil did not have to make changes in the squad and lined up with Barbosa, Augusto, Juvenal, Bigode, Bauer, Danilo Alvim, Zizinho, Jair, Friaça, Ademir and Chico. Uruguay had Máspoli, González, Andrade, Tejera, Gambetta, Pérez, Varela, Ghiggia, Schiaffino, Miguez and Morán.

The sensation that something wasn't quite right would not go away when Reader's whistle blew for the start of the match. The Brazilians tried to repeat the cavalier approach of their first two matches and had three shots on target in the first five minutes. But it was the Uruguayans who came closer in the opening exchanges. Barbosa saved a vicious shot from Miguez after 10 minutes and in the 16th Schiaffino missed an open goal after a meltdown in the Brazilian defence. Five minutes later a cross from winger Chico was met by a powerful header from Ademir that Máspoli tipped over the bar.

By the 26th minute, Brazil had had eight attempts on target against three from the Uruguayans – including a Chico shot that skimmed the outside of the post. Uruguay had a chance a minute later following a great save from Barbosa after Schiaffino had shown Augusto a clean pair of heels and invaded the Brazilian box, but Morán blasted the rebound over the bar.

Jitters were spreading through the stadium and it is quite possible that emotions impaired some people's judgement concerning an incident that would become an eternal source of debate about the game: after an altercation between Bigode and Ghiggia, who were having a private duel on the left side of the Brazilian defence, Varela was thought to have given the Brazilian defender what could be called a good old clip around the ear. Something had indeed happened, as Mr Reader forced both players to hug, but for radio commentators the scene had been of a clear act of aggression by the Uruguayan captain that had gone unpunished. The incident would later be used as evidence that big man Bigode had been intimidated by Varela. Logic would rule out that version immediately: Bigode was hardly a Zen master and had been sent off three times playing against the Uruguayans. Even with all the instructions given by Costa for his more physical players to avoid fighting, it is unlikely that Bigode would have taken a slap in the face quietly. What seemed much more clear was that Uruguay were willing to exploit the left side of the Brazilian defence with Ghiggia's speed – the winger would execute no fewer than nine runs in the first half alone.

Chico would spurn a great chance in the 36th minute after finding himself with just Máspoli to beat, but he allowed the goalkeeper to pounce on the ball. Uruguay then made the blood of the Brazilian support freeze on the 38th: Miguez latched on to a weak header by Bauer and whacked the ball against Barbosa's left post.

The first half would end with Brazil registering 18 shots to six from the Uruguayans, but the away team had come much closer to scoring. Still, the draw suited the hosts just fine. Brazil were 45 minutes away from a maiden World Cup title and they had one hand on the trophy when they managed to breach the Uruguayan barrier within two minutes of the second half: Ademir released Friaça, who penetrated the Uruguayan box on the right and fired a perfectly angled shot to beat Máspoli on the right side. Brazil were 1-0 up and Friaça had fulfilled the dream of any Brazilian kid from past, present or future: to score for the Seleção in a World Cup final at the Maracanã. The goal elicited a thunderous roar from the crowd who began to anticipate another rout. Friaça would later admit the joy of scoring had psychologically taken him out of the game. Play was stopped for almost two minutes because of the effusive celebrations but also thanks to a tantrum by Varela – who wanted the goal ruled out for offside – which was so fierce it forced the referee to call for an interpreter to have Varela's views explained. It did not change the decision but the Uruguayan captain had managed to buy some time to stem the momentum generated by the goal and avoid an immediate blitz by the Seleção. 'Obdulio was screaming at everyone and had the ball under his arm,' Ghiggia remembers. 'I approached to collect it and restart the game, but he immediately shouted at me, "We either kick up a fuss or they will kill us!"'

Still the Seleção went forward, spurred on by a crowd in celebratory mood, but did not manage to threaten Máspoli's goal. Meanwhile, Varela, who seemed an obvious target for the booing from the Brazilian fans, started acting like a man possessed. Screaming at his team-mates and even manhandling them, he demanded more commitment. Rattled but not desperate, the Uruguayans seized their first real opportunity in the half: Varela hit a long pass on the right for Ghiggia, who avoided the sliding tackle of Bigode and slipped the ball to Schiaffino, who beat Barbosa with a powerful shot. Scarier than the goal itself was the evidence that Bigode and Juvenal were struggling to make an impact on the game.

While Schiaffino and his team-mates celebrated the crowd fell eerily silent. That, Costa would later recall, had unsettled his players even more than the equaliser itself. 'The team froze with the silence.

All of a sudden they lost their confidence, like actors who lose a crowd in the theatre. I saw the boys get paralysed and no orders or shouts seemed to shake them off that.'

Uruguay had nothing to lose. Although technically the draw would still hand the Jules Rimet trophy to Brazil, it was apparent that the momentum had shifted. So shocked was he with the goal, reserve player Nilton Santos simply headed to the dressing room to hide from what some in the stadium started to sense as an impending doom. The crowd would later wake up again to cheer the Seleção, who almost scored by accident when Gambetta went too strongly to intercept a Jair cross.

Then, seven minutes later, Ghiggia received his 18th ball of the game. Once again he darted through the left side of the Brazilian defence. Once again Bigode gave chase. Once again Ghiggia outran his marker. The move looked a carbon copy of the first goal and Schiaffino was indeed closing in fast on the Brazilian box, just as he had done before. But so was Juvenal, who was desperate to try to succeed where Bigode had failed. Barbosa had to make a decision: he moved slightly forward to position himself for the anticipated cross to Schiaffino. Running towards the Brazilian box, Ghiggia looked up and saw that Barbosa's movement had left a narrow gap on the near post. His decision was almost instantaneous and although he mishit the ball, he got enough spin on it to wrong-foot the keeper. Remarkably, Barbosa managed to react. He dived to his left and managed to slightly slice the ball with his fingers. He fell to the ground praying he had done enough to send it round the post. The silence in the crowd told him otherwise.

Barbosa climbed slowly to his feet as the Uruguayans celebrated emotionally in the centre circle. The remaining 12 minutes would go in a blur for the goalkeeper and his team-mates. Shell-shocked, the Brazilians did not threaten Máspoli's goal again before Reader blew his whistle at 4:50 pm Rio time. While 173,000 or 200,000 people tried to understand what had just happened and the Uruguayans hoisted Ghiggia on to their shoulders, the Seleção staggered back to the dressing room, where they wept. Flávio Costa simply could not say a thing. The team wouldn't leave the stadium until around 9.00 pm, the team navigating their way through empty streets. The Seleção stars then scattered. After meeting his wife at São Januário, Barbosa drove to his house in the Rio suburb of Ramos, only to find an abandoned party on his street, which included a cake decorated with the phrase 'Brazil – World Champions'.

One of the longest post-mortems in the history of sport had just begun.

It didn't take long for scapegoats to be named: Barbosa, Bigode and Juvenal, either separate or together, were inevitably blamed for the 'Maracanazo' in newspaper reports and popular accounts of the game. The goalkeeper was judged to have failed to stop an easy shot by Ghiggia, while both the defender and the midfielder were exposed by the rings the Uruguayan winger had run around them – only years later would the spaces created in the Brazilian half by Flávio Costa's man-marking defensive tactics be properly scrutinised. That the three scapegoats were black should not go unnoticed. Bigode also had to deal with accusations of cowardice after the supposed 'slap' by Varela.

Nobody, however, symbolised the 1950 defeat more than the goalkeeper. He tried to resume a normal life, but after a tense encounter with a group of supporters outside a cinema, he decided to go back home and lay low for a few days. A month later, Barbosa was back in action for Vasco. He would remain one of Brazil's best goalkeepers for the next few years and, in 1953, was called up for the South American championship in Peru. At 32, he played in a 2-0 victory over Ecuador, his first game after the Maracanazo. It would also be his last Seleção outing; in a game against Botafogo a few months later the goalkeeper suffered a horrendous fracture in a challenge by striker Zezinho. He missed the 1954 World Cup – where he would probably have been a sub thanks to the rising form of his 1950 deputy, Castilho – but would still play club football for nine more years, only retiring at 41 and after 1,300 games.

Barbosa finished his Seleção days with 27 goals conceded in 22 matches. But the one scored on 16 July 1950 would matter more than any other. Not only for Barbosa, but for other black goalkeepers as well. After 1950, it took 56 years for a black goalkeeper to be a starter for the Seleção in a World Cup – AC Milan's Nelson Dida. The defeat to Uruguay also created the racist myth that black goalkeepers would be more error-prone than white ones, a diatribe that, shockingly, still has resonance in Brazil.

Playing at a time when footballers hardly made enough money for a decent pension, Barbosa accepted an invitation to work at Adeg in 1962, a Rio de Janeiro state organisation responsible for managing sporting venues. Their portfolio included the Maracanã. Although the former goalkeeper was responsible for the neighbouring Aquatic Park, he still had to look at the stadium every day. Barbosa was still in the job in 1986, when a TV crew popped in for an interview. The former goalkeeper agreed to talk but refused emphatically with the choice of location – the Maracanã pitch. 'I won't go there, sorry,' he said.

In time, life would deal him another tough hand: his long-time partner, Clotilde, fell ill and his life savings were used to fund her treatment. So when the BBC came knocking and offered a decent fee for an interview in 1993, the former Seleção star took it. The brief was simple: the BBC wanted to sit Barbosa down with the then Seleção goalkeeper, Cláudio Taffarel, before a decisive match against Uruguay at the Maracanã in the last round of the South American qualifiers for the 1994 World Cup. Once again a draw would do for Brazil. At 72, Barbosa expected some support from the Brazilian Football Confederation but instead was greeted with a denial for Taffarel's appearance at the interview, or for the request for photographs to be taken of them together. 'The highest sentence for a crime in Brazil is 30 years,' said Barbosa. 'I have already served that.'

On 7 April 2000, by now a widower and living off hand-outs given by Vasco, Barbosa died after suffering a heart attack. He was 79 and although penniless, seemed at last to have made peace with the Maracanazo curse. In the years just prior to his death he had appeared on TV and allowed Brazilian journalist Roberto Muylaert to conduct a series of lengthy interviews for an autobiography that helped shed new light on the events surrounding the 1950 final. They showed that a comedy of errors behind the scenes played a bigger part than the players' lack of 'bottle' in the most traumatic defeat suffered in Brazilian football history. Brazilian newspaper *Folha de S. Paulo* ran a headline that hinted at the keeper's rehabilitation: 'Brazil will witness Barbosa's second funeral. Inquisitors can now finally light up their fireworks.' In 2009, Juvenal, another man singled out after the Maracanazo, became the last surviving member of the first XI to finally rest in peace.

The Maracanazo left a huge mark on the Brazilian public's psyche. A young Pelé, after seeing his father cry while listening to the game, vowed to win the trophy one day 'to please the old man'. João Havelange, who only six years after the Maracanazo would take the reins of Brazilian football, promised he would 'bring the trophy to Brazil', while Mário Zagallo would for years be haunted by the scenes of sadness he witnessed so close to the crowd. The defeat affected the country immensely: at a time when Brazilians were not quite sure where they stood in the new world order, football had become tangled up with their notions of national identity and the defeat in Rio had hammered their self-esteem. Nelson Rodrigues, one of the most popular 20th-century writers in Brazil, would diagnose a 'stray dog complex' that pre-existed the Maracanazo but that was amplified by the events of 16 July.

Nevertheless, the 1950s would witness both a cultural and economic leap for Brazil. The process of industrialisation started by Vargas between 1951 and 1954 was picked up by his successor, Juscelino Kubitschek, and by the end of the decade Brazil had embraced its own version of the American dream at the same time it was about to get a brand new capital – Brasilia. Bossa nova, the fusion of samba and jazz born in Rio de Janeiro, would become the soundtrack of a cool Brazil. There would be more sadness too – Vargas' suicide in 1954 caused national commotion and forced his political nemesis

Carlos Lacerda (who had protested about the construction of the Maracanã so near downtown Rio but who had actually been a victim of an assassination attempt traced back to the president) to resort to a self-exile abroad in order to avoid the public fury.

Eight years after the Maracanazo, Brazil would finally fulfil what Brazilians thought was their destiny with an astounding World Cup win in Sweden. Pelé, at 17, became the youngest player to win the tournament after a campaign masterminded with military precision by CBD president João Havelange. Among the winners was full-back Nilton Santos and goalkeeper Castilho, both survivors of the 1950 squad – Castilho once again stayed on the bench but Santos became a Seleção legend, also taking part in Brazil's successful defence of the cup four years later. So did Zagallo, his national military service days long behind him.

After the 1950 defeat, Costa could not have convinced even his mother that he should have stayed in the job. He was replaced by Zezé Moreira, who would bring a major change to the Seleção by abandoning the man-to-man marking that had backfired so miserably in the game against Uruguay and adopting a zonal system that would help lay the foundations for the 4-2-4 variation Brazil would make great use of in later years. By the time Brazil travelled to the next World Cup, in 1954, they had already gone through another big change – the white uniform, which Brazil had worn for the previous 40 years, had been replaced by the bright yellow in which the Seleção would become immortalised.

There is great controversy about the reasons for the change. Officially, it obeyed the desire to increase the visual identification with the team and the country, hence the rules laid down in the public contest that was set up to choose the new design – it had to use the colours of the Brazilian flag, where green, yellow and blue predominate. But the change is still described in Brazil as a mixture of superstition and 'moving-on spirit'. It is difficult not to see a political slant here. The first half of the 1950s marked another polarisation of political forces in Brazil, often guided by intense nationalism, which would sustain the flag symbolism hypothesis. Brazil still played in white two years after the Maracanazo, when they contested (and won) the Pan-American Championship in Chile, but from 1953 onwards they started to use the yellow-green model with blue shorts and white socks designed by illustrator Aldyr Schlee. The white shirt was not radically 'retired': the Seleção wore it as late as 1957, when Brazil played in that year's Copa America – and there is a picture of legendary midfielder Didi on the cover of magazine *Manchete Esportiva* to prove it.

Flávio Costa returned to club football, winning Rio state titles with Vasco and Flamengo, but his reputation as the cleverest man in Brazilian football had taken a battering after the Maracanazo. Still, he would have a Seleção comeback: Costa managed the national team for 27 games between 1955 and 1956, including a 4-2 defeat to England at Wembley in which Stanley Matthews almost reduced Nilton Santos to tears. It was all part of a tour where Brazil, once almost as insular as England with regards to travel, decided to test themselves abroad as much as they could to 'study' their European rivals. Costa would later manage in Portugal (Porto) and only retired in 1970. He died in 1999, aged 93. Only 50 people turned up to his funeral in Rio.

Brazilians and Uruguayans would take almost two years to lock horns again after the Maracanazo; on 16 April 1952, as part of the Pan-American Championship, the two sides met in Chile. Both teams were still peppered with veterans from the previous World Cup – Bauer, Friaça and Ademir for Brazil and Máspoli, Pérez, Ghiggia and Miguez for the world champions. The Seleção triumphed 4-2 in a bad-tempered match that ended with the dismissals of Miguez and Brazilian Ely. Varela missed the match through injury. The legendary Uruguayan captain would retire in 1955, ironically enough after a game played by his club Peñarol at the Maracaná. Far from a hated figure, Varela had won the admiration of Brazilians after the 1950 final. Allegedly, the captain had strolled the streets around the team hotel in the hours after the Maracanazo and had even drunk beers with some disgruntled Brazilian fans. His career with the Celeste ended after the 1954 World Cup, when Uruguay were finally defeated for the first time in the history of the competition – Puskas' Hungary knocking them out in the semi-finals. The Hungarians won the match 4-2, the same scoreline registered in their troublesome win over the Brazilians in the quarter-finals, which had prevented a 'revenge game' for Brazil against their old rivals.

In 1970, though, the date with destiny happened. After seeing off the valiant Peru 4-2 in the quarter-finals, the Seleção found themselves with their neighbours once again filling the underdog role. Evoking memories of 1950 was inevitable and the ghosts of that defeat would prove how much power it still held over the Brazilians: on 17 June, in Guadalajara, Pelé, Carlos Alberto and co had a jittery start that became even worse after 19 minutes, when a mis-kick by Uruguayan midfielder Cubilla made Brazilian goalkeeper Félix look foolish and gave Uruguay a 1-0 advantage. The Seleção drew level right before the half-time whistle after defensive midfielder Clodoaldo had thrown himself forward and slotted home the goal. 'The press had spent the whole build-up to the Uruguay game talking about 1950 and that made us even more nervous for what was already a tense occasion – a World Cup semi-final, for goodness sake,' remembers Carlos Alberto, the Brazilian captain in the tournament. The players, however, were fired up by a Brazilian version of the hairdryer treatment from their manager. 'Zagallo was incensed when we entered the dressing room at half-time. He gave us a proper bollocking and told us to stop thinking about what had taken place 20 years before. I guess he was pretty livid Uruguay could be pickpocketing Brazil again,' laughs Alberto.

More settled and benefiting from a fitness regime that had invariably left their players with much more petrol in the tank during second halves in Mexico 1970, Brazil finally edged ahead 2-1 in the 76th minute, through Jairzinho. Seven minutes later, Rivelino put the result beyond doubt and only some divine injustice prevented Pelé from scoring a peach of a goal after a ballet dancer dribble over the goalkeeper and a shot that missed the net by centimetres. At the time, both countries had two world titles and whoever made it to the final would have a shot at keeping the Jules Rimet trophy (awarded to any team to win the World Cup three times). Brazil came out on top this time, but it still wouldn't be enough to lay the ghosts of 1950 to rest. As for Uruguay, it would take 40 years to reach that far in a World Cup again. But who can blame the public imagination? Drama and revenge are part of narratives that perfectly fit into sporting stories and in Brazil's case it wouldn't help that they kept meeting Uruguay for important occasions at the Maracanã.

In 1989, the two teams would decide the Copa America in Rio. Uruguay were aiming for their third straight title, while Brazil were then marking 40 years without continental superiority. Talk about the Maracanazo proliferated in the pre-match coverage, but Brazil won the title thanks to a sole Romário goal. Four years later, in the last round of the South American qualifiers for USA 1994, Brazil and Uruguay once again stepped on to the Maracanã turf for a decisive game: rattled by a shaky campaign, Brazil had the advantage of only needing a draw to qualify, while the Uruguayans were underdogs and needed a victory, just as they had in the 1950 final. In the end, 101,533 people saw Romário score a brace that not only guaranteed Brazil's bragging rights for being the only country to have attended every World Cup (a record that still stands), but also dumped the Uruguayans out of the competition.

Brazil would never again lose to Uruguay at the Maracanã after 1950. Still, when it had mattered most it was Varela and his men who had prevailed. Loathed before and during the 1950 World Cup, the captain had achieved a feat that in the minds of the Uruguayan people was comparable to the actions of the men behind the push for independence almost 90 years earlier. That the blue shirt with a red number 5 sewn on the back is the main piece displayed at the Centenário Stadium Museum – in fact it is the only shirt from the 1950 team exhibited – is a testament to how mythological Uruguay's victory became to the David country that had given their Goliath neighbours a hiding.

1966

TWO

1966
HAVELANGE AND ALL THAT

JEAN-MARIE FAUSTIN GOEDFROID 'JOÃO' HAVELANGE had a plan, and despite the succession of middle and last names, his intentions did not involve a plot against any European royal house. But Havelange, ironically enough, was indeed looking to interfere with a line of succession. More specifically the one that guaranteed the reins of football's governing body, FIFA. Founded by European countries in 1904, FIFA had, since its birth, been dominated by continental forces. Above all, France, in the figure of Jules Rimet, the man behind the creation of the World Cup and whose 33 years in the presidency still stand as a record. Since 1955, however, it was England that had taken control and after six years under Arthur Drewry, the man in office in 1963 was Sir Stanley Rous, whose lobbying and political influence had been instrumental in the success of England's bid to host the 1966 World Cup.

Little did Rous know that the Brazilian had his sights on the top job and saw the tournament as an opportunity to showcase his credentials. After eight years at the Brazilian Sports Confederation (CBD), Havelange had become a powerful man in his home country and his involvement with the success of the Seleção had become organic. For an ambitious man, the FIFA presidency was a natural step, particularly at a time when Brazilian football had taken the world by storm with back-to-back world titles in Sweden 1958 and Chile 1962. Brazilians could certainly be excused for feeling that the game invented by the English had been reshaped by Pelé, Garrincha and co. And Havelange had strong reasons to also puff out his chest. It was under his watch that the amateurish preparations for tournaments, which had cost the

Seleção dearly on previous occasions, would give way to a business-oriented approach that perhaps only Havelange could have brought to the table.

There would be no better way to showcase this prowess than in a World Cup hosted in England. The problem was that the success had inflated not only Havelange's ego. The Seleção were entering a period of civil war on and off the pitch that would have dire consequences for their plans in England. Curiously enough, though, the events of 1966 would end up being a crucial step for a turnaround in Brazilian football and its famous authority.

Jean-Marie 'João' Faustin Goedefroid de Havelange was not born in a typical Brazilian household. The son of a Belgian engineer turned arms dealer and with powerful connections among the Brazilian elite, Havelange was born in Rio de Janeiro in May 1916 and grew up with a middle-class background at a time when Rio was still the capital of Brazil and the de facto focal point of interest in the country. His rise in football and political spheres in Brazil was hardly predictable. In fact, one of Havelange's early dilemmas was to hide his interest in the sport from his father. In a controversial biography released in 2007, initially as an authorised project that he later rejected, Havelange tells tales of secret kickabouts at Fluminense FC where a whole system of vigilance would be in place to alert him to the arrival of his father. Although Havelange Senior was a supporter of Belgian side Standard Liege and had not flinched when his son played youth tournaments for Fluminense, the story changed when it became apparent that he might be able to make a career of it. 'My father never really saw a future in a career as a professional athlete,' says Havelange. So horrified was Faustin that he actually made Havelange promise to him on his deathbed, in 1934, that the 18-year-old would dedicate himself only to Olympic (and therefore amateur) sports.

Havelange focused his efforts on the water and as a swimmer made it to the 1936 Olympics in Berlin, although he failed to progress beyond the initial heats of the 400m and 1500m freestyle events. The trip, though, was something close to a gap year for the young Havelange – and must have felt about as long, thanks to the shambolic planning by the Brazilian Olympic Committee. The 94-athlete delegation was sent to Europe aboard the *President San Martin*, a cargo ship that not only had more stops than the Brighton–Bedford train service but also did not have a swimming pool as part of its amenities, which meant that the swimmers spent 21 days without being able to practise.

In 1952, however, Havelange's life couldn't be more different. After obtaining a law degree and joining the legal department of Viação Cometa in 1940, one of the biggest bus travel companies in Brazil, Havelange was occupying the chairman's office. He went on to compete in the Helsinki Olympics, this time as a member of the water polo team, before his career as a sporting director began to take off when he became one of the vice-presidents at CBD in 1956.

Two years later, he made the move for the presidency of CBD, winning a landslide vote (185 votes to 19) over opponent Carlito Rocha, then one of the most well-known men in Brazilian football. Havelange immediately imposed his ruthless business ethos on the CBD operations, with special focus on the national team. 'I applied my managerial experience in the corporate world to football. When I took over CBD, the Brazilian national team had only a manager, a fitness coach, a doctor, a kit man and a masseur. At Cometa the team minding the workers had more than that. It was no surprise we were the company with the smallest number of accidents. A bus and team of footballers are not that different.'

Above all, he was quick to understand that more professionalism in the players' preparations could be the difference between near misses and Brazil actually winning the World Cup for the first time. Morale could not be lower among the players, supporters and the media in the 1950s. After the Maracanazo and its festival of mistakes in 1950, the Seleção's following World Cup campaign, in Switzerland, was still marred by astonishing levels of amateurism. Despite taking Brazil to within a whisker of the title in Rio, only six players from the 1950 squad were recalled – goalkeeper Castilho, left-back Nilton Santos, midfielders Ely and Bauer, and strikers Baltazar and Rodrigues. Attentive readers will immediately notice the absence of the much-maligned trio of Barbosa, Bigode and Juvenal, and also Zizinho, who even after the tragedy was still one of most lauded footballers in Brazil and South America.

Blinded by the 'need' to make up for the Maracanazo, Brazil travelled to Switzerland as if some of the mistakes which had thwarted the previous campaign hadn't happened. The entourage in Europe was huge and included politicians who made sure they would belt out inflammatory speeches in order to rally the troops – indeed, before setting out for Switzerland, the whole squad was received by President Vargas and who told them that they were 'representing the skills, strength and resistance of a race'. Some speeches from hanger-on politicians even preached revenge for the death of Brazilian soldiers in the Second World War, albeit not taking into account that no military operation actually took place in Switzerland.

No surprise then that the players' nerves were in tatters. It didn't help either that the 1954 World Cup had a confusing system where each of the four groups had two seeds who would not face each other. Brazil and France were the named seeds in Group 1, but while the Seleção, wearing the iconic yellow shirt for the first time in a World Cup, hammered Mexico, France were defeated 1-0 by Yugoslavia. Thus, a draw between Brazilians and Yugoslavians would be enough to take both teams to the quarter-finals. Except nobody seemed to have told the Seleção. After conceding in the 48th minute in Lausanne, Brazil equalised through Didi 20 minutes later and proceeded to attack their Balkan opponents gung-ho style, despite desperate attempts from the Yugoslavs to warn them. When Scottish referee Charlie Faultless blew the final whistle, several players wept, as they thought the Seleção had just been knocked out.

They hadn't, but instead of relief came a sense of superiority that seemed as risible as their naïve hubris, for Brazil's opponents in the quarter-finals were Hungary, a formidable side spearheaded by Ferenc

Puskás and one that would lose only one of 47 matches between May 1950 and February 1956 – that match being the 1954 World Cup final against Germany. 'I am not interested in other teams,' was the swift answer from Seleção manager Zezé Moreira when asked about the dangerous opponents they would face in Berne on 27 June.

He wasn't that smug after the Hungarians scored twice in only seven minutes. Outclassed, the Brazilians lost their composure in both a tactical and behavioural sense: Nilton Santos picked a fight with Bozsik and both got their marching orders in the second half and Brazil were reduced to nine men soon afterwards when Humberto hit Lorant with a kung-fu kick. The Magyars won 4-2 and also had to face the Brazilians in 'extra-time' when a general punch-up broke out after the final whistle. Even Moreira was involved, throwing a boot at his Hungarian counterpart's face. Brazilian journalists and broadcasters also got involved in the melee and that ensured supporters back home also followed the (very partial) description of the 'Battle of Berne'. Incensed, a small crowd in Rio decided to take matters into their own hands. The reason why they decided to trash the Embassy of Sweden building remains a mystery to this day. Now Brazil were losing games and also seen as thugs.

Enough was enough for Havelange. As a result, Brazil went to the 1958 World Cup with a level of sophistication in their preparations that was unheard of even by European standards. Players were submitted to a series of medical exams that revealed a daunting picture: several of the athletes had conditions such as worms, anaemia and so many cavities that all 33 players pre-selected for the tournament had at least one tooth extracted – reports also speculated that one of the players was diagnosed with syphilis. A pedicurist was also at hand to make sure ingrowing toenails and calluses wouldn't bother the players. 'I was ridiculed for submitting players to the pedicures,' Havelange explains. 'But the amount of dead skin and calluses removed was enough to fill a huge bin liner. A footballer's tool is his feet so for me it was quite obvious they needed that kind of attention.'

The new CBD president also brought a psychologist on board for the first time in the history of the Seleção, although the decision almost backfired spectacularly when the professional in question produced a report in which he claimed Pelé, then only 17, should be excluded from the squad – the same Pelé that took the tournament by storm and scored a hat-trick in the semi-final and a brace in the final.

Havelange's masterstroke, however, was to appoint Paulo Machado de Carvalho as his second-in-command. Not only a kindred spirit as media mogul, Machado had already occupied the presidency of São Paulo FC and was an influential figure in Brazilian football. Carvalho's appointment was a peace offering from Havelange to soothe the apparently eternal bickering between Rio de Janeiro and São Paulo. Previous divergences had resulted in Brazil sending weakened teams to the 1930 and 1934 World Cups and even later campaigns were marked by fierce debates about a player being picked ahead of others. Machado was also bestowed with the role of leading the mission to Sweden. In the end, Brazil mesmerised the world and finally lifted the Jules Rimet trophy.

Some of the glory rubbed off on Machado, who was nicknamed 'Marshall Victory'. Havelange got less exposure, partly because he did not even travel to Sweden. Instead, he remained in Brazil and listened to the games on the radio while jumping from meeting to meeting to raise money to make sure the delegation would be able to fund their stay as they kept advancing in the competition. 'There was too much to do back home. We didn't have support from the government so it was my responsibility to sign the paperwork at banks, for example.' His style, however, hovered above the team in Sweden. Just like Havelange never showed much patience with the press, the Seleção stayed isolated from the Brazilian journalists in their hotel.

Brazil's lightning struck again in Chile in 1962, which meant that for the first time since Italy 1938 a country had managed to win back-to-back World Cup titles. The Seleção and Havelange had the right to feel invincible and the CBD started thinking this prestige could be used to tackle the Eurocentric FIFA. Especially if Havelange could upstage Stanley Rous in his own backyard. No other stage would be as appropriate for a show of force as the 1966 World Cup. The Jules Rimet trophy, the original World Cup grail, would be permanently given to the first country to win it three times. No other nation in the world looked closer to that feat than Brazil after 1962.

Brazil's momentum, however, also put Havelange and Machado on a collision course. Cracks in their relationship had started to appear in 1965 when they clashed over the release of players to the national team. Santos were at the eye of the storm as they wanted to tour the world with Pelé in exchange for hefty match fees. The 'Marshall' defended the formation of two different versions of the Seleção, one with Rio-based and the other with São Paulo-based athletes so that club and national team tour agendas could be synchronised. Havelange torpedoed the idea by arguing it would antagonise the two football centres of power.

It has also been alleged that Havelange felt upstaged by the 'Marshall'. A media-friendly figure, Carvalho endeared himself to the collective imagination in Brazil after it transpired he could rally the troops as effectively as the manager. When Brazil were told on the eve of the 1958 final that the Swedes would be allowed to play in their yellow kit, thus forcing Brazil to play in blue, Machado immediately told the players it was a good sign because they would be playing 'in the same colour as Mother Mary's shroud'.

His credentials were enhanced by a very peculiar episode in the 1962 campaign. Despite his exploits on the pitch, which became even more important after Pelé injured himself in Brazil's second group stage match (a goalless draw against Czechoslovakia), Garrincha was an unpredictable character. Brazilian fans of several generations are familiar with his tales of mischief, including a compulsive desire to disobey instructions and attempt to dribble past whatever appeared in front of him. But breaths were being held all over the country after the winger managed to get himself sent off in the semi-final win over

Chile – tired of having lumps kicked out of him, Garrincha retaliated by kicking an opponent on the backside.

FIFA rules meant that Brazil would have to face the Czechs in the final without the player who had guided them through much of the tournament. However, the linesman who witnessed Garrincha's aggression, Uruguayan Esteban Marino, was nowhere to be found when the disciplinary hearing was heard. The fact that Marino had on several occasions officiated in Brazilian football, including in games organised by the same São Paulo Football Federation that once had the 'Marshall' as vice-president, didn't go unnoticed. The Spanish media, aggrieved by poor refereeing during their defeat to Brazil in the group stages, even insinuated a bribery scheme had taken place. Marino was the linesman who failed to award Spain a penalty after left-back Nilton Santos fouled striker Enrique Collar inside the Brazil box – Spain were 1-0 up when it happened and defeat would have sent the Seleção packing; instead they recovered to record a 2-1 victory. Marino's absence from the hearing guaranteed Garrincha would be on the pitch in the final.

All the credit for this went to Machado and that stung Havelange. He now saw the partnership as an obstacle in his plans for world domination. Therefore, Brazil's shot at a third straight title would take place without the 'Marshall', who quit his post in January 1966 after more disagreements with Havelange, who would travel to England as Brazilian football's absolute sovereign, combining his and Machado's former functions. Little did Havelange know, however, that the changes would upset the apple cart.

After years waiting for a World Cup triumph, Brazil had secured two in a row and all eyes were now focused on the possibility of leaving behind all the years of hurt by getting an eternal hold on the Jules Rimet trophy. Havelange's political aspirations apart, the symbolism of a victory in England, the land where football was invented, thrilled the Brazilian players, fans and media. Lifting the trophy at Wembley would crown the definite ascension of the Seleção to the pantheon of legends.

But in reality, the task was tougher than in any previous campaign. This started on the pitch, with Brazil experiencing a changing of the guard in the team. The 1962 World Cup squad still ranks as the oldest that ever represented the country and after the triumph in Chile a huge number of players simply had to retire. Gone, for example, were influential left-back Nilton Santos, as well as gifted midfielder Didi. Garrincha was already 33 years old and his alcoholism was finally starting to take its toll. It also didn't help that years of physical abuse at the hands of opposition defenders had pretty much crippled the winger. Even Pelé, who was 21 by the time Brazil won their second World Cup, had already showed signs of being jaded due to the excruciating number of games he played for his club Santos.

Brazil needed to find a team for 1966. The CBD (and Havelange) did not ignore that. In fact, preparations for England started as early as April 1963, when the Seleção toured Europe for a series of friendly matches supposed to give newcomers some international experience and at the same time lay the foundations for a new team. They could barely have travelled more exposed and opponents promptly pounced: although the Seleção beat France and West Germany and drew with England at Wembley, there were four defeats, including 3-0 at the hands of Italy and a 5-1 drubbing against Belgium. It could not have been a heavier comedown and manager Aymoré Moreira was put to the sword by Havelange. The choice of replacement betrayed the confusion going through the mind of the future FIFA president. Vicente Feola, who was in charge of the 1958 team, was brought back in the hope that he could galvanise both the players and public opinion. The Seleção found themselves using nostalgia as hope.

That trip down memory lane, though, also summoned ghosts from failures past. Political lobbying and pressure from club directors meant that Feola could not even pick his own players. When the training camp started, 47 players had been called up as a means to placate regional interests and the desires from clubs to have their athletes valued by joining the Seleção. To accommodate all these players, the Seleção was split into four teams that would spend several months playing each other in practice sessions that took place in five different Brazilian cities to give people a chance to see their heroes.

Among the players called up was a promising 19-year-old midfielder who had attracted a lot of attention for regularly scoring at Cruzeiro, in the landlocked state of Minas Gerais, which was one of the few teams outside the Rio–São Paulo axis to actually get noticed by the greater public. Eduardo de Andrade, nicknamed Tostão ('little coin' in Brazilian slang), had made his professional debut at 15 for America, who poached him from Cruzeiro's youth academy. The year was 1962 and it took only another 12 months for Cruzeiro to lure him back, with club director Felicio Brandi arriving late at his own wedding after making sure Tostão had signed. He would form an exciting midfield trio with future Seleção regulars Wilson Piazza and Dirceu Lopes.

Two things immediately stood out for Tostão about the preparations for 1966. One was the distracting environment at the training camp, with politicians and assorted authorities vying for the attention of the players. 'Things were shambolic at the preparation for that World Cup,' recalled Tostão. 'We were being paraded to fans and authorities instead of concentrating on our jobs. It seemed clear to me, young as I was, that what we were doing was not the right way to prepare ourselves for a competition as serious as a World Cup. There was a general feeling that all we had to do was travel to England to collect the Jules Rimet, as if no opponents would try to knock us off of our perch.'

He was also taken aback by the amount of players trying to make it to the World Cup, a quantity inversely proportional to the information they received from the technical staff, let alone the manager. 'We were basically clueless about what was going to happen. The only clear thing was that Brazil could not travel to England with 47 players in the squad. That also meant there wasn't a chance for us to gel and people were constantly thinking they could be dropped at any moment. How they expected us to work effectively in an environment like that beggared belief.'

With the players aware that they would not all make it to England, training sessions became more competitively brutal than usual – and then the bitching started. The swollen Seleção were struggling to find team spirit. 'We could only guess what was going on and the management decided to keep the players apart as much as they could to avoid the antagonism becoming rife. Then we started making assumptions. The team that had Pelé obviously became the one that everyone thought had the most likely starters. Conversely, everybody was saying that my team was going to be decimated by the cull before the World Cup.'

It was also hard for the players to catch a breath, literally. 'Marshall' Machado was not the only major staff change prompted by Havelange. Paulo Amaral, the fitness trainer who had prepared the 1958 and 1962 squads, was made a director and replaced by Rudolf Hermanny, who had never worked in football before and whose methods had only been tested in the preparation of judo athletes. So in an era where the fitness levels of teams were becoming even more important in the game thanks to sports science advancements in Europe, Brazil were tampering with the stamina of their players not only with untested methods but also while those players were under intense psychological pressure.

In May 1966, the Seleção started a frenzied tour of friendly matches in Brazil and abroad, but even after three months of preparations, Feola had no idea of which XI he would pick in the World Cup. His anxiety wasn't soothed by a difficult draw that placed Brazil alongside Bulgaria, Hungary and Portugal. 'We were not feeling sharp enough and a week before the World Cup none of us had a clue about who was going to play,' remembers Lima. Like any returning manager, Feola finally resorted to surrounding himself with players he trusted – even if it meant banking on some players from 1958 who were surviving on reputation rather than current form. 'The 1958 and '62 veterans were there because of their names, not for their form,' said Tostão. 'Apart from Pelé, they were all past their prime and their presence unsettled rather than comforted some of the players. And it riled many of us because it was felt that the veterans were getting special treatment.'

This ragged regiment of former stars included Garrincha, whose career had started to nosedive after his glorious World Cup in Chile. Hunted by opponents, the winger had serious knee problems and frequently resorted to painkilling injections so that he could play. 'Garrincha was basically walking when he was on the pitch,' said Tostão, 'and I remember that he would spend hours every day doing special exercises so that he could stand on his aching knees.' But even with his knee trouble, Garrincha's true nemesis was the alcoholism that between 1966 and 1972 would limit him to playing just 17 matches – and for five different clubs.

So when the Seleção arrived in England spirits were damper than the weather and matters weren't helped when they discovered that the bus scheduled to pick them up from Heathrow to take them to Lymm, the village in Warrington that would serve as their base, simply wasn't there – it would turn up two hours later.

When they eventually arrived in Lymm the players unpacked, stretched and headed for the training pitch – only to discover that it was locked up and nobody could locate the groundsman. When they finally did make it on to the pitch they discovered that the surface was unkempt and the grass horribly overgrown – for a week, until it was rectified, they had to practise at a nearby secondary school pitch.

An opportunity to get the feelgood factor going in the camp was allegedly also passed up. According to Pelé, Brian Epstein, the manager of the Beatles, contacted the Seleção to organise a visit from John, Paul, George and Ringo, but the offer was turned down by supervisor Carlos Nascimento. 'I met John Lennon in New York years later when I was playing for the Cosmos and he told me the story,' said Pelé. 'Nascimento had felt that "those four hippies" would be a distraction to our preparations.'

Tempting as it is to immediately tut at the narrow-mindedness of the CBD officials, it is very likely that the story is a product of hearsay, not least because the Beatles were still in the middle of their 1966 Asian tour and were not in any way football fans. But the story nevertheless underlines the feelings of disquiet and discontent among the players camped out in Lymm. The atmosphere could be cut with a knife and there was still a sense that they were grossly underprepared for the tournament. 'We were about to play a World Cup without even having fielded the same team twice. Not even the players had faith in the team,' he wrote.

The Seleção opened their campaign at Goodison Park on 12 July 1966, Valentine's Day in Brazil. Bulgaria's tactics were obvious from the outset – unenamoured with the grace and guile that Pelé could bring to a game, they focused more on dishing out tough love to him than actually trying to play much football. With a line-up that featured six survivors from the 1962 World Cup – goalkeeper Gilmar, full-back Djalma Santos, defenders Bellini and Altair as well as Garrincha and Pelé – Brazil took on the East Europeans in a fairly brutal encounter. The 2-0 win flattered the world champions, who scored through free kicks from Pelé and Garrincha, in the 15th and 63rd minutes. The result could have given Brazil a boost, but in fact the team finished that game in tatters.

Pelé was ruled out for the second game, against Hungary, and with only three days between the two fixtures several players failed to recover in time – not helped by the team's sub-par fitness standards. The lack of more experienced players meant newcomers Gérson and Tostão were drafted in to try to inject some energy into the squad. Tostão, who had replaced Pelé, seemed undaunted in filling the iconic player's position in the team and scored a crucial equaliser to cancel out the Hungarians' first-minute strike. But a jaded Brazil could not hold on and Hungary soon retook control of the match. Two more goals settled proceedings and left Brazil in a very delicate situation. Not for the first time in a World Cup the Seleção would play the last group game with qualification still in the balance. This time, however, they not only needed to win against an impressive Portuguese outfit, but also hope that Hungary would fail to defeat Bulgaria.

Portugal boasted eight players from the Benfica side that had lifted the 1962 European Cup and would prove to be a dominant force throughout the decade. The star of their team was Eusébio, the goal-scoring machine who would net 317 goals in 301 games for Benfica and 41 in 64 for the national team during his illustrious career. Having come top of their group in the European qualifiers, Portugal hit the ground running at the 1966 World Cup, defeating Hungary 3-1 and Bulgaria 3-0. Their story was even more interesting because a Brazilian had plotted their rise.

Born in Rio de Janeiro in 1917, Otto Glória is still a rare case of a Brazilian manager with a successful record abroad. After a stint at Rio sides Botafogo and Vasco in the late 1940s he was hired by Benfica in 1954 and oversaw a transformation at the Lisbon club both on and off the pitch. Glória helped develop new training facilities for Benfica and pestered the directors to scout for talent in the former Portuguese colonies in Africa, a move that would later result in the discovery of Eusébio in Mozambique. Between 1954 and 1959, Benfica went on to win the Portuguese League twice and lift the Portuguese Cup three times. Glória wasn't at the helm when Benfica won the European Cup, but he had laid the foundations for that success. In 1968, the Brazilian was back in charge when Benfica took on Manchester United at Wembley in another European Cup final – they lost, thanks to the genius of George Best and Bobby Charlton – but Gloria's return to Benfica had been stimulated by his stint with Portugal at their maiden World Cup.

Feola was obviously aware of the danger represented by the Portuguese. In an attempt to counter them he decided to completely reshuffle his team for the decisive game. With nine changes, including the dropping of the fading Garrincha, many felt that the Seleção had lost the match before they had even stepped foot on to the Goodison Park pitch on 19 July.

In much better shape and state of mind, the Portuguese followed Bulgaria's tactic of targeting Pelé. By today's standards their roughhouse tactics would have resulted in a collective GBH charge for the Portuguese players (including Eusébio), but on the day, it drew no real reaction from English referee George McCabe. With lumps kicked out of him, Pelé could barely walk by the end and only stayed on the pitch because no substitutions were allowed at the time. Within just 15 minutes Portugal went 1-0 ahead, after reserve goalkeeper Manga fluffed a speculative Eusébio cross and managed to almost literally place the ball on the head of António Simões. It only took another 12 minutes for Eusébio to head in the second and put the game virtually beyond the reach of Brazil.

Rildo's 73rd-minute strike gave the Seleção a glimpse of hope but their ten-and-a-half-man team were finally put out of their misery by a thumping Eusébio strike five minutes from time. Bruised and beaten, the Seleção saw their dream of a third title replaced by the nightmare of a first-round exit that had not happened to them since 1934. In just three matches, Brazil had used 20 out of the 22 players they had taken to the competition. Only Zito, injured right before the competition, and youngster Edú did not see any action. Portugal went on to register an impressive campaign that ended in a close defeat to England in the semi-finals.

Havelange had a taste of how supporters felt about the Seleção when he was still at Goodison Park. Brazilian fans watching the game converged on the area near the tunnel to the dressing rooms and started angrily berating the CBD president. Nobody needed to be a clairvoyant to know much more heated scenes would take place in Rio de Janeiro when the team returned.

Fearing a hostile reception at the airport, Havelange called on the support of Commander Guilherme Bungner, the pilot of the DC-8 that would take the Seleção home. Bungner was also at the cockpit when the team flew from Chile four years before, and he came up with a solution: delay the departure from Heathrow for several hours so that the plane would arrive in Brazil in the middle of the night – a manoeuvre disguised as a technical problem. Even then the players were rushed through the airport at Rio de Janeiro and those waiting for flight connections were swiftly moved to other planes. 'It was like a military operation,' Pelé remembers.

Despite their early exit from the tournament, the players were treated to crocodile leather wallets and golden key rings by Havelange as a thank-you for their participation. The president also gave Feola a seven-day, all-expenses-paid holiday in London so that the manager, terrified by news that supporters had stoned the windows of his house in São Paulo, could compose himself – but this proved to be a golden handshake as the president terminated his contract upon his return home. It would prove to be the manager's last job before his death in 1975; his career and health never recovered from the aggressive scrutiny post-'66.

Brazil had come back empty-handed and the Seleção's fall from grace mirrored a troubled political landscape at home. Two years before, a military coup had seized power by deposing President João Goulart, whose flirtation with radical left-wing economic reforms had scared the Brazilian middle classes enough for conservative groups to march on the streets of Rio and São Paulo in rallies that attracted more than 1.5 million people. Goulart's ascension in itself was a consequence of a political crisis triggered in 1961 by the resignation of the then president, Jânio Quadros. Thanks to the quirkiness of an electoral system that allowed separate votes for the two top jobs, Goulart had been elected Quadros' vice-president in 1960. Since assuming power, however, he had struggled to maintain his grip on it, facing a referendum to change the Brazilian political system to a parliamentary democracy. The March 1964 putsch put an end to Goulart's reign and the army-led takeover quickly descended into a dictatorship, with suspended political rights and the cancellation of free elections.

At the time, the generals and assorted officials did not immediately turn their attentions to the activities of the national team, in contrast to the Vargas regime decades before. The Seleção, for example, hosted the Soviet Union for a friendly at the Maracanã in 1965 – ironically, another game in which Manga the goalie dropped a clanger by taking a poor goal kick that ricocheted off the head of a Russian striker and hit the net when Brazil were leading 2-1. But the fury caused by the Seleção's fiasco in England started to change the political picture. Figures close to the Brazilian president, General Costa e Silva, wanted a full inquiry into the World Cup preparations but thankfully for

Havelange the idea didn't take off. Decades later more direct political meddling in Brazilian football would actually take place, ironically, in a democratically elected parliament. But while the generals were kept at bay, Havelange still had a lot of work to do.

Brazil's shambles in England had not done the CBD president any favours in his potential challenge for the top job at FIFA, but his plans for ascension to that throne had to be put aside while he tidied up his office in Brazil in order to avoid another pathetic performance in Mexico in 1970. The early return from England was manna from heaven for Havelange's enemies in Brazil. Before his decision to travel to England as supreme commander, Havelange claimed he invited several substitutes for the *chef de mission* role before deciding to lead the troops in person for the first time. The Brazilian media, however, had a field day and thanks to the popularity of the 'Marshall' it all became a story of how the CBD president had decided to hog the limelight.

Behind the scenes, Machado was reportedly preparing an insurgent campaign to unseat Havelange in the 1967 CBD elections, having enlisted Pelé as a possible lieutenant to win votes – although the player would, years later, happily stand by Havelange's side during his proper push towards the FIFA presidency. After dreaming of establishing a legendary status for Brazilian football with a third consecutive World Cup, Havelange had woken up with the old divisions rekindled in his country and a hate campaign mounting against him in the press, in which he was accused of either being a dictator or of being too weak to successfully steer Brazilian footballing affairs.

The whole debacle got under his skin and decades later it would still haunt the godfather of Brazilian football. 'I have over 12 hours of interviews with Dr Havelange and the only time there was proper regret in his words about his work was when 1966 became the subject,' says biographer Ernesto Ribeiro.

Havelange soldiered on. But first he had to deal with another kind of potential crisis. The excruciating number of games for club and country and the violent treatment at the hands of his markers in England had taken its toll on Pelé. In an outburst right after the defeat to Portugal he had announced his intention to retire from the Seleção. 'The whole competition had lost some of its allure for me. My legs had taken a battering and I had found the violence and the lack of sportsmanship as dispiriting as the weak refereeing that allowed it to go unchecked for so long,' he wrote. Giving the man a break was urgently required if there was to be any hope of making Pelé change his mind. Brazil's most famous player had his doubters, though. After his injury in 1962 and the 1966 woes, Pelé's reputation had been affected back home. 'Pelé was only 25 but there were already people thinking the Seleção needed to start to move on – which was a ludicrous idea,' said Carlos Alberto Torres. 'But it was clear the whole 1966 experience had affected him badly. Even with the shambles of our preparation, nobody really expected Brazil to perform so badly in England.'

Torres would go on to captain Brazil in Mexico, but he had been one of the more puzzling absentees from the final 1966 squad. 'Carlos Alberto was one of our fittest players and nobody really understood why he was left out of the squad,' said Pelé.

What became clear to the players was that Brazil had been overrun by European opposition not simply because of the problems relating to their fitness routines pre-World Cup but because football as a game at international level had changed in terms of physicality and strategy since 1962. 'That World Cup raised the bar in terms of athleticism and the Seleção didn't know how to cope,' said Carlos Alberto. 'Two years after the World Cup, we played West Germany in Stuttgart and still weren't up to their fitness standards.' Tostão remembers the game for other reasons. Although he agrees with his former team-mate that Brazil lost the muscle battle in 1966, it was the tactical imbalance that alarmed him more. 'We had stopped in time after 1962 and expected the world to simply do the same. But when we arrived in England for the World Cup we could see that the Europeans were playing in a much more compact and organised way than us.'

Tostão remembers an impromptu team meeting after the game in Stuttgart where he and future 1970 stars Gérson and Rivelino debated for hours what, in their opinion, had been a rout at the hands of the Germans, albeit only a 2-1 scoreline on paper. And they decided to take matters into their own hands. 'The three of us pretty much mutinied. During the next game, against Poland in Warsaw, we formed a midfield line that would protect us a bit more and at the same time support the strikers – because we couldn't simply pretend that nothing was going on. But the stimulus for the evolution in our tactics had been 1966. Without that train wreck I don't think we would have shaped up in time for 1970. Honestly. Oh, and we beat Poland 6-3.'

Neither the Germany nor Poland games featured Pelé, who endured a two-year absence from the national team, although the striker still featured in Santos' demanding tours of international friendlies, which included a visit to Nigeria in the middle of its civil war with Biafra. He would return to the Seleção in July 1968 for a match against Paraguay, announcing his comeback with a brace of goals.

Away from the pitch, Havelange was trying to sort out the mess that his political ambitions had created. He publicly assumed responsibility for the 1966 failure, but for decades also vented his anger at what he considered a biased attitude towards Brazil from referees and organisers in England. In a 2008 interview with Brazilian newspaper *Folha de S. Paulo*, marking the 50th anniversary of the 1958 victory, the former CBD president revealed what he considered an obvious conspiracy in favour of Alf Ramsey's England team in 1966, which resulted in them lifting the World Cup. Havelange ignored the limitations of the Brazilian squad but still found 'evidence' of wrongdoings. 'We had basically the same team that had won in 1962,' he said. 'The FIFA president was Stanley Rous, an Englishman; the World Cup was in England; two out of our three group matches had an English referee. Why? So that they could help kill my team. Pelé was fouled repeatedly and no action was taken. I met Stanley Rous shortly after the World Cup in an event and refused to shake his hand. I told him he needed to take a good look at himself for the blatant sabotage against my team.'

Brazil needed to regroup for Mexico 1970 and rebuild the team. Easier said than done; between 1967 and '68, the Seleção still looked far from convincing on the pitch and the press had their knives out again after an embarrassing 2-1 defeat to Mexico at the Maracanã. The decision to bank on another returning manager – Aymoré Moreira, who coached the 1962 World Cup team – was clearly not working and many people in Brazil began to look towards the South American qualifiers with trepidation. Moreira was duly relieved of his duties at the end of 1968 and the successor Havelange named for the vacant spot stunned even some of his closest allies: Brazil would challenge for a place in the 1970 World Cup with a journalist at the helm. A journalist known for his links to the Brazilian Communist Party at a time when the dictatorship had entered its most vicious period after the ascent of General Emilio Médici.

In February 1969, João Saldanha was unveiled as the new 'professor' in charge of the Seleção's destiny. Saldanha's appointment was even more surprising given the fact he had been one of the fiercest critics of the team's failure in England – in a highly charged article, Saldanha had given Havelange (although without mentioning him specifically by name) the mother of all dressing-downs. 'It is time the command of Brazilian football shaped up,' he wrote. 'They need to be less patronising, more humble and work their socks off so that Brazilian football can rise from the ashes of Liverpool.' Now Saldanha, whose coaching career had been limited to a stint at Botafogo in 1948, had been asked to help with that rise. 'It was a masterstroke,' said Carlos Alberto. 'Havelange was being criticised in the press and now he had brought one of them to power. Saldanha was also a very popular man and the appointment bought time with the supporters, which was crucial.'

The more surprising reaction, however, came from the government, which did not oppose Saldanha's appointment despite his political leanings. Despite the apparent cosiness that Havelange shared with the dictatorship, the CBD president was far from a feted figure within the military. First of all, one of his best friends was former Brazilian president Juscelino Kubitschek, who governed the country between 1956 and '61 but was exiled in 1964 after his political rights were suspended by the coup. Havelange also had a cordial relationship with 'Jango' Goulart. While one can certainly be uncomfortable with the way the future FIFA president seemed to be at ease in the company of dictators, it is also curious that Saldanha, whose political principles were very open, didn't seem too bothered about working for a regime that was torturing and killing fellow Marxist sympathisers.

In any case, Saldanha's appointment was a huge gamble and after the initial shock, the Brazilian press began to prophesise doom for the qualifiers. But the players could not have responded better to the new arrival: the Seleção steamrollered their opponents, winning all six matches. Led by Tostão and Pelé, they scored 25 goals and conceded only two. In the final game of that campaign, a record attendance (which still stands today) of 183,341 people filled the Maracaná to watch the 1-0 victory over Paraguay. The Seleção had won back their supporters.

As Brazil finished 1969 it seemed that they were at last ready to leave 1966 and all that behind. But not so fast. Never a humble character, Saldanha seemed to let the success go to his head. While skirmishes with fellow journalists didn't really bother anyone, the manager raised some eyebrows when his relationship with the players became less than cordial. The situation was made even more delicate by the fact that Saldanha was bickering with none other than Pelé. In March 1970, they had a showdown in front of the other players and technical staff after the striker stood up and erased the manager's tactical plan from the blackboard, a few days before a friendly against Argentina. As well as confronting the players Saldanha also went public, saying Pelé had eyesight problems. The atmosphere soured even further when the manager reportedly refused to give team instructions before a meaningless friendly against Bangu, a minnow Rio side, on 14 March, which ended in a 1-1 draw.

Havelange felt compelled to act and called the manager for a meeting, only to get little sense from Saldanha, who constantly tried to change the subject or talked endlessly about irrelevant matters. Players and technical staff would later report that the manager was prone to heavy drinking binges, a theory that doesn't seem that absurd in the case of a man who once invaded the Flamengo team hotel with a gun in his hand in order to have 'an eye-to-eye' conversation with manager Dorival 'Yustrich' Knipel, who had been criticising his methods. Three days after the Bangu game, Saldanha inflamed the situation further by dropping Pelé from the starting XI for a friendly against Chile. Another meeting was called, this time at the CBD headquarters in downtown Rio and Havelange, in front of Saldanha, demanded a report from supervisor Antonio do Passo. After asking the manager if what Passo said was true, which was confirmed, the president announced that Saldanha was to be relieved of his duties. Saldanha promptly started to berate Havelange furiously, to which the president calmly replied: 'You are still under contract to CBD. If you have any criticism, please go outside and do it.'

And that's exactly what Saldanha did. In front of a waiting media scrum, the manager reported that his sacking had been motivated by a refusal to accept the imposed call-up of Atlético Mineiro striker Dario, who General Médici had wanted in the World Cup squad. Havelange, Saldanha claimed, had bowed under pressure from the dictator and had demanded that the manager should bring the player into the group. 'I had them tell the president to mind his business with the ministries while I took care of the Seleção,' Saldanha vented to the reporters. He missed a chance to point out that he wasn't absolutely wrong over his decision to drop Pelé. While the striker had reached the 1,000-goal milestone the previous year that galvanised his legendary status, his form for the national team had been relatively poor and the media criticism seemed to be getting under Pelé's skin, especially after the crowds started booing him at some Seleção games. When Saldanha dropped him for the Chile game, even Mario Zagallo supported the decision publicly by stating that, 'Pelé's performances recently have been detrimental to the Seleção.'

A lot of the hullaballoo was motivated by Pelé's recently signed new contract with Santos, which would pay him the equivalent of £180,000 for two years, a huge sum for 1970s Brazil. The fee commanded by the King of Football obviously raised huge interest from the public and satirists promptly pounced: a famous newspaper cartoon had Pelé sitting on money bags while giving an interview in which he pleads for the country to look after poor children – a gag inspired by the famous message the striker had given to a sea of microphones after scoring the milestone goal a year before. 'Neither the media nor the public know anything about football,' complained Pelé in 1970, 'but they are always looking for reasons to analyse our games. Supporters think we have to rout teams at every game because of what they read in the newspapers.'

The Dario story, nonetheless, was obviously too good to be ditched. After all, contrary to many of his predecessors, Médici was indeed a football fan who had actually tried to play professionally at Grêmio de Bagé, a small side from Southern Brazil. He never shied away from posing for pictures with a ball or in the Maracanã VIP stand. Médici was also more than a hard-line general. He understood the value that the Seleção could add to his efforts to win the hearts and minds of the general public in Brazil and perhaps the sole reason for his silence during the whole Saldanha crisis was the fact that his government was busy trying to contain a public relations disaster after reports of torture against political prisoners had reached the American media and even Pope Paul VI. But he made himself much more available to Havelange than his predecessor, General Castelo Branco, and the CBD called upon more financial resources than ever before to fund preparations for the trip to Mexico.

One thing Médici didn't have to worry about was whether Saldanha's replacement was going to be another volatile character. Havelange picked Mário Zagallo, a man who had two World Cup -winning medals as a player and who was famed for his love of the Seleção and Brazil. Having retired from the national team in 1964 with 36 caps and 29 victories, Zagallo took over the manager's job at

Botafogo three years later and the Rio side went on to end a six-year trophy drought by winning two Rio State Leagues and one Brazilian Cup in the space of two seasons. But the main reason for bringing him to the Seleção was that he knew the players well – and in the case of Gérson and Pelé had actually played alongside them – and he was highly regarded as a footballer who had thought outside the box.

In 1958, it had been Zagallo who had detected the flaw in the 4-2-4 system Brazil would use in the World Cup. 'We were getting exposed in midfield with only two men so it was fundamental that one of the wingers came back to reinforce the line. I was the one doing that for Brazil,' says the man who the press nicknamed 'the ant' for his tireless tactical work – he could score too, having netted the fourth goal in Brazil's 5-2 demolition of Sweden in the 1958 World Cup final. Whether General Médici had an influence or not over the new Seleção order, the fact is that when Zagallo took over Dario became part of the squad. 'Dario had been the top scorer everywhere he played. That's why I called him up,' explained Zagallo.

Whatever the Dario situation, there is no doubt that the regime was following the developments closely. Education minister Jarbas Passarinho, to whose office the CBD was legally subordinated, had several meetings with Havelange and in one of these he imposed the presence of Brigadier Jeronimo Bastos as *chef de mission*. His arrival, alongside the presence of men with military backgrounds in the technical staff, such as Captain Cláudio Coutinho, who oversaw the fitness regime, would later be used as an example of the militarisation of the Seleção – although this claim does seem a bit exaggerated. Coutinho, for example, was one of the biggest authorities in Brazil when it came to new fitness and had even spent a season in the United States in an exchange programme with the feted Dr Kenneth Cooper; he was also was a fine manager who would take the Seleção job to the 1978 World Cup and could have won more trophies than the 1980 Brazilian championship with Flamengo had he not drowned in a scuba diving accident in Rio de Janeiro that same year. His input proved to be crucial in getting the players physically prepared for

Mexico. Unlike the previous tournament, Brazil's preparation was thorough and included a lengthy period of altitude adaptation and five staff dedicated to improving fitness levels. 'It was a scientific job and each player had an individually tailored programme,' said Carlos Alberto Parreira, who was also part of the fitness team and who went on to manage the Seleção in two World Cups, including USA 1994, when Brazil lifted their fourth title.

As for Zagallo, he did not make the same mistakes as Feola. Although his initial reaction was to drop Tostão, a player he considered incompatible with Pelé, he would later reconsider and turn the 'Little Coin' into one of the first false number 9s in the history of football. Tostão's tactical awareness and ability to create space was perfectly exemplified by the run he made which set up Jairzinho for the winning goal against England in the group stages in Mexico. The mention that part of the move included nutmegging Bobby Moore brings a little giggle from Tostão before he addresses the cloud of uncertainty under which the Seleção had departed for Mexico. 'Everybody was still talking about 1966, so traumatising had that experience been. But we players knew from the start that the preparation this time was spot-on. It also helped that we did not have 40-odd players in the training squad.' Ironically, none of the centre-forwards taken to Mexico actually convinced the manager that they could do a better job than Tostão, who he shoe-horned into the position – including the controversial Dario, who didn't even make it to the bench for any of the six games Brazil played in the tournament.

The disparity in the approaches adopted for 1966 and 1970 was so vast that it seemed as if 40 years instead of four had passed since the debacle in Liverpool. Even the team shirts were redesigned to prevent collars from gathering sweat in the Mexican heat and each player's kit was bespoke. The Mexican World Cup was the first one broadcast live on television in Brazil, although unlike European and American audiences the resounding majority of Brazilians still had to sit in front of black and white TV sets. Among them was João Havelange.

Technically, he had not returned to his habit of distancing himself from the players, since he had flown to Mexico for the opening ceremony, but he flew back without watching Brazil's debut at the tournament – a 4-1 drubbing of Czechoslovakia.

On the afternoon on 21 June 1970, when another 4-1 score gave Brazil their third world title and a permanent hold on the Jules Rimet trophy, the phone rang at the CBD president's apartment in Leblon, the charming seaside neighbourhood in Rio de Janeiro. On the other end of the line was Emilio Médici. Like Kubitschek in 1958 and Goulart in 1962, he wanted to host the world champions at the presidential palace. His wish was duly granted: Havelange and the team met with the general in Brasilia (the new national capital, founded in 1960) and took pictures with the trophy before flying to Rio for a rapturous reception on the streets of the city that curiously divided opinion – some thought the regime were using the carnival atmosphere of the victory to divert attention from the brutality of its political oppression, while others argued the streets were symbolically reclaimed by the people during the celebrations.

Fours year later, the lives of the two presidents – Havelange and Médici – would take very different turns. And Brazilian football would find itself a victim of its own success.

1974

THREE

1974
THE KING IS GONE BUT
(DEFINITELY) NOT FORGOTTEN

WHEN BELGIAN REFEREE Vital Loreaux blew the whistle for half-time at the Maracanã on the afternoon of 18 July 1971, 138,000 people in the stands felt as if the world had come to a standstill. Brazil were playing Yugoslavia and it was Pelé's last game in a Seleção shirt. After 14 years and 123 games, he had decided that his international career was over. Visibly moved by the screams of 'Stay!' coming from the crowd, he did a lap of honour around the pitch and soaked up the adulation. It was a much more emotional affair than his first farewell a week earlier in São Paulo, after a game against Austria, although the crowd at the Morumbi Stadium could brag to their Rio counterparts that they had at least witnessed Pelé's 95th and last goal for Brazil.

At 29, Pelé was hardly damaged goods and his physical conditioning could certainly have allowed him to go on for another couple of years, perhaps even to a fourth World Cup. Only he didn't want to. 'The World Cup win in 1970 made me think about retiring from football, beginning with the national squad, to spend more time with my family,' he said. 'My father always told me that one should leave by the front door. It was time for me and for the Seleção to move on.'

If the man Brazilians called 'the King' felt the time was right for him to retire, the rest of the country certainly did not. And even if the Seleção had been preparing carefully for the inevitable day when Pelé would quit or his body would quit on him, there wasn't any way that the departure of such an important and iconic player and personality could be easily managed. And to make matters worse for the Seleção management, his was not the only noticeable retirement as the beautiful dream team of 1970 began to break apart.

From 1971 to 1973, Brazil would also see Clodoaldo, Carlos Alberto, Gérson and Tostão exit the stage. Already in his thirties, Gérson fell victim to the physical evolution of the international game, while Carlos Alberto had to eventually admit defeat to a chronic knee injury. Tostão's retirement was a different matter altogether and much more dramatic. In 1969, he was hit twice in the left eye by clearance kicks that led to lesions forming on his retina. Surgery in the United States had not only made it possible for him to be Brazil's top scorer in the World Cup qualifiers but also ensured that he would go on to win the tournament alongside Pelé and co in 1970. In 1972, Vasco broke the Brazilian transfer record to sign the midfielder from Cruzeiro, but just ten months later, the risk of losing his eyesight led to his complete retirement from football. He was only 26.

The loss of such key players made the already herculean task of defending a World Cup in Germany in 1974 all the more arduous. The Seleção would have to blood several new players and try to regroup without the guidance of their most valued senior players in order to stand any chance of defending their crown. Few people believed they would have the means or the men to do it. Matters would not be helped by political intrusions off the pitch, starting with a much more open declaration of intent than ever before from the military government to use football as a political tool. While the association of governments and sport was a strong characteristic in the development of football in Brazil, it took just half a decade for the 1964 revolutionaries to follow suit – thanks in large part to General Médici's love of the game. Success in the 1970 World Cup, however, had taken things to a whole new level. While it is condescending to suggest that Brazilians ignored the actions of a violent and repressive regime every time a football rolled, there is no doubt that the exploits of the Seleção in Mexico contributed to a goodwill factor that played perfectly into the hands of political spin doctors working for Arena, the governing party. In the parliamentary elections of November

1970, Arena won a landslide victory that included 223 of the 310 seats in the Brazilian version of the House of Commons.

The early 1970s marked a period still officially known as the 'Brazilian Miracle', in which the country experienced an unprecedented economic boost, with GDP growing at over 10 per cent a year and colossal levels of investment made in huge infrastructural projects, such as Brazil's first nuclear power plant and the 13-kilometre bridge linking Rio de Janeiro to the neighbouring coastal city of Niterói, which for decades was one of the longest bridges in the world. Interestingly, construction of the bridge was started in 1969 with the blessing of Queen Elizabeth II, whose official visit to Rio included a meeting with Pelé at the Maracaná before a friendly between Brazil and England.

Sport remained a high political priority and between 1969 and 1975 there was a boom in stadium construction around the country. Areas where football was still semi-professional suddenly had huge arenas. In total, 30 new grounds popped up across Brazil. As part of the government's efforts for 'national integration' in the football landscape, it imposed the creation of the first Brazilian Championship in 1971. Up until then, Brazil was the only major footballing nation that did not have a tournament properly contested by teams from across the country. There were a number of logistical problems that had prevented its inception earlier, key among them the vast geographical distances that needed to be travelled, and for that reason alone both clubs and players had been happy for the game to remain regionalised.

State championships dragged immense crowds to stadiums, especially in Rio and São Paulo, and six out of the ten most attended games in the Maracaná's history were Rio state championship games. In 1976, for example, 174,599 spectators witnessed Flamengo's 3-1 win over Vasco – a crowd number that was only outstripped by the 1950 World Cup final and the Seleçao's 1-0 win over Paraguay in the 1970 qualifiers.

Mirroring Brazil's political and economic structure, where the south-east of the country had historically experienced greater development, Rio and São Paulo had the country's biggest clubs and the embryonic version of a national championship had taken place in the 1950s and '60s, with teams from both states contesting the tournament. But in 1959, Conmebol, South America's football governing body, decided to emulate the European Cup by forming the Copa Libertadores; in turn, the CBD created the Brazilian Trophy, a cup whose winner would be the Brazilian representative in the Copa Libertadores – as only champion clubs would compete in the new tournament. In that same year, EC Bahia caused a legendary upset by defeating Pelé's Santos over three games in the final – to give an idea of how unlikely the result had seemed, it took the north-eastern Brazilian club 29 years to win a major national trophy again. Santos, however, would win the tournament five times in a row (1961–65), bagging two Libertadores and Intercontinental titles along the way. Interestingly, their 1962 triumph was against Eusébio's Benfica, whose main players would later have the last laugh against the King in the 1966 World Cup.

The Brazilian Trophy evolved into another tournament between teams from five southern states: the Roberto Gomes Pedrosa trophy, named after the Brazilian goalkeeper at the 1934 World Cup. In 1971, however, 20 teams from eight states were contesting what was playfully nicknamed 'Médici's trophy'. Teams were divided into two groups of ten, playing 19 matches in a league format before the top four of each group advanced to a second round where teams would be placed in three groups of four, in a double round-robin format. Each pool winner moved to a top three final round, where three single games decided the champion – in this case, Atlético Mineiro, with a 1-0 victory over Botafogo at the Maracanã. The format was confusing but guaranteed a festival of matches around the country, something that the CBD and Havelange delighted in since, by law, the governing body was entitled to 5 per cent of gate receipts of every match taking place at an interstate level in Brazil.

While London with its ten or more professional clubs is a football abnormality in Europe, a plurality of participants in Brazilian cities was much more common, although mostly in Rio and São Paulo, which were able to organise heavily populated state leagues with results that were much less predictable than in places like Porto Alegre, where Internacional and Grêmio have, respectively, 42 and 36 state crowns. The logistical challenge of playing a nationwide tournament was also hard on supporters. Travelling fan bases are a relatively recent phenomenon in Brazil, a country whose transport infrastructure still lacks a proper railway system and where air travel has only in the last few years become more accessible to the working class. Which is why episodes like 'The Corinthian Invasion of 1976', when more than 50,000 supporters from São Paulo club SC Corinthians descended upon the Maracanã for a semi-final tie in the 1976 Brazilian Championship, are still the stuff of legend.

Not surprisingly, the Brazilian Championship has never reached the attendance level registered at state competitions. It has never reached the 25,000 spectators per game mark and attendances have experienced a steep decline since the 1980s, although other variables are responsible for this. The combination of political interest and financial greed led to a swelling of team participation in the early years of the Brazilian Championship. The First Division, which started with 20 teams in 1971, featured 40 teams three years later. In 1978 there were 74 clubs and 1979 marked the year when 94 teams, a total greater than the four English professional leagues combined, took part in the competition, including teams from regions and cities where the government wanted to please local authorities or to gather public support.

But the government also saw football as a powerful PR tool for Brazil's international image. Amid the concern abroad about news of torture and repression ravaging any opposition to the military, President Médici's court decided that a great way to publicise normality – or to at least try – was to throw a huge football party. In 1971, Havelange was summoned to Brasilia to meet Médici, who then explained his idea for an international tournament that would officially serve as a celebration of the 150th anniversary of

Brazil's independence from Portugal. According to Havelange's own memories, General Médici already had the whole plan for the Independence Cup in mind and began to explain it in detail the minute he opened the door to his office. He envisaged a tournament that would be contested by 20 teams from around the world – with England and Germany as the main international attractions – that would tour the main Brazilian cities. In Havelange's calculations, the whole enterprise would cost around US$66 million in today's money, but the hefty bill didn't seem to concern the president.

It was a different story when the time came to invite the teams. England, Germany and Italy declined to travel to Brazil. Many people are still unsure as to whether these decisions were based on human rights principles or the politics of FIFA. Havelange had used a 1971 lunch in central London with the governing body's president, Stanley Rous, to formalise his decision to stand against the Englishman in the 1974 Congress. In Brazil, the refusal from the major European nations to attend the tournament is still seen as an act of sporting retaliation from Rous. Another European nation that refused to attend the 'Minicup', as the Independence Cup quickly became nicknamed, was Holland. At the time, Brazil's most famous football magazine, *Placar* (*Score*, in Portuguese), sarcastically declared that the Dutch would not be missed. The irony of that statement would resonate strongly at the 1974 World Cup.

In the end, Britain was represented at the Independence Cup by Scotland, who joined Czechoslovakia, the Soviet Union, Yugoslavia, Ireland, France and Portugal as the European contingent. There were also the likes of Argentina and Uruguay and assorted South American neighbours, alongside Iran and multinational teams representing Africa and the CONCACAF area. Twelve cities hosted games, including Manaus, with all its Amazonian heat and humidity.

To the joy of generals and fans, Brazil won the tournament thanks to a last-gasp goal by Jairzinho in the final match against former colonial ruler, Portugal. The game attracted almost 100,000 people to the Maracanã, but it was hardly the kind of crowd that used to greet the Seleção in the days of Pelé. The organisers knew it and the tournament became the first official attempt to lure the King out of retirement. In his 2007 biography, Havelange says he personally invited Pelé to come back for the tournament in order to help raise interest from the public and media. According to him, Pelé demanded a special appearance fee in return for his participation, which the player would later deny. It marked the first shaky moment in the relationship between the two men, which would break down spectacularly 20 years later.

In the early '70s, however, Havelange could not afford a proper fallout with the King at the time when he was finally making his move on Rous. As soon as the 1970 World Cup was over, Havelange had a meeting with Mohand Maouche – the president of the Algerian FA – and his Ethiopian counterpart, Ydnekatchew Tessema, who were both flown to Brazil by Elias Zaccour, a savvy Lebanese immigrant who in the mid-1960s had the profitable idea of organising tours of Brazilian football teams through Africa and the Middle East and, apart from making a comfortable living, ended up meeting the CBD president during the World Cup in England in 1966.

This time, however, Zaccour was trying for something else: to broker a deal for the African football bigwigs to have a greater say at FIFA. The list of demands included more power and more World Cup places for nations from Africa, and the expulsion of South Africa altogether, where apartheid still ruled. The South African regime had already been punished by FIFA, but Stanley Rous was irking Tessema. There was a precious opportunity for Havelange to gather support among what we can call FIFA's gagged majority – the African continent's membership share in the world governing body in the early '70s amounted to less than a third. Havelange went for it, clocking up air miles despite his almost pathological fear of flying, meeting and greeting federation presidents in the four corners of the world. On some occasions, he took the Seleção alongside him, which explains the team's visits to Algeria and Tunisia in 1973. In total during his campaign, Havelange visited 86 countries.

While Stanley Rous initially had the endorsement of adidas supremo Adi Dassler, Havelange had Pelé. The King was duly drafted in to the Brazilian's campaign, joining him in meet and greet opportunities. If saying that it was Pelé who won the election is a bit of an overstatement given that Havelange's dealings with the Soviet bloc were crucial to making gains into the European vote, having the most famous player in the world by one's side was certainly a big help. In Havelange's own account, during his campaign for the presidency he came across more than 40 federation presidents who had asked to meet Pelé. His charm offensive did not go unnoticed: Havelange would later repay Pelé by pulling some strings with influential and rich friends in Brazil to help bail the player out of a bad investment he had made in a car parts factory.

The reasons why the Brazilian powerbroker wasn't sparing any effort to reach the FIFA presidency have been scrutinised to exhaustion. What few people have focused on, however, is the fact that in 1974 Jean-Marie Faustin Goedefroid de Havelange was a political 'dead man walking' in Brazil, having fallen out of favour with the Brazilian army cardinals. In March, President Emilio Médici had given way to Ernesto Geisel, who had quickly moved to install his own supporters in influential positions within the government. One of them, Admiral Adalberto Nunes, the all-powerful navy minister, was adamant that Havelange should pay for a previous 'offence' – the sacking of his brother, Admiral Heleno, years before.

Never Mr Popular with the military because of his friendships with two exiled ex-presidents – and also due to Nunes' perception that the CBD was spending too much money – Havelange knew he had it coming when Médici departed. Admiral Nunes was also certain that the CBD supremo often used the job for financial gain and believed he had found enough evidence to prove it. Before travelling to the FIFA congress in Frankfurt, where he would be elected as the first non-European president of FIFA, Havelange had already been warned by sources in Brasilia that regardless of the result his reign at the CBD had come to an end. His departure opened the way for an unlikely return for Admiral Heleno, who would preside over the ruling body from 1975 until 1980.

Brother Adalberto's revenge wasn't over, though. In January 1975, Nunes arrived at President Geisel's office in Brasilia with a dossier outlining his accusations regarding Havelange's financial activities. Alongside claims of embezzlement and assertions that he had used public money to help fund his presidential campaign, Havelange was accused of giving Pelé handouts, as early as 1965, to help cover creative tax returns. Furthermore, it hadn't gone unnoticed by the navy man that Havelange had blatantly disregarded the Brazilian government's official anti-communist stance by advocating China's reintegration to FIFA. There was enough ammunition for the military to make Havelange's life extremely uncomfortable – and Admiral Adalberto Nunes pressed for an investigation. President Geisel, however, decided to put a lid on the case: although Havelange was relieved of his duties in December 1974, the general authorised the use of the public purse to cover debts left by the CBD. It would come at another kind of cost, however: between 1975 and 1989, the most powerful man in football would be *persona non grata* in the sport's power circles in his own country, a significant irony for somebody who would stay in the FIFA presidency for 24 years.

It is hardly a surprise that this background environment would affect things on the pitch, and the Seleção had urgent matters to attend to in 1974. Things were not going well in their preparations for their title defence. Without the need to qualify for Germany, the Seleção's schedule had been radically curtailed. Pelé's farewell in Rio in 1971 marked the start of a period of almost 11 months without international games, which certainly did not help in the team's rebuilding process. Victory at the Minicup was celebrated as a positive sign, but the team still had Tostão, Gérson and Clodoaldo on board at the time.

A new generation of players capable of filling the huge shoes left behind was eagerly needed and so great expectations were placed on the Olympic squad that would contest the Munich Games in 1972.

A team featuring young guns Zico and Falcão, then mere promising players at their respective clubs, Flamengo and Internacional, qualified for the Olympics after an unbeaten run in Colombia. Only Falcão made it to the Summer Games: the rules preventing the presence of professional players in the Olympics forced Brazil to send a second-string team to Munich and it crashed and burned spectacularly, losing to Denmark and Iran and drawing with the Hungarians. Neither Zico nor Falcão made the squad for the 1974 World Cup.

After the Minicup, the Seleção reconvened in May 1973, with a 5-0 thrashing of Bolivia. In the following four weeks they managed to beat the Germans in Berlin and the Russians in Moscow, but they also experienced defeat against Italy and Sweden. The team played nine games in nine different countries in Europe and Africa. The mixed bag of results led to a lot of criticism from the media and things quickly descended into a showdown between players and journalists following the tour. After another lukewarm performance, this time against Scotland at Hampden Park, the Seleção stars released the 'Glasgow Manifesto', in which they stated their decision to stop giving interviews – with the blessing of the CBD command. In retaliation, the media stopped mentioning the players' names in their reports, albeit making it clear to readers who they were bashing. Tempers were flaring and the situation didn't get easier when footballers and hacks boarded the same aeroplane to fly back home – according to reports, goalkeeper Leão threatened to thump a member of the travelling press, but thankfully things didn't escalate any further than angry words.

In fairness, both Leão and the hack were probably angry for the same reason: the style of play of the Seleção circa 1973 did not bear any resemblance to the panache and fluidity that had marked the 1970 team. They had obviously suffered a huge loss of personnel and the absences led Zagallo to choose caution instead of audacity in his tactics. Spurred by his then exclusive place as the only man to have won the World Cup as both a player and a manager, Zagallo was understandably confident in his abilities. Indeed, his tactical tinkering had worked wonders in 1970, where he not only had succeeded into solving a tactical conundrum of being without an outstanding number 9, but had also played to the gallery by fitting all his star players into the same XI, which had helped bring the media and the fans onside. For better or worse, the picture was very different now.

Without the backbone that the team had had four years earlier, Zagallo reckoned the best approach for the title defence was built upon a solid defensive display. It should not be forgotten that the 1970 team had the worst-ever defensive record by a Brazilian winning side, shipping seven goals in six matches. Pelé and co had simply compensated brilliantly up front by scoring 19. This time around, however, Zagallo and many people in Brazil were not quite sure the Seleção had enough attacking firepower to balance their defensive frailties.

In fairness to Zagallo, he gets very little credit for also sorting out the defensive system of the 1970 team. Many people will immediately cite Tostão's 'false 9' role and instead forget the centre-back partnership of that side also relied on improvisation. In order to compensate for all the attacking players he had selected and the marauding full-backs (Carlos Alberto's goal against Italy in the final being an example of how Brazilian players in that position love going forward), Zagallo decided to use Wilson Piazza, a defensive midfielder, as a centre-back, which also allowed the gifted Clodoaldo to slot into midfield to protect the back four. Piazza was once again playing in that role for the Seleção in the build-up to Germany '74, but his partner from 1970, Brito, gave way to Luis Pereira, a behemoth of a defender who was an integral part of Palmeiras, a club side that in the early '70s was laying down a marker for a long domination of domestic football.

Founded by members of the huge Italian diaspora in São Paulo, whose cultural influence in the city (and in the country, as a certain Luiz Felipe Scolari will attest) was strong enough for the *paulista* accent to sound Italian, the club played second fiddle to Santos for most of the 1960s, pretty much like every other side in Brazil. But by the end of the decade, there was a sea change. Santos, even before Pelé retired from the national team, were already struggling to fend off challengers for their crown. After winning the 1968 Gomes Pedrosa and the 1969 São Paulo championship, Santos would only lift the 1973 championship before an 11-year dry spell. Their performances were certainly not helped by a gruesome calendar of global exhibition tours that were needed to balance the books at home.

And, boy, did Santos travel: the King himself clocked up a staggering 1,114 appearances for the club between 1956 and 1974. Of these, only around 640 were competitive games. Pelé averaged 58.6 games a season during his 19 years at the club, and in only five of those seasons did he wear the Santos shirt less than 60 times. Good as they were at attracting top talent in Brazil, Santos were not immune to the effects of time. Alongside Botafogo they had been the greatest provider of players to the 1958, '62 and '70 teams and suffered accordingly with the changing of the guard.

Meanwhile, Palmeiras had been building what their fanatical supporters would nickname 'the Academy'. They announced their arrival by twice winning the Gomes Pedrosa and the Brazilian Trophy between 1967 and 1969 and took the early '70s by storm with back-to-back Brazilian titles (1972–73) and two São Paulo state crowns (1972 and 1974). In Leão they had arguably one of the best Brazilian goalkeepers of all time, while Luis Pereira did more than merely defend: he scored more than 50 goals in a career that included six seasons in Spain at Atlético Madrid. Ademir da Guia, son of legendary defender Domingos da Guia, was an attacking midfielder whose composure would earn him the nickname 'Divine'.

Little surprise, then, that Palmeiras ended up having the greatest representation of any club in the Seleção squad in Germany. Six out of the 22 players called up by Zagallo hailed from the Academy, among them striker João Leiva, whose nephew Lucas would, three decades later, become a Liverpool FC regular. They joined the likes of Rivelino and Jairzinho, who together had 128 caps for Brazil, although none of them had yet reached 30. In theory, a good balance between newcomers and veterans. In reality, however, the team did not seem to gel and in a run of 12 friendlies before the World Cup they came through with a series of unconvincing 1-0 wins and some embarrassing results, such as a draw against French side Racing Strasbourg and a hard-fought 3-2 'triumph' over a Southwest Germany XI.

Four years earlier, the Seleção had also travelled to Mexico with some less than encouraging results under their belts, but this time the King would not be leading his men into battle and some of his most battle-hardened knights had also exited the realm. 'The 1974 squad was a very good team. But they weren't as good as our 1970 team,' reflected Carlos Alberto. 'The problem was that a lot of people demanded that they were. Defending a World Cup title has never been an easy thing. From 1930 to 2010 only Brazil and Italy have managed to do it. And how can you underestimate the effects of the absence of a guy like Pelé on any team? Those guys in 1974 had a lot on their plates even before the World Cup started and they had to measure themselves against their predecessors.'

It didn't take a World Cup-winning captain to figure that out, mind you. Any person with the slightest knowledge about the game was aware that Pelé's departure had left the Seleção orphaned. And a few months earlier General Geisel had tried to intervene and had his daughter, Amalia, phone Pelé's apartment. 'Pelé, my father is asking you to play in the World Cup. This is important,' she said.

Thirty-two years later, Pelé recalls giving a short answer, explaining that he had already retired from the national team and reminded the president's daughter that there had even been two farewell games to mark the occasion. But the pressure placed on the King to reconsider his decision continued and the next attempt to coax him out of retirement came in the form of banker Antônio de Almeida Braga, a friend of Havelange's who had briefly served as director at the CBD and during his tenure in 1968 had given Pelé a helping hand by allowing him to miss some Seleção friendlies so that he could travel with Santos to earn special appearance fees. In an interview published in Havelange's 2007 biography, Braga explains that he asked Pelé directly if money would convince him to return to the Seleção. Pelé once again answered with the argument that he wanted to quit at the top. A decade later Pelé would mention for the first time that his refusal to return was also in protest at the lack of a fair democracy in Brazil. 'I was feeling fit to play but the reason I refused to come back was that I was too unhappy with the situation in my country,' explained the King in a TV interview in June 2013. 'The dictatorship was demanding too much from the people.'

The problem with Pelé's stand against the oppressive regime in Brazil is not in doubting his sincerity for wanting the freedom of democracy for his countrymen, but where his plea ranked in comparison to personal and financial interests. The King's inner circle, particularly Pelé's brother Jair, were horrified that he could be held responsible for the failure to win a fourth title for the Seleção – the 'Tetra', as Brazilians nicknamed it. Pelé also felt aggrieved that, in his opinion, the public and media in Brazil hadn't put up enough of a fight to keep him involved with the national team when he had announced his intention to retire. Last but not least, the King had found out that retirement would actually represent a very interesting business opportunity, since companies were reportedly falling over themselves to get his endorsement during the World Cup. Pelé would go on to make more money off the pitch than on it and would work in Germany doing PR for Pepsi during the tournament. 'Pelé was very private and he never mentioned to me any issues with the military,' said Carlos Alberto. 'In fact, we the players never really got involved with the politics. We had a job to do and that was playing football. So it comes as a surprise to me that he said anything about his retirement being a political statement. He was, however, saddened by how people accepted his retirement. At the time of his Seleção retirement there was this ludicrous argument that at 29 he was getting old. Rubbish.'

Regardless of the real reasons going through his head, Pelé's refusal caused another rift with Havelange, who wanted the player to grace his first World Cup as FIFA president. In his biography, Havelange claims that Pelé later admitted he had made a mistake. 'He told me that accepting my invitation could have earned him a fourth world title and that he regretted it.'

That, however, did not prevent the new FIFA supremo from lending Pelé a helping hand. It was thanks to Havelange's lobbying that the player got his big deal with Pepsi and Havelange's influence also put in motion Pelé's famous move to America and the New York Cosmos, which may have failed to make the Americans fall in love with soccer but represented financial salvation for the King – the deal to play for the Cosmos for two seasons, after he had officially retired from football, is reported to have earned Pelé US$9 million and 50 per cent of every commercial deal using the name he had trademarked as early as 1965. Pelé was therefore compensated for the decades when he could not even dream about leaving Brazil to play abroad. There were just too many pressures from several levels, to the point where the player was officially declared a 'national treasure', which legally forbade his departure; and thanks to bad advice and the shady dealings of agent Pepe Gordo, Pelé was virtually penniless at the beginning of the 1970s. That seemed to be occupying a much bigger part of his thoughts than any induced U-turn to rescue the Seleção in Germany and the whole protest argument has never been echoed by any of his team-mates, even the ones with more leftist tendencies such as Tostão. 'We didn't get involved with politics and much of that happened because a lot of people in Brazil were kept in the dark about what was going on in the country at the time,' said Tostão. 'We were never told what to say or felt at any time that we were being used, although everybody knew we lived under a dictatorship.'

It is tempting to speculate about what impact Pelé would have had in Germany. Football had been moving fast towards a much more physical game and even in Brazil Pelé was, at least statistically, slowing down. In his last full year as a professional player (1973), the King had scored his lowest total of goals since 1966. It was still an astounding total of 45 in 66 games, but his averages were decreasing.

Alongside brother Jair, one of Pelé's closest advisors had been Júlio Mazzei, one of the most respected fitness coaches in Brazil and a man who would also manage the Cosmos. He had been against the return and may have pointed to his declining powers to state his case.

On the other hand, it is valid to think that the presence of Pelé would certainly have had a positive effect on morale, both inside and outside the Brazil camp in Germany. 'Tell me a single player who would say he'd fancy marking Pelé, please,' jokes Carlos Alberto. His experience would also have helped settle the nerves in the team that was burdened by expectation back home to repeat the feats of 1970.

In the end, Pelé did go to Germany – but to walk around wearing Pepsi's colours and to work as a commentator for a Brazilian TV channel. He also took to the pitch in the opening ceremony, as part of a 'trophy exchange' gimmick with Germany's Uwe Seeler, who had also retired after 1970. Pelé would pay visits to his former team-mates and was clearly moved by the experience of not 'fighting' alongside them anymore. One episode, though, made his heart drop. During a conversation with 1970 squad colleague Paulo César, who had remained in the fold, Pelé claims César expressed his worries about getting more money from a deal he was negotiating with Olympique Marseille. 'Paulo cornered me to say he had a dilemma, but rather than worrying about tactics he couldn't decide whether to hold out for more money,' he recalled in his 2008 biography.

After allocating so much time and so many resources into football, the government wanted a Seleção victory as an endorsement of their vision for Brazilian society. 'Newspaper opinion pieces in 1974 invariably rambled on about the benefits of order and organisation in Brazilian football,' explains Brazilian writer and historian Marcos Guterman, whose work focuses on the use of football in the propaganda of the Brazilian authorities. 'It was quite common to find comments on how discipline would make Brazilian football invincible, uniting skill with European discipline.' The disciplinarian approach would mean isolation for the Seleção, whose headquarters in Feldberg in the Black Forest never really made the players feel comfortable – and nor did the extensive security put in place by the German authorities in reaction to the kidnap and murder of Israeli athletes during the Munich Olympics two years earlier.

It had not occurred to Zagallo and his staff to enquire about the weather in the month of May when they visited Feldberg – a well-known ski resort in Germany – the year before in order to choose where to base the Seleção for a training camp before moving to Frankfurt, where Brazil would play during the group stage. 'It was cold and many players had niggling injuries during training because of the low temperatures,' said Jairzinho. 'We shouldn't really have gone there.'

Veteran Brazilian journalist Sergio Barbalho was one of the first representatives from the national media to arrive at the German village and he remembers the scene. 'The day we arrived the Seleção were still in Brazil, where they would play a friendly in Rio. It was over 30 degrees back home and 48 hours later they arrived at a place that was covered in snow. We obviously thought preparations would be disturbed.' Indeed they were, with several sessions cancelled or rescheduled and Clodoaldo suffering an injury ten days before the start of the tournament. The 1970 world champion was duly sent home and Zagallo found himself juggling alternatives to try to make his mind up on his starting XI.

Brazil had been drawn in a curious group with Yugoslavia, Scotland and World Cup debutants Zaire. 'There were clear mistakes made in that campaign, especially in comparison with 1970, where every detail seemed in place for us to challenge for the title,' said Roberto Rivelino. 'But I still think people tended to dismiss our team quite quickly, when we had actually assembled the best squad possible with the players we had available in Brazil at the time.'

Yugoslavia would be the Seleção's first opponents in the tournament on 13 June. For the first time in a World Cup, the defending champions would officially play the opening game. When the Seleção finally stepped on to the Waldstadion pitch, Brazilian fans and media were shocked to see that Zagallo had picked an XI that had never played together – and it showed. The Yugoslavians took the initiative early, hit the post twice and forced Leão into a series of crucial saves. The goalless draw flattered the defending champions, who struggled to create chances and left the pitch clearly disappointed with their performance. It would not be the first or the last time in that tournament. In his address to the Brazilian press corps, Zagallo would hail the team's determination and point to the importance of the result for their qualification prospects – hardly the attitude the Brazilian supporters were looking for.

Scotland were the Seleção's next opponents and the expectation that there would be a change in gear quickly faded when it became apparent that Brazil would be taking a cautious approach to the game. The Scots started brightly and with a little more luck could have caused real trouble for the Brazilians. Once again Brazil seemed happy with the point they earned from the 0-0 draw – the first time in the Seleção's history that they had failed to score for two games in a row. And when in the same round Yugoslavia thumped Zaire 9-0, it became clear that Brazil would be scrapping for second place in the group. As things stood, Yugoslavia and Scotland, who had beaten the Africans 2-0 in their opening match, were going through. But surely Rivelino, Jairzinho and co would not only beat Zaire but also put on a convincing display that would finally show what Brazil had come to Germany for? Right?

No sports bloopers show would be complete without one of the weirdest scenes ever to take place on a football pitch on 22 June 1974. As Jairzinho is lining up to take a free kick for Brazil in the 77th minute of match number six in Group 2, Zaire's Muepu Ilunga breaks ranks from the defensive wall and boots the ball like an avid kid in a school yard. For decades it has been used as 'exhibit A' to illustrate the amateurish state of African football at that stage, while later football historians would mention how Ilunga's impulsive run was an attempt to waste time and avoid a drubbing at the hands of Brazil, which reportedly could have resulted in severe punishment at the hands of bloodthirsty dictator Mobutu Sese Seko. Whatever the truth, Brazil had been fast approaching a humiliating group-stage exit that would have made the 1966 shambles look heroic in comparison. At 2-0 up, Brazil desperately needed a third goal to pip Scotland to second place behind Yugoslavia.

Things had looked to be going the Seleção's way when Jairzinho seized on a loose ball to open the scoring after just 12 minutes, but half-time would arrive with Brazil still leading by just a single goal. It was only in the 66th minute that a thunderous Rivelino strike put Brazil 2-0 up. By the time Ilunga had bizarrely punted the ball away from Jairzinho, Brazil were getting desperate. Then, with 11 minutes to go, Valdomiro elicited a huge sigh of relief from the Brazilian bench when he managed to outfox Kazadi Muamba with a speculative shot from the right to put the Seleção 3-0 up. Brazil were through, but with a mediocre campaign, a mediocre brand of football and the knowledge that the dreams of emulating 1970 were hanging by a thread. Worse: the results meant they would share a second-stage group with Argentina and the Netherlands, who had already become the sensation of that tournament with their reinvention of tactics and strategies. Everybody was bedazzled by the exploits of Cruyff and co.

Everybody apart from Mário Zagallo.

In 1624, when Brazil was still a Portuguese colony, an invading Dutch expedition crossed the Atlantic and took over Salvador, the Brazilian capital at the time, with an army of over 1,500 men. Six years later, the Dutch would come again. This time the target was Olinda, also on the north-eastern coast. After hammering the local resistance, the expedition established a base for what become an enclave with its own government and laws. The invasion was far more than a mere overseas venture to re-establish sugar trade with the Brazilian northeast, a line of supply that had been cut off by Spain during the years their crown merged with the Portuguese. In fact, the Dutch would send Prince John Maurice of Nassau, from the dynasty that still answers for half of the name of the Dutch Royal House, to command an expeditionary force that went even further into Brazilian territory.

The Dutch, though, didn't only use the sword: under Nassau, investments in infrastructure never made under the Portuguese took place and his government was exemplified by a liberalism that saw the first synagogue in the Americas built in Recife. The whole adventure lasted until 1644, when Portugal managed to gather enough support to mount an insurrection that 11 years later would kick the Dutch out. The Netherlands would go on to secure a South American foothold in Suriname and their colony would, centuries later, famously help provide them with some of their most famous footballers, such as Ruud Gullitt and Frank Rijkaard, both sons of Surinamese immigrants who settled in Holland.

Brazil in the '70s was still a very insular country and so, for the majority of people, any reference made to the Netherlands would rouse historical references to belligerent Dutch participation in Brazilian colonial history rather than to contemporary football analysis. This meant, therefore, that very few Brazilians were familiar with the powerful emergence of Dutch football in the early 1970s and the revolutionary impact it would have on the game.

Brazilian clubs were not, at the time, making much of an impact on the world stage and it would take until 1976 for a Brazilian team (Cruzeiro) to win the Copa Libertadores again – 13 years after Pelé and Santos had won back-to-back titles. Triumphing in South America's most prestigious team tournament represented one of the few chances for clubs to measure themselves against their European counterparts and so very little was known about them or their players. Neither did the media pick up properly on the feats of Feyenoord and Ajax, who won all editions of the European Cup between 1970 and 1973.

At a time when television was not even showing domestic games properly, nobody could see the Dutch play, even when they came to Argentina for the Intercontinental Cup games. Furthermore, the Dutch were not, historically, a regular participant at the World Cup.

Apart from appearing at the 1934 and 1938 tournaments, Holland had failed to qualify for any other World Cup until 1974 – and their ticket to Germany had hardly been earned with much authority to spare: the Orange went through on goal difference over the course of the qualifiers at the expense of Belgium (with whom they had shared two 0-0 draws).

All of this contributed to the shock and awe experienced by the Seleção and their supporters when they first encountered Total Football in action in the World Cup. The style first developed at Ajax by Rinus Michels became immortalised through the way Johan Cruyff and his team-mates toyed with Uruguay in their opening group game. In the words of veteran Brazilian journalist João Máximo, people witnessed a miracle in Hannover on 15 June 1974. 'The Dutch players were simply multiplying themselves, with each player moving around every single bit of space on the pitch. It was enough to make everyone dizzy. When a Uruguayan player had the ball, three or four opponents surrounded him, but if the same was attempted by the Uruguayans, there always seemed to be a free Dutch player to receive the ball. The scariest thing of all was the calm and authority that Holland simply executed over Uruguay, who still had some of the players from their run to the semi-finals in 1970.' In the end the 2-0 scoreline flattered the double world champions: the Dutch had 17 shots on target against a single one from the Uruguayans, and also had a goal wrongly ruled out. Thanks to a series of acrobatic saves from keeper Mazurkiewicz, Uruguay did not leave the pitch totally humiliated.

A famous story regarding that game reveals how the Dutch caught opposition teams so off-guard. Forward Pedro Rocha, famously pictured in that World Cup surrounded by Dutch opponents, remembered in an interview in Brazil, where he played for almost ten years, how confused his team became during the game. Montero Castillo, a fearsome midfield enforcer, was given the task of keeping Cruyff under surveillance by Uruguay manager Roberto Porta. At half-time, with Uruguay trailing 1-0, Rocha asked his team-mate why he couldn't close the Dutch number 14 down. 'Montero answered, "How could I mark him? He didn't stop running and moving around the pitch. I chased him wherever I could but didn't even get close enough to whack him."' In the second half, the midfielder at least managed to hit his opponent – earning a red card in the 67th minute.

'Even the numbers they wore were unconventional,' says Máximo, referring to the then unusual shirt numbers worn by the Dutch players – goalkeeper Jongbloed, for example, lined up with the 8 on the back of his shirt. Four days later the Dutch would disappoint in a goalless draw against Sweden, which suggests that at least in Western Europe teams were more prepared for the movement of the Clockwork Orange. Cruyff and co then hammered Bulgaria 4-1, qualifying at the top of Group 3 ahead of the Swedes, who had only managed a 0-0 draw with the Bulgarians before beating Uruguay 3-0.

The Dutch performances had not gone unnoticed by hosts West Germany, whose 1-0 defeat to East Germany in their Group 1 game was marred by accusations that Beckenbauer and his team-mates had eased off so they would avoid crossing the path of the Dutch – although both countries took to the pitch in Hamburg having already qualified for the second round. The result meant the East Germans would join Brazil and the Dutch in the round robin for a place in the final, alongside an Argentina side that survived a group with Olympic champions Poland, 1970 runners-up Italy, and surprise package Haiti. The Dutch would be Brazil's last opponents in the order of play, so there was to be plenty of time for observation and analysis by Zagallo and his technical staff.

In the meantime, however, Brazil could not afford to look ahead too much given what had taken place in the first round. The dramatic way in which they had just scraped through to the next round irked the press and led to further accusations of excessive caution by the manager. Zagallo defiantly dismissed what he defined as media panic, saying that the first round was water under the bridge and the Seleção would now show the world real Brazilian football. But the first hurdle was far from simple. East Germany, in their only World Cup, had managed to assemble a very decent team that had finished with a bronze medal in the Munich Olympics. Led by midfielder Jürgen Sparwasser, they negotiated their passage to the second round in the World Cup with relative ease, beating Australia 2-0 and holding Chile to a 1-1 draw. Questionable though it was, their victory against their Western counterparts in the last round had raised spirits and they were certainly not willing to roll over and die in the presence of a Brazilian team whose results had been less than convincing. In fact, the East Germans had outscored the Seleção in the group stages.

On 26 June, Brazil met East Germany in Hannover. Zagallo had once again made changes, dropping captain Piazza and replacing him in midfield with Paulo César Carpegiani – who 24 years later would manage Paraguay in the 1998 World Cup. Leivinha made way for Valdomiro and Dirceu Guimarães replaced Edú, which meant Brazil would start their fourth match in Germany with their fourth different line-up.

The match was a scruffy affair, with three yellow cards in the first 30 minutes. Neither team properly threatened each other until the 60th minute, when Rivelino used his left foot to fire a free kick past Jürgen Croy that had a priceless contribution from Jairzinho – the forward dropped down to open a gap in the wall and the ball flew directly through it and into the net.

East Germany had a very good chance to level through Martin Hoffmann but Brazil held on and eased some of the pressure for the derby against Argentina four days later in Gelsenkirchen. The Seleção had won only one out of the last four meetings against their continental rivals and it would be the teams' first meeting in a World Cup. After missing out on qualification for Mexico 1970, there were hopes back home that Argentina could improve on the fifth place they had managed in England eight years earlier, by then their best result in the tournament. But their faltering first-round campaign had been made worse at the start of the round robin: a 4-0 massacre at the hands of Holland, with a brace by Cruyff. If they were to leave

Germany with at least a top-four finish, Argentina needed to beat Brazil. The Seleção, however, seemed to have finally woken up in Germany and for the first time in the tournament took to the pitch with the proverbial bit between their teeth. Rivelino scored his third goal of the tournament with a long-range effort after 32 minutes only for Argentine captain Miguel Brindisi to equalise four minutes later with a sublime free kick.

Jairzinho put Brazil ahead again four minutes into the second half with a header, but the game remained tense until the end. With the final whistle, Argentina were out of the tournament and the Seleção found themselves a win away from a fourth World Cup final – provided they could find a way to stop Holland from ticking. But they had a mountain to climb and years later Zagallo would admit that he knew it.

In the company of assistant coaches Carlos Alberto Parreira and Cláudio Coutinho, Zagallo had attended the Dutch masterclass against Uruguay earlier in the tournament. In interviews with the Brazilian media, the manager revealed their astonishment by declaring they had not been able to draw a tactical model of what they had witnessed in Hannover. A couple of weeks later, though, Zagallo was light-hearted when discussing what Brazilians were calling the 'Carrossel Holandês' (the Dutch Carousel). It started with a dismissive comparison between the Dutch team and Rio club America, famous in city folklore for faltering at crunch times. 'The Dutch have a very good team,' he said a few days before the showdown, 'but they lack tradition in football. I am not really worried about Holland, my preoccupation is how we are going to face Germany in the final.'

It is often reported in Brazil that after reading a report from observer Paulo Amaral in which his attempts to explain the Clockwork Orange movement on paper resembled a collective drawing from a bunch of three-year-olds, Zagallo said that Cruyff and his team-mates behaved like people playing in a Sunday kickabout.

Decades later, he would argue that his behaviour was part of an intense pep talk for his players through the media. 'We had lost half a team since 1970 and that included Pelé,' he explained in March 2006, just months before he returned to Germany as Parreira's technical assistant at Germany's second home World Cup. 'I knew we had lost our bite but couldn't say anything because the commander can't ever put his team down. I did what I had always done with my teams: I bigged them up while putting down opponents that everybody was talking about. But I was absolutely aware that Holland and Germany were playing better than we were.' If so, Zagallo was very convincing in his mockery. 'I don't see anything special in these guys [the Dutch],' he declared in his last press conference before the match.

Pelé, however, was not so sure. 'It was clear to me that Brazil had good players but the team were struggling even before they were paired with the stronger sides at that tournament. Even the result against Argentina had flattered us.'

On 3 July, Brazil and Holland met in Dortmund. The Westfalenstadion was packed with tens of thousands of Dutch fans, possibly also attracted to the game by the stature of the opposition. It also seemed that the Dutch players were a bit star-struck: the Seleção took the initiative and rightly so, since a draw would send the Dutch to the final on goal difference (after putting four past Argentina, the Orange won 2-0 against East Germany). Valdomiro had two good chances and Paulo César missed a glorious opportunity after managing to elude the offside trap that had worked so well for the Dutch defence in previous games. The Seleção were knocking at the door but also knocking seven bells out of the Dutch, the amount of X-rated challenges turning the game into an ugly affair – with four yellow cards issued in the first half.

Five minutes into the second half, however, it was Holland who broke the deadlock after Johan Neeskens beautifully diverted a cross from Cruyff over Leão. The goal changed the dynamics of the game. 'Brazil at that time were changing,' recalled Cruyff years later. 'In the '50s and the '60s they would send the skilled guys to the World Cup but in 1974 they were pure force. They were still Brazil, but Holland were better at that point in footballing terms. We were what Brazil had once been.'

Fifteen minutes later, Cruyff killed the game, turning in a cross from Ruud Krol. Whatever the Seleção had left of their composure went out the window: another barrage of horrendous tackles ensued and in the 84th minute Luis Pereira got his marching orders from German referee Kurt Tschenscher for trying to break Neeskens in half with a flying challenge. Incensed, the Brazilian defender made matters even more embarrassing by arguing with Dutch supporters while clutching the CBF crest as if to show Brazil were triple world champions. Pereira had just made history by becoming the first Brazilian player to get a red card – they were only brought into the game in 1966, as any football trivia enthusiast will remember. It would take another 16 years for another player to receive the dubious honour (defender Ricardo Gomes, for a tackle from behind on Diego Maradona).

Four years after enchanting the world in Mexico, Brazil had crashed down to earth with a vengeance and the knives were quickly out. Zagallo's house in Rio was vandalised by angry supporters. The mood was so dark that not even a cash incentive paid in advance by Havelange cheered up the team enough to do anything more than just show up for the third-place match against Poland, who duly won it with a Lato goal. 'For everything that happened to us in that World Cup cycle, I think the Seleção went as far as they could,' reflected Rivelino. 'The team was good but never really clicked. We had our chances against the Dutch in the first half and things might have been different had we scored first. At the end of the day, Holland and Germany were the best teams at that World Cup and deserved to make it to the final. Instead of trying to find scapegoats, we should have recognised the merit of those who had beaten us.'

For those who had wanted to benefit politically from the exploits of the Seleção, the German World Cup was disastrous. 'If the 1970 win was a boost for the military government, the 1974 defeat helped sour the public mood towards the dictatorship,' Marcos Guterman explains. In November, the government lost considerable ground to the opposition in the parliamentary elections that put even more pressure on the demand for democratisation – although that led, in turn, to an even greater increase in the use of football for politics.

Unlike in 1966, the Seleção wasn't simply a victim of bad planning. For the first time since their irresistible rise to three World Cup titles within 12 years, Brazil had to cope with the idea that the rest of the footballing world was catching up faster and faster with them.

The Seleção had also found out the mere sight of the famous yellow shirt was no longer enough to win them matches. They would have to take a good look at their tactics and style. Their first test without the King could have gone much worse, but by Brazilian standards it was still a failure. Pelé also felt the pain, even though he didn't play. 'People would stop me on the streets and say that the Seleção lost because I didn't come back. It was a difficult period for me.' Difficult enough to actually speed up his club retirement – at least until Cosmos and Time Warner came knocking. On the night of 2 October 1974, in the 22nd minute of Santos' home match against Ponte Preta in the São Paulo state league, Pelé picked up the ball and kneeled down in the centre circle. He would never play an official match on Brazilian soil again.

1982

FOUR

1982
THE YEAR FOOTBALL DIED

KUALA LUMPUR IN the final week of May 2002 was enjoying what some could call World Cup fever by proxy. In a matter of days, the first World Cup on Asian soil would kick off with title holders France facing newbies Senegal in neighbouring South Korea, the country sharing hosting privileges with Japan. As part of their preparations to synchronise players' and technical staff's body clocks to Far Eastern time zones, the Seleção had stopped in Malaysia on their way to the tournament, where they would also fulfil commercial commitments by playing a warm-up friendly against the Malaysian national team after a US$1 million cheque signed by the Asian Tiger government had landed at the CBF headquarters in Rio.

Following the caravan was the press corps, including the army of people regularly shipped by TV Globo to wherever the Seleção were playing. Among the troupe collecting bags and trying to negotiate passage from the luggage to the arrivals hall was Paulo Roberto Falcão. Age had treated him well, even though his once trademark long crop of hair had been considerably deforested by the passing of time. Falcão was exhausted after the long-haul flight from Barcelona – from where the whole circus had departed following a bizarre friendly against 'überminnows' Andorra arranged by sponsors Nike. It had been a mismatch so pointless to World Cup preparations that even Falcão had struggled to refrain from openly criticising it, ultimately only holding his tongue because his pundit job for TV Globo, who owned the World Cup broadcasting rights, walked hand in hand with the Brazilian FA. He wasn't in the best of tempers, therefore, and his mind was probably wandering somewhere else when he handed his passport to the immigration officer. Said officer took several looks at both passport and passport holder for what seemed an eternity to Falcão. Suddenly, the official fired the question:

'How come Brazil lost that game?'

Falcão does not remember what he answered, but the immigration officer had acted as an unlikely trigger for old emotions. That game. THAT game. The game that defined the most feted generation of Brazilian footballers since Pelé's golden generation. It just refused to go away. Twenty years had passed since the 1982 World Cup but the tournament still seemed unfinished to Falcão. So it arguably did to a whole nation, although the intensity of the 1982 outrage had calmed over the two decades. 'That episode in Kuala Lumpur was just different. It was the realisation that the impact of that World Cup was much stronger than any of us players could even imagine. But that question also got me thinking again about what had taken place 20 years before. It's not that I had ever put those events to the back of my mind but all of a sudden they came flooding back.' A nudge was all it was, but it would still take another decade for the man once known as 'the King of Rome' to finally face his demons.

Yorkshire in November is colder than any place in Brazil will ever be. It is definitely not a comfortable setting for a Brazilian to play a football match, especially a Brazilian past his physical prime and whose diet of fags and booze had made even playing in warmer climes a considerable test. But there was Sócrates Brasileiro Sampaio de Souza freezing on the bench for Garforth Town FC, then in the depths of non-league football but connected enough to Brazil for the former Seleção captain to make the most unlikely of cameos in 2004.

He played for a couple of minutes in Garforth's 2-2 draw against Tadcaster Albion as part of an outrageous publicity stunt pulled of by Simon Clifford – a Teesside man obsessed with permeating the academy system in English football with Brazilian skills, an idea that seemed to have caught Sócrates' imagination even without the whole VIP treatment he was pampered with during his visit to England. During the course of a week, Sócrates also took part in a Q&A in a Brazilian bar in London, received an honorary degree from the University of Leeds and was the recipient of a guard of honour during a visit to Manchester United's Carrington training ground, where a smitten Sir Alex Ferguson played host. In one of his final nights in Britain, Sócrates would finally retreat to a quiet Leeds pub for a pint – almost a dozen of them, which needed to be matched by the punters who accompanied him. Guards and notepads were down and the man Brazilians referred to as 'the Doctor' – thanks to the fact that he actually held a degree in medicine – chatted about football in a sincere and honest way. It was at that place, so far from his comfort zone, that Sócrates made an observation surprising enough for even the most dedicated analyst of the Class of 1982: to that day, Sócrates had never watched Brazil v Italy. He just couldn't bear it.

After the last remnants of the great 1970 team crashed and burned against the mighty Holland in Germany 1974, discipline once again became an obsession for the men holding the reins of Brazilian football. Which was easier said than done.

Mário Zagallo was replaced by Osvaldo Brandão, who had managed the Seleção in the 1950s but whose career had been given a second wind with Palmeiras' exploits in the early seventies (back-to-back Brazilian titles in 1972 and 1973). Brandão lasted almost three years before a sequence of lukewarm results and his insistence in denying Admiral Heleno Nunes' wishes that the Seleção should play with wingers led to a situation where Brandão jumped before he was pushed.

To ensure that Nunes now got what he wanted, Cláudio Coutinho was chosen to take over the team in the middle of the qualifying campaign for Argentina 1978 (and the return of the World Cup to South America). Coutinho had been the army official who, in 1970, had overseen the highly successful fitness regime that underpinned the Seleção's assault on the Jules Rimet trophy in Mexico. He had cut his managerial teeth when given command of Brazil's Olympic team for the 1976 Montreal Games, and the fourth place in Canada was at the time the best ever obtained by the Seleção at the event. He had also worked as fitness coach for Olympique Marseille. Still, Coutinho was hardly the most qualified man to take over – Internacional's Rubens Minelli had just won back-to-back Brazilian titles in a team boasting a young Paulo Roberto Falcão. But Coutinho was much more able than any competitor to use his military connections to lobby for the job. He may have lacked experience but he had a lot of nerve: in one of his first interviews, the new manager announced the need for Brazilian football to embrace the European emphasis on tactical discipline and group sacrifice over the reliance on individual brilliance.

Having been part of Zagallo's staff in 1974, Coutinho had been thrilled by the Clockwork Orange and wanted to emulate Rinus Michels' Total Football experiment below the equator. His first official game in charge was a 6-0 drubbing of Colombia at the Maracaná, against the same opposition that had previously held Brazil to a goalless draw under Brandão. The Seleção would qualify for the World Cup but the lack of convincing results against European teams put the manager under pressure and nudged him into a more conservative style. Nothing could have expressed that change more than the decision to leave Falcão in Brazil and travel to Argentina with midfield chopper Chicão in his place.

After draws against Sweden and Spain in their first two group games, the Seleção qualified for the second round with a meagre 1-0 victory over Austria. Under pressure from Nunes, Coutinho dropped Zico and Reinaldo, arguably the two most technically gifted forward players in Brazil at the time, and replaced them with powerful forwards Roberto Dinamite and Jorge Mendonça.

Brazil duly beat Peru 3-0 but after a goalless draw with Argentina the team played Poland a day before Argentina faced the Peruvians.

A 3-1 win over Grzegorz Lato and co wasn't enough for the Seleção as the hosts thrashed the Peruvians 6-0 and qualified for the final on goal difference.

Brazil had to settle for third place after beating Italy 2-0 in the play-off.

Remarkably, Brazil had lost the title even though they finished the World Cup unbeaten – Coutinho would return home proclaiming the Seleção were 'the moral tournament champions'. For the third time in a row, Brazil had finished in the top four, a performance that almost any country in the world would be proud of. But for Brazilians, it meant a second frustrated attempt to claim the 'Tetra'.

Coutinho was berated by both the public and the media but still held on to the job for another year, until a semi-final defeat to Paraguay in the Copa America sealed his fate. By the time the Seleção reconvened, in April 1980, spirits were low. Brazilian football had gone through some changes; six months earlier, a government decree had split the CBD into independent sport federations, including the Brazilian Football Confederation, as part of an effort to modernise the organisation.

The new governing body would have to hold elections for its presidency and the centralising hardliner Admiral Nunes was defeated comfortably by businessman Giulite Coutinho, who won the vote with the promise of a new deal for Brazilian football. Modernisation for an entity that seemed trapped in time and which had failed to address the financial woes of its affiliate clubs was part of the package of Coutinho's promises: in 1941, the Getúlio Vargas government, then a dictatorship pure and simple, ratified the presence of the state in the sports arena by granting the CBD a monopoly in the organisation of football games and competitions in Brazil. The legislation forbade the creation of rival leagues and associations and established that the CBD would get 5 per cent of the gate receipts from every inter-state match and every game involving the Seleção on Brazilian soil. Under Brazilian law, football clubs were also forbidden to function as companies and to this day are still defined as non-profitable organisations. Even a moderniser like Coutinho would not meddle with this status quo and the legal base that sustained it – the income it generated for the CBD and its control over football matters gave him no incentive to do so.

With that, alongside further adjustments in the 1970s that would give clubs the same voting rights in local federations regardless of size or importance, the seeds were sown for a system of horse-trading which strengthened the governing bodies while weakening the financial and institutional power of the clubs – which was the polar opposite to the structure in European football where the clubs hold much more power. The creation of the national championships, while a strategy rooted in the military dictatorship's political plans, also came in handy for the CBD, whose gains were ring-fenced and then increased steadily thanks to the swelling in participation in the Campeonato Brasileiro. From 20 teams in its first edition in 1971, the tournament was contested by 94 clubs in 1979 – more than the number of participants in England's top four divisions combined. For the CBD, more games represented more money, pure and simple. That would not change radically in Coutinho's tenure, when football became a separate body and the Brazilian Football Confederation (CBF) was created. His first Brasileiro still had 44 clubs in the first division.

Neither did Coutinho seem to worry about the problems faced by clubs. It was easier to create a national championship than to play it. Going up and down the country was a logistical and financial nightmare for teams in a country as huge as Brazil. Besides, they still had to plan for the state championships, which were still attracting more fans to their stadiums than the national tournament, especially in traditional football cities such as Rio and São Paulo. In these tournaments, the big clubs would be subjected to a fixture pile-up that mirrored the craziness of the Campeonato Brasileiro. This time, with local federations interested in having as many derbies as they could at the same time, they wouldn't limit the occasions the big guns would face the minnows – after all, local federations needed to please smaller clubs when elections took place at their respective governing bodies.

The big clubs did not profit from TV revenues either, because the ruling body pretty much gave away the broadcasting rights for free until the mid-1980s. Even if they wanted to, the authoritarian organisational structure would not allow them to. Sport governing laws passed by the military in the 1970s meant that the voting process in state federations gave powerhouses and amateur clubs the same weight. It would be the same as Manchester United and Manchester City having the same voting power as Bury and Oldham if they wanted to challenge decisions affecting their schedule. Unlike Brazil, however, English football was never designed to make the Football Association despotic and neither did it encourage the formation of county associations to meddle with professional football issues.

That's not to say that clubs were not also responsible for their woes. Brazilian football has been historically marked by the amateurism of club directors and tales of shady business deals have often come to the fore. Operating in a similar system to Spain, where even giants like Barcelona and Real Madrid are owned by their thousands of 'socios', who have the power to elect boardrooms, Brazilian teams sat tight for decades and did not push towards a scenario of more autonomy and accountability. But the president, Coutinho, never really wanted to stage a revolution. He knew, though, that things could not be run as carelessly as in the days of Nunes and his cronies. So Coutinho put a lot of effort into commercial developments, symbolised by a sponsorship deal with the Brazilian Coffee Institute (IBC) that put the company logo on the new Brazil crest – a blatant violation of FIFA rules that would go unnoticed until 1990. It was also during his tenure that Brazil printed the kit maker's logo on the shirt for the first time.

This constricting environment for the clubs worsened in 1979 with a more significant succession: Brazil had a new president and General João Figueiredo replaced Ernesto Geisel with the mission to oversee a smooth return to democracy but at the same time to also try to plug the holes in the Brazilian economy caused by the aggressive expansionism implemented by his predecessors. But Figueiredo's plans were blown away by the Second Oil Crisis that would leave Brazil on the brink of bankruptcy at the beginning of the 1980s.

The financial woes opened further cracks in the popularity of the military government, who at the time also had to handle dissent within their own party – in 1981, an army captain and sergeant tried to detonate a bomb during a crowded music festival headlined by leftist artists in Rio, but fortunately only succeeded in blowing themselves up instead. But the incident put even greater pressure on Figueiredo, who tried to placate matters by ending the strict two-party system in Brazilian politics – only for the opposition to later make substantial gains in the 1982 elections. Before then, however, football was already serving as a front for pro-democracy rallies. And who else could be at the helm if not the footballer named after one of the founding fathers of philosophy?

Sócrates was born in 1954 in Belém, the capital of the Amazonian state of Pará. His father, Raimundo, was a civil servant and an avid reader of Greek philosophy, which helps to explain why his first two children were named after masters of thought (Sócrates' younger brother was called Sophocles). It was hardly the usual background of a typical Brazilian footballer, and his approach to the game was always considerably more thoughtful and measured than most of his fellow professional athletes in Brazil. While some players would later recall tales of deprivation and poverty while growing up, one of Sócrates' most traumatic childhood memories was the vision of Raimundo making a bonfire with his beloved books after the Army Coup in 1964.

The family had already moved from Pará to Ribeirão Preto, which had been one of the biggest and wealthiest cities in the state of São Paulo since the 19th-century coffee boom. Given the presence of immense farmlands, it was hardly a region synonymous with political dissent, but Ribeirão Preto had curiously staged a revolution of its own in 1887 when their city council abolished slavery almost a year before the national abolition law was signed. It was there that Sócrates fell in love with the game while studying at the traditional Marist Catholic school.

In his teenage years Sócrates would be spotted by Botafogo – not the famous Rio de Janeiro side, but a tribute club founded in Ribeirão Preto that would sometimes give the capital city-based powerhouses a good run for their money. By the time he was 17, however, Sócrates needed to make a decision. He had finished his formal education and was interested in the prospect of studying medicine, an occupation that would provide a sound safety net given the constant need for doctors in both the public and private sectors in Brazil. Raimundo had also made him promise that he would not simply forfeit his education for the game he loved so much. But Sócrates fancied his chances of making a successful career for himself in football and it just seemed a matter of time before he would not only break into Botafogo's first team but also own it. Divided as he was, Sócrates borrowed a leaf from Solomon's book: he chose both.

The way Sócrates juggled his excruciatingly demanding university studies and the life of a professional athlete was almost as impressive as his skills with a ball at his feet. For a start, he was forced to do a lot of training on his own after lectures, usually when most of his team-mates had already gone home. He would miss tactical sessions and regularly arrive in the nick of time for Botafogo games, often still wearing his white coat. The most remarkable thing is not that Sócrates had already passed his residency exams by the time he made a final decision about which road to travel in early 1978, but the fact he had also managed to play 269 games and score 101 goals for Botafogo in four years. But the efforts had taken their toll. 'Things reached a point where I simply had to choose, it was not humanly possible to keep fighting on two fronts,' he said. 'But I love football and medicine almost as much as I like beer!'

The lanky midfielder was finally nudged toward professional football because of a simple reality: even at minnows Botafogo he was already making ten times the average entry-level doctor's salary. His earnings would increase months later when Corinthians came knocking after Sócrates had led Botafogo's gung-ho challenge in the 1977 São Paulo league, when they finished fourth after some impressive displays from their star midfielder against high-class opposition that had included his new club. By the time he was unveiled by one of Brazil's most-supported clubs, details about his unusual background had already fired the public's imagination. Sócrates became known simply as 'the Doctor'.

He quickly rose through the Corinthians ranks but was overlooked by Seleção manager Cláudio Coutinho when he picked his squad for the 1978 World Cup, and would have to wait another year to win his first cap.

His career at Corinthians was not all plain sailing, however. After winning the 1977 state title the club won the trophy again in 1979 but then hit a slump that by April 1982 still didn't seem likely to end any time soon. That was the month the Corinthians socios voted in a new president, Waldemar Pires, who made the left-field appointment of social scientist, Adilson Monteiro Alves, as football director. Alves' approach to the job revolved around listening to the players rather than bossing them around like schoolchildren. As part of the revolution in the way the club was run, Alves actively encouraged the players to help run things by introducing a universal suffrage system where even the kit man would have a vote in decisions such as line-ups, team hotels and even signings. In 1980s Brazil, where a dictatorship was still in power and civil rights were still curbed under emergency legislation, it was a startlingly egalitarian philosophy. 'We voted for everything, even for how many times the team bus would stop during trips,' said Sócrates. 'But we also decided on important things such as the need to end the systems where players were locked away in isolation at the hotels before matches.'

Corinthians also made sure that this philosophy was confined to their sport operations: thanks to the intervention of one of their most famous supporters, Brazilian advertising guru Washington Olivetto, the experiment was christened the 'Corinthian Democracy' and players would soon be playing with political messages printed on the back of their shirts at a time when even sponsorship messages were considered taboo in Brazilian football. It did not take long for the movement to be noticed by the military government and army contacts tried to lobby Corinthians into toning things down.

But if the army's message was delivered to Sócrates, he didn't seem to care at all. In fact, he increased his rebellion. In a famous 1982 episode, he came up on stage alongside team-mates Casagrande and Wladimir during a show by controversial Brazilian rocker Rita Lee, who at the time had written 'Vote Me', a satirical song about political freedom in Brazil. Sócrates had clearly been drinking and as he giggled like a child beside Lee he contravened every image of the spartan footballer so idealised by the military.

He pushed things still further with his goal celebrations. He never screamed in delight or set off on a wheeling celebratory run, but instead calmly gave a Black Panther-inspired salute. But there was little the regime could do when Corinthians started to enjoy a run of success again. The club would win back-to-back São Paulo titles in 1982 and 1983 and reach the Brazilian championship semi-finals in 1984. They also would attract large enough crowds to earn good money and balance their books. Before all that, however, Sócrates dreamed of going to his first World Cup, even if his dreams also included the chance to make a political statement against the army rule.

One would think that a loose cannon like Sócrates, who also smoked and drank heavily, would not get anywhere near the Seleção. But his footballing skills and his ability to read the game were just too sublime to ignore. By the time Brazil had to start thinking of the 1982 World Cup qualifiers, there was no way that any manager could consider leaving him out of the squad again.

After the 'scientific' brand of football that had nearly taken the team to a 1978 World Cup final in Argentina but hardly endeared the team to the fans, the CBF looked for somebody who would be able to bring the best out of what was clearly a spectacular generation of skilful footballers that had emerged since 1978. Telê Santana was unveiled as Coutinho's replacement in early 1980 to do just that.

Few people in Brazil looked as able as Santana to shepherd this array of burgeoning greats, because few people had earned as much respect from the players as him. First of all, unlike Coutinho, Santana had been a footballer and a good one. In nine years for Rio side Fluminense, he netted 165 goals and still ranks as their third-highest all-time scorer. Santana had seen his international career curtailed simply because he had played on the right wing in the 1950s at the same time as world-class talents such as Julinho, Joel and Garrincha. As a consequence, he was only selected once to start for the Seleção – in a friendly against Portugal – and wasn't even able to enjoy it as he had to pull out due to injury. Still, even opposition fans, impressed with his talent and fair play, respected him. Santana was never sent off in his 12-year professional career and would later demand the same behaviour from his players. As a manager he had coached Atlético Mineiro when they won the first ever Campeonato Brasileiro in 1971 and also won state titles in Rio, Minas Gerais and Rio Grande do Sul.

His mission now was to earn back some self-esteem for the Seleção and the first chance to put his plans into practice was in the Mundialito. To mark the 50th anniversary of the 1930 World Cup, FIFA organised a celebratory tournament in early 1981 to be contested by all world champion nations. Only England declined, being replaced by Holland. It was not the most auspicious of starts for Santana; after his team had spent most of 1980 playing friendly after friendly without any significantly impressive results, they drew 1-1 with Argentina in their first game of the Mundialito and lost 2-1 to Uruguay in the final game. The only bright spark had been a 4-1 thrashing of West Germany sandwiched between the other underwhelming results.

Qualifiers for Spain 1982 started with Brazil scraping a 1-0 away win against Venezuela, where only a penalty kick separated the teams. Another away game against Bolivia ended with another tight win (2-1) before the team finally clicked into gear for the

Above: Arthur Friedenreich, affectionately known as 'the Tiger'. Despite his genius on the field, he tried to disguise his non-whiteness by patiently using a combination of paste and hotel towels to flatten his curly hair.

Left: Leonidas da Silva who played football for Brazil in two World Cups and was the top scorer of the 1938 World Cup, featured on a vintage postcard advertising Vinho de Jurubeba, a cure of rheumatism and syphilis, dated 11th July 1938. *Getty Images*

Above: Brazil celebrate their 6-1 victory over Spain on 13 July, 1950.

Below: Friaça fires home the opening goal in the title-deciding match against Uruguay in 1950. It was Brazil's only score of the match, which became known as the 'Maracanazo'.

Above: 1950 Uruguayan captain, Obdulio Varela. *Getty Images*

Above: Juan 'Pepe' Schiaffino (C) scores Uruguay's first goal against Brazil in the 1950 final. *Getty Images*

Below: As President Juscelino Kubitschek looks on, Joao Havelange hoists the Jules Rimet trophy aloft after the Brazil had become world champions in Sweden 1958. *Getty Images*

Above: Pelé signs autographs for fans before Brazil's match against Hungary at Goodison Park at the 1966 World Cup, a game they lost 3-1.

Below: Pelé gets set to take a free kick against Portugal at the 1966 World Cup in England.

Above: Portugal's roughhouse tactics against saw Pelé and his Brazil teammates kicked out of the World Cup – both figuratively and literally. *Getty Images*

Below: Barely able to walk at the end of the match, Pelé showed his class by congratulating Brazil's conquerors.

Above: Mario Zagallo offers advice to his players during a training session in 1973. *Getty Images*

Below: Jairzinho and Paulo Cesar leave the field after defeating East Germany 1-0 at the 1974 World Cup. *Getty Images*

Above: Paulo Cesar is robbed of the ball by Argentina's Carlos Babington (l) and Rene Houseman (r) during their 1974 group game. *Press Association*

Below: Jairzinho heads home Brazil's winner against Argentina in Hanover.

Above: Socrates deftly dribbles the ball against Argentina in 1982. *Getty Images*

Below: Socrates joins Falcao and Cerezo to celebrate their third goal, by Junior, in their 3-1 victory over Argentina in 1982. *Getty Images*

Above: Paulo Falcao celebrates after scoring Brazil's second goal against Italy in Barcelona. *Getty Images*

Below: Paolo Rossi celebrates his winning goal, his third of the match, which sent Brazil crashing out of the tournament. *Getty Images*

jornal da tarde

Cr$ 50,00

O ESTADO DE S. PAULO

Terça-feira, 6 de julho de 1982. Número 5.085. Ano 17

EX-LIBRIS

O ESTADO DE S. PAULO

BRASIL

Barcelona, 5 de julho de 1982.

Above: The image of José Carlos Junior weeping at fulltime appeared on the cover of *Jornal da Tarde* and became an iconic image of Brazil's 1982 campaign.

Above: The 1998 team line up before playing Morocco in Nantes. Back-row from left to right, Claudio Taffarel, Rivaldo, Cesar Sampaio, Aldair, Junior Baiano, Cafu; front-row from left to right, Ronaldo, Roberto Carlos, Bebeto, Leonardo, Dunga. *Getty Images*

Below: Ronaldo slips the ball past Holland's goalkeeper Edwin Van Der Sar to put Brazil 1-0 ahead in the 46th minute of the semi-final against Holland. *Getty Images*

Left: Out of sorts in the final after suffering a fit on the morning of the match, Ronaldo's cause is further hindered after this violent clash with French goalkeeper Fabien Barthez. *Getty Images*

Right: Mario Zagallo consoles his star player after the final whistle. *Getty Images*

Above: Ronaldo, Nike boots slung across his shoulders, looks on dejectedly as France lift the 1998 World Cup. *Getty Images*

Below: Dunga takes Kaka aside during a team training session at St. Stithians College in Johannesburg during the 2010 World Cup in South Africa. *Getty Images*

Above: Felipe Melo and Julio Cesar fail spectacularly to defend a cross from Wesley Sneijder of the Netherlands which ended in an own goal. *Getty Images*

Below: Felipe Melo stamps on Netherlands' striker Arjen Robben during the World Cup quarter final, which earned him a straight red card. *Getty Images*

Above: Daniel Alves collapses with disappointment after Holland knock Brazil out of the World Cup, while the Dutch players celebrate their triumph. *Getty Images*

Below: The rise of Neymar. As the World Cup cycle turns and the tournament returns to Brazil, so the pressure mounts on the shoulders of the Seleção's new star. *Getty Images*

home games, beating the same opponents 5-0 and 3-1 respectively. The return game against the Bolivians in the Maracanã marked the first national team hat-trick for Zico, which finally validated the forward's inclusion after some underwhelming performances. Born in Rio de Janeiro in March 1953, Arthur Antunes Coimbra (Zico) became a true working-class hero. Raised in the outskirts of the city, he endured a gruelling routine of studies and travel in order to rise through the ranks of Flamengo's youth system, which also included a demanding physical fitness programme to ensure his body could withstand the rigours of professional football. In fact, when Zico was first introduced to the youth academy coordinator in 1967, he was almost turned down: thin as a stick, Zico only measured 4'9". The club put him on a specially tailored diet and gym programme, which he repaid faithfully by taking the club to heights they could only have dreamed of before his arrival.

Nicknamed the 'Little Rooster' thanks to his thin frame and unruly mane of blonde hair, Zico did not boast the revolutionary spirit that possessed his Seleção team-mate Sócrates. On the contrary, Zico dodged controversy as smartly as he would evade his markers playing for Flamengo or the Seleção. He was a natural-born leader but he preferred to exert his influence away from the public eye. 'Zico would always lead the charge when it was time for the players to demand anything from the directors, even when it did not concern him,' remembers his Flamengo and Seleção team-mate Leandro.

Flamengo did not have the 'Corinthian Democracy' but their organisation was a close-knit bunch that in the first half of the 1980s would win a hat-trick of Brazilian championships and a Rio state title before lifting the 1981 Copa Libertadores and trashing the great Liverpool side of Kenny Dalglish, Graeme Souness and co in the Intercontinental Cup final. Impressing the world with their skill and their hunger, Zico and his Flamengo team-mates' exploits provided a crucial morale boost for the Seleção.

Zico, right-back Leandro and left-back Júnior would make it to the 1982 World Cup squad. Júnior would become an interesting case in his own right: he was a rare case of a Brazilian player who had honed his skills on the beach. One of the biggest myths concerning Brazilian football involves sandy beaches and a festival of kids kicking balls around, when in reality the seaside has historically been off-limits to poor and working-class kids. Moreover, a great number of Brazilian footballers, Pelé included, were either born or bred in landlocked regions. It has always been much easier to find kids kicking a ball on the streets or on a futsal court: the indoor version of football originally played with a heavier ball was developed in Uruguay in the early 1930s but was adopted in Brazil in the following decades and became a much more fertile breeding ground than the sands. While beach football can boast only 1970 reserve Paulo César as a World Cup winner, names like Ronaldo, Romário and Rivelino all hail from futsal, and many sport experts believe the game helped to enhance the dribbling and passing abilities of the Brazilian players, with Rivelino's outrageous 'elastic dribble' developed on a futsal court.

Júnior, a graduate from Juventus, a traditional Copacabana beach Sunday league, would now have the chance to emulate Paulo César. But his presence in the Seleção also created a jigsaw for Santana. Following the Brazilian tradition of cavalier full-backs, Júnior almost worked as a winger, just like his counterpart Leandro on the right side, which meant the manager had to find a way to balance the make-up of the rest of the team.

Santana had a good chance to experiment in the second week of May 1981, when Brazil were scheduled to play England, France and Germany away in the space of only five days. When Brazil flew back home, they brought three famous scalps in their luggage, including their first-ever Wembley victory and an epic triumph in Stuttgart in which goalkeeper Waldir Peres saved two penalties from Paul Breitner as the Seleção came from behind to win 2-1. Fans and media back home marvelled at the results and the style imposed by Santana – a flowing brand of football where no player seemed to touch the ball more than twice before passing it around. It was beautiful to watch. It felt even greater to play. 'We were adamant that Brazil had to abide by the style that had made it famous,' said Zico. 'We felt it would be wrong for us to take to the field feeling scared of losing or to feel hostage to the result. We wanted to enjoy what we were doing. Responsibly, of course, and nobody could ever say that as a team we didn't work our socks off. But we felt that something really special was going on.'

Santana's team was a radical departure from the Coutinho years in so many ways and their style rekindled patriotic fervour that had seemed lost over the previous two World Cup campaigns. In the build-up to the 1982 tournament, Brazilians did not hesitate to decorate the streets with the national colours in expectation of a huge party and there were official contests to award prizes to the most original decorations. The players got into the spirit as well and Júnior released a World Cup single ('My Happy People') that sold 600,000 copies.

There was a special bond between the players that was helped by the fact that most of the team were playing for Brazilian clubs and the amount of money thrown into the game was still not enough to create the bubble in which the game would immerse itself decades later. A trip to a supermarket in Rio could be rewarded with more than good deals: one's trolley could literally bump into Zico's. 'Brazilian football was always known for this culture where fans felt close to players,' said Fernando Calazans, a revered sports columnist based in Rio. 'They could see them around, not only on a football pitch.' In fact, informality is so ingrained into Brazilian football that calling a player by his first name or nickname became much more common than anywhere else in the world, whether by totally invented names, such as Pelé (which has no meaning in Portuguese at all), puerile reductions such as Kaká or by the well-known practice of adding the diminutive suffix 'inho' or the augmentative 'ão' to first names. Or you could just have the shortening of the shortening: Zico, for example, derives from Arthurzinho, the player's childhood nickname.

The informality between supporters and players could sometimes be quite humbling to the players, though. 'Supporters would never hold back from giving us an earful,' said Zico, 'but at least they identified with the Seleção because we were all playing in Brazil at the time, while these days players pretty much jump on a plane and fly abroad almost immediately after they play with the national team.' Being an exception to this rule could prove costly. Moving abroad had historically been taboo for Brazilian footballers and remained so in the early 1980s, even though players had already been going abroad as early as the 1930s. Fausto, the midfielder who scored the Seleção's first-ever World Cup goal, joined Barcelona in 1932. Anfilogino Guarisi, a Brazilian right-back nicknamed Filó, went to Italy and actually made it into the national team that won the 1934 World Cup. Even proto-superstar Leônidas da Silva was poached by Peñarol in Uruguay a year after he made his Seleção debut. But those departures had much more to do with Brazil's reluctance to embrace professionalism than some kind of career plan. And Leônidas had already returned to Brazilian football by the time he took the 1938 World Cup by storm.

The Seleção simply didn't 'do' foreign-based players. Although there was no written rule preventing expats from joining the team, for decades players went abroad pretty much knowing that doing so would burn bridges with the national team. That was the rationale, for example, that led José Altafini, a world champion with Brazil in 1958, to accept the offer of an Italian passport and a place in the Azzurri. Signed by AC Milan right after playing a part in Brazil's maiden win in Sweden (although he lost his place to a young Pelé in the starting XI two matches into the tournament), Altafini was dressed in blue by the time the Seleção started their defence of the title in Chile. 'At that time you simply ended your career at the Seleção if you moved abroad,' said Altafini, who went on to be one of the most prolific strikers in Serie A history. 'That was it. But I was 20 years old when I joined Milan, too young to not consider playing again at the World Cup. So I accepted the invitation to play for Italy.'

This exile wasn't necessarily written in stone, though: Vavá, Brazil's invaluable striker in 1958, played for the Seleção in a 1960 friendly in Rio after signing for Atlético Madrid. But mostly the transfers would be publicly seen as a sign of greed and lack of patriotism and both the public and media could be quite antagonistic towards players heading for the airport. However, there were also practical reasons: European clubs often refused to release Brazilian players for national team duty, including World Cup qualifying games.

In 1980, AS Roma offered Internacional £900,000 to sign Falcão. It was huge money in inflation-ravaged Brazil; to give an idea, it was enough money to cover 11 years of Sócrates' wages – and the Doctor was the highest earner in Brazilian football at the time. A sign of things to come.

Falcão was then one of the biggest stars in Brazilian football, having won three Brazilian titles with Internacional, and bade farewell by helping them to the Copa Libertadores final. Still, he left with boos from his fans still ringing in his ears, accused of having played with less intensity than usual so that he wouldn't get injured and jeopardise his transfer. It was an accusation that irked him. 'It was a minority of fans,' he remembers. 'I always felt appreciated for what I did for the club and many people understood I was perfectly entitled to do what was best for my career.' Nonetheless, the midfielder did gamble his place with the Seleção when joining the Giallorossi. Roma, as expected, did not release him for more than 90 per cent of the 33 games Brazil played between Santana's arrival and the 1982 World Cup. Falcão did not even train with his Seleção team-mates for almost two years and that could have been time enough for somebody else to simply slot into his place – it's not that Brazilian football was lacking in defensive central midfielders at the time. But Falcão was already one of the most talented midfield enforcers to ever wear the Brazil shirt and the manager could afford to wait for him. Falcão's case was strengthened by the fact Santana had so far struggled to establish a balance to what on paper was a squad designed to attack the opposition relentlessly.

Falcão's great strength lay in his ability to close down players and mop up play. Those attributes had been finely tuned while playing in Serie A, a league that had been attracting some of the world's best players since the reopening of international transfers in Italian football in the late 1970s.

Santana knew how valuable Falcão's contribution could be. At the end of the 1981/82 European club season, he was finally free to join the Seleção in May 1982 and Santana was able to put together his ideal line-up for the first time in a friendly against Switzerland in Recife. Winger Paulo Isidoro made way for the Roma player, who would assume defensive duties alongside Toninho Cerezo, with Zico and Sócrates leading the creative charge. They also alternated in roaming the right side of the field, while Éder, by no means a classic winger, patrolled the left side. After his heroics in 1981, Peres had earned the number 1 shirt and his defence would be marshalled by Oscar and Luizinho, with whom the manager had worked at São Paulo and Atlético Mineiro. Leandro and Júnior were the full-backs.

What Santana seemed to be struggling with was the selection of his number 9. In his dreams, Reinaldo would wear the shirt. Arguably one of the best centre-forwards in the history of Brazilian football, Reinaldo started playing professional football at 16 for Atlético Mineiro but had been plagued by knee injuries almost ever since. They didn't prevent him from setting a scoring record in the Campeonato Brasileiro in 1977 (28 goals in 18 games, an average 1.55 per match) that would stand for 20 years. Reinaldo scored 14 goals in 37 games for the Seleção, including the opener in the 1978 World Cup, but his frail knees kept letting him down. He still played a part in the legendary 1981 tour of Europe and had a goal against England at Wembley wrongfully disallowed by Austrian referee Erich Linemayr, but when 1982 dawned, he was already out of the running for a place.

São Paulo FC's Serginho, Vasco's Roberto Dinamite and Guarani's Careca were competing for two places and the latter made considerable gains for the starting shirt. Careca was also the best fit for the kind of game envisaged by Santana, where a roving striker could complement the flow provided by his 'magic midfield four'.

Before travelling to Spain, Brazil played a last home friendly and duly thrashed Ireland 7-0. Even centre-back Luizinho scored (one of only two strikes in his 36 games for the Seleção) in a match that served as a festive send-off for the Canarinhos (Little Canaries). Brazilians were in love with the Seleção again and TV coverage seized the moment, with a flood of coverage and gimmicks such as animations where players' autographs would show on screen following their goals. Although Santana ran a pretty tight ship over media access to the players, many of the Seleção stars had diaries serialised in newspapers and magazines.

The 1982 World Cup would have significant format changes in comparison to 1978. The number of teams had increased from 16 to 24, which forced changes to the format of the knockout stages. The best two teams from each of the six groups would advance and then be bundled into four groups of three for a round-robin. Brazil had been drawn in Group 6 alongside the Soviet Union, Scotland and newcomers New Zealand. They would be based in Seville. Thanks to their international exploits, the Seleção arrived in Spain with a fearsome reputation.

Some 68,000 people turned out to watch Brazil's debut at the Ramón Sánchez Pizjuán against Russia. Just three days before the game, though, the Seleção had been dealt a blow: during practice, Careca had suffered a serious thigh injury and had been ruled out of the tournament. Santana drafted in Dinamite as a last-minute replacement and decided to give Serginho the number 9 shirt. History would be unkind to the controversial centre-forward: Sérgio Bernardino stuck out like a sore thumb in that team full of 'fantasistas', but to dismiss his more workmanlike attributes is to undermine his ability as a footballer. Serginho still figures as São Paulo FC's all-time top goalscorer, with 242 goals in 401 games, and although he was never as graceful on the pitch as many of his contemporaries, he still managed to be a threat with both feet, in the air or at set pieces.

But apart from questions about his tactical suitability within the team, there were also fears about Serginho's behaviour. He had missed the chance to play in the 1978 World Cup thanks to a 14-month suspension for kicking a linesman, and in the 1981 Campeonato Brasileiro final he caused a national outcry for putting a boot to goalkeeper Leão's face. The same Leão who had also been called up to the World Cup squad. Needless to say, Santana felt it necessary to have several pep talks with Serginho in order to try and tame that side of his character and so prevent the striker from adding to his collection of red cards – a move that, in hindsight, would actually neuter his performances.

On that evening of 14 June, though, the manager had other worries. After initially making his mind up to not use a right-winger, Santana backtracked for the USSR game; but instead of using Paulo Isidoro, who had featured constantly in the starting line-up during the qualifiers, he selected Dirceu, a veteran in his third World Cup and, alongside Falcão, the only player based abroad (at Atlético Madrid) in the 22-man squad. Having hardly played for Santana for the same reasons as Falcão, but without the same rapport with the other players, Dirceu looked uncomfortable on the pitch against the Soviets, but not nearly as out of sorts as Waldir Peres: with 34 minutes gone, a long-distance speculative shot by Andrei Bal went pathetically through the goalkeeper's legs. Eight out of the 11 players that started the match, Peres included, were playing their first-ever World Cup match and nerves seemed to have got the better of them. But in the second half, with Isidoro replacing Dirceu, the Seleção started putting more pressure on their opponents, who also had to deal with the energy-sapping Spanish heat. In the 65th minute, Sócrates escaped two markers and drew the score level for Brazil with a wondrous long-distance shot.

Then, three minutes from time, in a sequence of moves that echoed the Seleção circa 1970, came pure magic: Isidoro stole the ball near the Soviet box and rolled it to Falcão, who instead of having a go opened up his legs, wrong-footing half of the defence and allowing Éder to pounce and hit a raking volley past the great Rinat Dasayev. Brazil had survived the debut jitters and would face a Scottish team that had assembled a squad that was arguably even stronger than in 1978.

Scotland had started their campaign by putting five past the Kiwis but also conceding twice. Manager Jock Stein had reportedly told the squad they should not even worry about the game against Brazil and instead concentrate on the Russians. But to everybody's surprise, Scotland found themselves in front after 18 minutes, courtesy of a powerful shot by David Narey, who legend says was mockingly told off afterwards by his team-mates for making the Brazilians angry. After the scare against the Russians, Santana had opted to bring back Cerezo to reinforce the midfield in lieu of Isidoro. There was 15 minutes of relative unease among the Brazilians after falling behind for the second game running before Zico hit a perfect free kick to equalise. Four minutes into the second half, Júnior used his right foot to swing a vicious corner into the Scottish box for Oscar to rise above his fellow defenders and head Brazil in front. Éder scored the third after 65 minutes by chipping the ball over a disheartened Alan Rough. Falcão completed a rout that pundits in Brazil believed had made the Seleção favourites for the title.

In all fairness, it was easy to get carried away. While Brazil were unbeaten and had now already qualified for the second stage, other traditional powerhouse teams were struggling. Champions Argentina had been beaten by Belgium in the opening game; Germany were humbled by the valiant Algeria; and hosts Spain were held to a 1-1 draw by debutants Honduras. Only England had managed to look good in a 3-1 victory over France. But while the mood was buoyant in Brazil, an old connoisseur of the game and the country expressed his reservations.

Many other people would have slid into obscurity after a high-profile dismissal and a breakdown. But João Saldanha was a unique creature. After losing the Seleção job three months before the 1970 World Cup, Saldanha had resumed his punditry duties and was an ever-present in the commentary box for every Seleção game. He became one of the leading analysts of the game in Brazil and actually benefited from his controversial exit, playing up his supposed clash with the Brazilian dictatorship over attempts to influence his team selections. Saldanha was a voice of dissent in 1982, criticising what he saw as Santana's stubbornness in the whole 'no right-winger' experiment. For Saldanha, the Seleção were overcomplicating things in Spain and might be caught out by more organised and dangerous sides than the ones they had faced so far in the tournament.

That certainly wasn't the case with New Zealand, however. Within 30 minutes of their meeting on 23 June, Brazil were already 2-0 up thanks to a Zico brace. Falcão scored the third and Serginho finally opened his account at the tournament to complete a comprehensive win. At the end of the group stage, Brazil had qualified with maximum points for the first time in three World Cups and the early scares seemed to have been put behind them. Apart from Brazil, only England had managed to win all their three group games, but even their impressive displays against France and the Czechs weren't enough to strip the mantle of favourites from the Brazilians.

The underwhelming performances from other traditional contenders didn't result in any early exits but had upset the apple cart enough to set up some juicy encounters in the second stage. England, for example, were grouped with Germany and hosts Spain, who had only managed to qualify behind a surprising Northern Ireland. Brazil would have to see off Argentina and Italy if they were to get to the semi-finals. Argentina, featuring Diego Maradona, who had a huge point to prove after being left out of the 1978 World Cup-winning team by César Menotti. The same manager was in charge of the team in Spain and had recovered from the opening-day defeat to the Belgians by beating Hungary 4-1, but then only managed a 2-0 triumph against minnows El Salvador. Compared to Italy, however, they had been in fine form. Having won two World Cups in a row in the 1930s, Italy had gone quiet on the world stage until 1968, when they won the European Championships. In World Cups, though, they went through a mediocre spell, the nadir of which saw their elimination from the 1966 tournament at the hands of lowly North Korea. The Italians were so ashamed by their Middlesbrough fiasco that the game's authorities took the drastic measure of closing Serie A to foreign imports in an effort to strengthen their home-grown talent pool.

Coincidence or not, they went on to win a continental title, made it to the 1970 World Cup final and finished in the top four in Argentina 1978 before reopening the market for international transfers in 1980. But in that same year, Italian football was plunged head-first into controversy when a match-fixing scandal involving five top-flight teams was uncovered. Players were arrested in dressing rooms and investigations led to severe punishments. Among them was Paolo Rossi, then the most expensive player in the world. Initially suspended for three years, he had his ban reduced to two years on appeal. That meant Rossi didn't play a single game until two months before the World Cup and few people in Italy expected manager Enzo Bearzot to include the striker in his World Cup squad. Bearzot did more than that: Rossi was named in the starting XI for Italy's first game at Spain 1982. His impact, however, was negligible. Italy drew all their group stage matches and neither of their meagre two goals were scored by Rossi. Their campaign had been pitiful and they only managed to edge past Cameroon for the second spot in Group 1 on goals scored. Lambasted by the home media, the Italian players decided to stop talking to the press and the mood in their camp was sombre by the time they came to prepare for their match against Argentina.

With the exception of Poland's 3-0 routing of Belgium, the second round began with a number of evenly contested matches. England and Germany cancelled each other out in a goalless draw and France came through with a 1-0 win over Austria. On 29 June, Italy and Argentina opened their pool and during the first 45 minutes it seemed as if the Italians were more concerned about not losing the match than winning it. Argentina, however, failed to capitalise on the lack of ambition being shown by their opposition and were then hit by a combination of sucker punches in the second half: having zeroed in on the spaces left by Argentina on the right side of their defence, the Azzurri drew first blood when Tardelli finished a neat one-two in the Argentine box with a vicious left-foot shot.

Argentina went forward with all guns blazing and Maradona, kept quiet for most of the game by a masterclass in man-marking by

Claudio Gentile, managed to strike the post with a free kick before Italy cruelly hit the South Americans again on the break, this time through Cabrini.

Passarella scored for the defending world champions seven minutes from time but Italy held on for their first win in Spain at the fourth attempt. It was a result that suggested the Azzurri were at last starting to click.

The Brazilians, however, were understandably more worried about their derby with a wounded Argentina. After the defeat to Italy, Maradona and co would have to beat their neighbours in order to stay alive in the tournament and the threat of that scenario was enough to focus the minds of the Seleção both on and off the pitch. The players knew that they had fallen behind too easily against relatively weak opposition in their opening two matches of the tournament; to do so against a more formidable opponent like Argentina might prove deadly.

On 2 July, Brazil and Argentina met in a World Cup for the third time in eight years. Just before kick-off, Argentine midfielder Daniel Bertoni, who played for Fiorentina and had forged a cordial relationship with Falcão, whispered a warning to his fellow Italy-based South American.

'Mind your legs, mate.'

The game did not become quite the pitched battle that Bertoni had forewarned, but it was still marred by some ugly moments. It was also a cracking game. Argentina flew out of the blocks and very nearly opened the scoring during the opening exchanges through centre-back Galván before Brazil stole the initiative with just 11 minutes gone: Éder fired a howitzer of a free kick that bounced on the line and fell into Zico's path, who buried it in the net.

Momentum was firmly with the Seleção and they were soon attacking from everywhere, but they could not press home their advantage. It took until the 66th minute for the second goal to be scored. Argentina had by now thrown caution to the wind, and as Passarella swarmed over the centre circle he was dispossessed by Serginho, who started a move that in seven touches would end with him heading home to put Brazil 2-0 up. Nine minutes later, a Zico pass split the Argentine defence for Júnior to slot the ball through goalkeeper Fillol's legs; he celebrated the third goal with some samba steps for the crowd.

Ramón Diaz pulled back a consolation goal for Argentina in the 89th minute, but it was too little too late. It was a consummate performance. 'At the end, some of the Argentine players were even wearing the Brazil shirts they exchanged with us,' remembers Falcão.

All that separated Brazil from a third consecutive World Cup semi-final, therefore, was Italy.

'You play there. Is there anything you want to say about them?'

Santana waited until the end of his team-talk to address Falcão. Of all the 22 Brazilian players in the 1982 World Cup, the curly-haired midfielder had most reason to feel anxious about the winner-takes-all game to be played on 5 July. Living and working in Italy, he would be facing well-known opponents. And Falcão was worried that his team-mates had got the wrong idea after the Italians had stumbled past the finishing line to get out of the group stage. 'Some of the lads were teasing me and saying it must have been quite easy to earn a living in Serie A,' he remembers. 'But I did tell them Italy were a much better team than their results had suggested – which was something the lads could finally see when we went to watch Italy v Argentina.'

When prompted by the manager, Falcão expressed his worry about the possible threat of left-back Antonio Cabrini, who had added to the Azzurri's attacking armoury. 'I knew Claudio Gentile would try to mark Zico out of the game the same way he had done with Maradona,' said Falcão. 'So I suggested Zico should try to veer more to the right so that he would force Cabrini to stay back more. In the end, though, it was decided that we would keep things as they were, with Zico more centralised.'

It was typical application of the 'if it ain't broke don't fix it' principle and few could blame Santana for thinking he was doing things right. Brazil had convincingly disposed of the Argentines and up to that moment had a tally of 13 goals to three in four matches, while the Italians had conceded the same amount and only scored four. In the knockout stages, both teams had beaten Argentina but Brazil had a better goal difference, which meant that they only needed a draw to progress. This had had a bearing on Falcão's tactical advice.

Had Italy been in the same position, they would certainly have parked the bus. Bearzot, their manager, had developed a system that improved on Italy's famous catenaccio. He knew how to close down the opposition. But Bearzot also knew his team had a formidable opponent to overcome in Barcelona and that Italy's victory over Argentina couldn't hide the fact that Paolo Rossi, his main striker, had yet to score in the competition, giving grist to the mill for those who had questioned his presence in the squad from the outset. The Italian media were screaming for the manager to drop the disgraced striker. Rossi was not feeling too good about himself either and his confidence had not been helped by Brazil's momentum. 'They did not look from this planet,' said Rossi. 'That Brazil side was the best I had seen. Those players could have worn blindfolds and they would still have known where each other were. As for me, I felt like I was still learning to play football again after the two-year suspension.'

In the other camp, the mood couldn't be more different. Defender Oscar would later remember that while some players had made observations about how Poland, already qualified for the semi-finals and the next opponent for either Brazil or Italy, were hit by an injury crisis, no one was looking past the challenge of the Italians. 'But it was never in our minds that the result was a foregone conclusion,' said the defender.

'In the dressing room before the game against Italy, Telê [Santana] mentioned the fact that a draw would be enough to see us through – but only to remind us not to relax,' said Zico. 'He would never tell us to hold back. Our commitment was always to go for the win. That was the true Brazilian way.' While there been no 'clairvoyant' headlines like there had been before the 1950 final, Brazilians were still pretty sure that their team would leave the Sarrià having made it through to the semi-final. Actually not only the Brazilians: on arrival at the stadium in Barcelona, FIFA president João Havelange met Artemio Franchi, the Italian who was then the number one at UEFA. Franchi promptly joked with Havelange that he already felt like a winner. 'Not losing to your guys today will be a victory for us,' he reportedly told the Brazilian.

5 July. The crowd packed into the Sarrià had barely taken their seats after the national anthems when Francesco Graziani broke down the left side of the Brazilian defence. Closed down by two Brazilians, he quickly had a glance infield and saw that Cabrini was advancing unopposed on the far flank. He flicked a cross-field pass to Cabrini, who had ample time to whip a cross into the area. Paolo Rossi escaped the shackles of Luizinho and scorched to meet it head on. With five minutes gone, Italy were 1-0 up and Rossi had broken his duck just when the team needed him most. So shocked did they seem by their sudden, early advantage, the Azzurri nearly conceded an equaliser just minutes later when Zico broke free into the box only for Serginho to block his way and send the ball wide.

Chased relentlessly by Gentile who was like a second shadow, Zico would finish the first half with his shirt torn after it had been tugged so much by his marker. But in a rare escape from Gentile in the 12th minute, the Rooster provided Sócrates with a perfect assist for the equaliser.

The Italians, though, were succeeding in rattling Brazil and disturbing the fluidity of their movement in midfield that had been so crucial to the Seleção's previous success in the tournament.

Under pressure from the swarming defence, Cerezo managed to mishit a pass in the 27th minute that worked as an assist for Rossi, who fired the ball past Valdir Peres to put Italy back in front. For the second time in that World Cup, the Brazilians were behind at half-time and would need to chase the result.

The fact they could still rely on the draw was encouraging for those watching the game, but the Seleção dressing room was a charged atmosphere. Frustration and anger shared space with Cerezo's tears. The midfielder was so distraught by his mistake that he couldn't stop crying. Cerezo only calmed down after a long pep talk by Sócrates. Meanwhile, while the rest of the world waited for the second half, Brazilian photographer Reginaldo Manente, who was on the pitch working for São Paulo newspaper *Jornal da Tarde*, was killing time by inspecting the crowd. His eyes rested on a good-looking woman in the VIP stand. It wouldn't be the last time she would attract the photographer's attention.

As the second half kicked off, Brazil pressed hard for another equaliser. Zico slipped a delicate through-ball to Cerezo that forced veteran goalkeeper Dino Zoff into an impressive clearance dive. Shortly afterwards, Zico provided another ball, this time to Serginho, who was only able to attempt a feeble back-heel that Zoff was able to clear again.

Then, after a brilliant piece of counter-attacking, Rossi missed a precious chance to finish Brazil off.

On 68 minutes, the momentum swung again. A great sequence of moves by Zico and Cerezo pulled the Italian defence out of shape and opened space for Falcão, who fired a piledriver past Zoff to equalise for the Seleção. His emotional celebration became almost as iconic as the powerful left-foot shot that looked to be sending Brazil to the semis. With the jugular vein almost popping from his neck, Falcão ran towards the Brazilian bench to celebrate and almost choked on the piece of gum he had been chewing. 'Some of the Italian players would later ask why I was scowling at them during the celebration, but I was just trying desperately to clear my throat,' remembers the midfielder with a smile.

With the game tied, it seemed certain that the Seleção would now settle down and play with an eye on securing the draw, but for the next six minutes they gave no impression of wanting to change their tactics. Santana replaced Serginho with Paulo Isidoro, which would in theory balance the defence a bit better, but Brazil still pressed for a winner, with right-back Leandro playing almost as a centre-forward.

Italy's creative midfielder Antognoni used the space created by Leandro pushing forward so relentlessly to win his team's first corner of the game, in the 74th minute. He took the corner, and the poor clearance fell to Tardelli. His shot was nothing special but still made it to the Brazilian box where Rossi had been left alone by a botched attempt to spring the offside trap; with time and space on his side, the striker made no mistake in burying the ball in the net to secure his hat-trick, becoming only the second player ever to do so against the Seleção in a World Cup game.

Brazil now had no other option but to continue to throw themselves forward for the remaining 16 minutes. But they struggled to create anything as the Italian defence drew back tightly, and they were lucky not to fall even further behind when the Azzurri broke and Antognoni scored, only for Israeli referee Abraham Klein to – wrongfully – rule it out for offside.

In the 89th minute, Oscar appeared in the Italian box and hit a bullet of a header that Zoff collected miraculously on the goal line. It was the last move of the game. Brazil were once again on the end of a massive World Cup upset and the shock of their exit hit them and their fans in the stadium hard. Amid the scenes of heartbreak, Manente once again looked for the pretty lady he had spotted in the crowd. She was crying wildly, tears and make-up running in dark streams down her cheeks. The photographer vaulted the pitchside barriers to take a picture of her. It was only when he arrived within touching distance that he saw a young boy named José Carlos Junior whose stricken expression was a much more poignant summation of all that had happened than the tears of the beautiful Vilma Villella.

The next morning, the teary image of the boy was on the cover of *Jornal da Tarde*, without a headline. It became one of the most iconic images in the history of Brazilian journalism and months later won Manente the Esso Prize, the most important media accolade in the country. José Carlos symbolised the tears of a nation that had not prepared to weep in 1982.

Just like in 1950, Brazil had woken up on cloud nine, only to crash from the heights by the end of the day. But while recriminations immediately began, with Cerezo and Serginho becoming targets of particular criticism, the general reaction could not have been more different to 32 years before. While the generation of Barbosa, Zizinho and Ademir had reached a World Cup final, the class of 1982 had fallen even shorter from the title; but the difference was that they had fired the public's imagination to the point that they are often spoken of in more revered tones than squads that actually won the trophy – the 1994 team, the habitual loser in direct comparison, much to the irritation of players from that generation such as captain Carlos 'Dunga' Verri.

'There is nothing wrong in losing with dignity, it is a part of the game,' said Zico. 'We were obviously saddened by the result but everybody had clear consciences. The Seleção were going home but we had stood by our convictions till the end. We didn't allow the win-at-any-costs mentality to compromise our belief in the Beautiful Game.'

At the press conference after the game, Santana was applauded when he arrived and when he departed. The manager didn't offer any excuses and simply gave credit to the Italians for their performance. In the desolation that had been the Brazilian dressing room Santana had told the players they had to be proud of what they achieved: 'The whole world was enchanted by you. Be aware of that.'

The fans also acknowledged it. They headed en masse to Rio de Janeiro's international airport to welcome the team back home. Santana was particularly moved by the reception but while he refused to publicly acknowledge his grief, especially when consoling some of his most distraught players, inside the manager was heartbroken. So heartbroken that just a few weeks after returning from Spain he accepted an offer to work in Saudi Arabia. 'It was a self-imposed exile for my father, who had been really shaken by that defeat,' explains Renê, Santana's son.

Critics, nevertheless, lashed out at Santana for not holding his players back after the second equaliser, an argument that over the years has morphed into a kind of 'exhibit A' of Brazil's tactical naivety and their tendency to concede as often as they scored. The main voice opposing this line of thought was that of Falcão, who was in a much better position to judge the reasons behinds the 'Sarrià Tragedy' – the nickname the Brazilian press promptly adopted to describe the match – than any commentator. 'I find it laughable that people say that our team couldn't defend properly,' he said. 'In five matches in that World Cup, we scored 15 goals and conceded five. Against Italy we made more tackles than the Italians and they scored their third goal when we had pretty much everybody back in our area for that corner. We lost to a team that seized their opportunities, but even some of my Italian team-mates couldn't believe the Azzurri had knocked us out.'

Few people felt that defeat as deeply as Falcão, who would have to resume his life in Italian football after the World Cup, although he managed to salvage some pride when Roma won the 1982/83 Serie A title, leaving Juventus in second place. It was a small measure of revenge over the 'Juventinos' (Zoff, Cabrini, Gentile, Scirea, Tardelli and Rossi) who had played in the Sarrià Tragedy.

The defeat also hit Sócrates hard. In order to arrive at the tournament in perfect condition he quit smoking and drinking for several months; after the defeat in Barcelona, he fell spectacularly off the wagon. Twenty-two years later in Leeds, Sócrates would still struggle to express his feelings about that game. 'We had a hell of a team and played with happiness. Then we came across the Italians. Rossi had three touches and scored a hat-trick. Football as we know it died that day.'

While Sócrates' statement appears bitter, particularly in light of the heroics of Rossi and his team-mates – they would go on to win the tournament and the striker would score another two goals in their semi-final against Poland, as well as one in the final – it also makes some sense. While Brazil's 1982 World Cup campaign lacked the shambles in preparation that had so famously plagued other unsuccessful attempts, the legacy of that specific defeat has been arguably more damaging to Brazilian football. For a start, it provided ammunition for the pragmatists in Brazil and abroad. The Beautiful Game, they claimed, had become obsolete and it was time that the Seleção caught up with what the Europeans were doing.

That would not happen in the following World Cup, though: for Mexico 1986, the Seleção once again had Santana at the helm, summoned from his desert exile to take over a team that was struggling to balance veterans with new arrivals. This time, however, there was an added problem: while the Seleção's 1982 defeat had curbed a lot of their gung-ho attacking style, their performances in Spain had caught the attention of European clubs. In the next two years, seven players from the 1982 squad would sign with Serie A clubs, including Zico, Júnior, Cerezo and Sócrates. The Doctor's departure was the most dramatic: unlike his peers, Sócrates dreaded the idea of going abroad but announced that he would only stay at Corinthians if the legislation to grant free presidential elections for Brazil in 1984 came to fruition – a cause that had taken millions to the streets of big Brazilian cities. When the proposal was narrowly defeated in parliament, Sócrates accepted an offer from Fiorentina. His departure crowned a series of disappointments for Brazilians on and off the pitch: in January 1983 they lost the legendary Garrincha, finally defeated by his addiction to alcohol, and the year would end with thieves breaking into the CBF headquarters to steal the Jules Rimet trophy, Brazilian football's most important conquest. The economy continued its downturn and by 1983 Brazil was virtually bankrupt and formally defaulted on its foreign debt, resorting to an International Monetary Fund rescue package that came with draconian conditions that would hold back economic growth for 25 years.

The return of Santana to the Seleção was followed by an attempted rehabilitation of the class of 1982. His squad for Mexico 1986 featured no fewer than eight players called up for the previous tournament, including Sócrates, Zico and Falcão. All of them were in the twilight of their careers. Sócrates was the only one who made it to the starting line-up; Santana opted for a midfield combination that excluded Falcão, and Zico was desperately trying to get fit after months of struggling with a knee injury.

While failing to recreate the dazzling brand of football of four years earlier, the Seleção still aced the group stages and hammered Poland 4-0 in the round of 16. Then came a classic and dramatic clash with European champions France, in which Brazil went ahead, conceded an unlucky equaliser and saw Zico miss a penalty in the second half before capitulating in a penalty shoot-out that started with Sócrates missing his attempt. Redemption on the pitch denied, the class of 1982 would spend the following years trying to move on. There were some interesting episodes along the way: in June 1990, in order to celebrate Júnior's retirement from Pescara, the club organised an Italy v Brazil masters friendly. Santana and Bearzot were back in the dugout and both sides resembled the 1982 squads – although Italy didn't have Zoff, Cabrini, Tardelli or the recently deceased Scirea. Brazil won 9-1.

At the time, Santana was still trying to find his feet again in club management. After Mexico 1986, he club-hopped until 1990, when he ended up at São Paulo and built a team that in four years won 11 trophies, including two Copa Libertadores/Intercontinental Cup doubles (their triumph over Johan Cruyff's Barcelona in 1992 impressed even rival fans) and a Brazilian championship. In 1996, however, a stroke forced Santana into retirement and ten years later he died from an abdominal infection. To this day he is still remembered in Brazil as a romantic who fought for the preservation of the essence of Brazilian football and whose anti-violence agenda still strikes a chord with both the public and the media.

In 1989, Paolo Rossi visited Brazil for the first time since the events of Barcelona in order to take part in a São Paulo masters tournament – the 'Bambino D'Oro' (Golden Boy) had retired in 1987 – and was quickly reminded that the events of the Sarrià hadn't been forgotten. First, he got kicked out of a cab when the driver recognised the 'Executioner of 1982', as Brazilians nicknamed him. Worse would happen when Brazil and Italy met at Pacaembu stadium: the crowd treated Rossi with a pelting session involving objects as varied as monkey nuts, banana skins and coins every time he approached the touchline. 'I was a bit scared by the way some Brazilians, especially the ones in the press, were obsessed about the past,' said Rossi. 'In general, however, Brazilian people were nice to me. But I do understand some of them have a little resentment towards me.'

Tempers, though, cooled down with the years and in 2013 Rossi was flown to Brazil to star in a commercial for a credit card company, in which he plays himself as he walks into a barbershop. Upon presenting his credit card, the Italian legend is recognised by the barber. That part was played by José Carlos Junior, the weeping boy in the iconic photo. Thirty-one years later, two unlikely related characters of the 'Sarrià Tragedy' had been reunited.

For the Brazilian players, closure would come with a mixture of admiration and vindication. The 2.8 goals per match average registered in 1982 hasn't been matched in subsequent tournaments, even after FIFA increased the number of teams to 32 in 1998. Two of the following five World Cups, including the tournament won by Brazil in 1994, had to be decided on penalties. 'The quality of the game has been compromised by this fear of losing,' vented Sócrates in one of his last interviews before his death. 'It pains me to see teams much more worried about neutralising the opposition than trying to create something.'

The Doctor died of septic shock in December 2011 – the same day Corinthians won the Campeonato Brasileiro. Players from his former club marked the minute's silence by imitating his famous Black Panther-style goal celebration. Sócrates was 57 and had had the chance to vote in six presidential elections in his lifetime.

A few months later Sócrates' former Brazil team-mate Falcão tried to exorcise his own demons by releasing *Why Did We Lose?*, a collection of mini-essays by him and other Seleção players in commemoration of the 30th anniversary of the Italy game. It's an interesting collection of anecdotes and reflections that ends with a touching sentiment. 'We lost that game but won a place in history,' wrote Falcão. 'Of course all of us suffered a great deal with the defeat but I am also grateful that I was part of one the greatest games in the history of football and part of a team that is associated with great football. It was a privilege to play alongside those guys.'

1998

FIVE

1998
BOY MUST BE MAN

EVEN BY THE the standards of official celebrations in Brazil, the fanfare around the 1994 World Cup-winning team, the first in 24 years to win the trophy, after a much maligned campaign, was over the top.

Having flown from Los Angeles a day after an unbelievably tense final with Italy, decided only after a penalty shoot-out – a tie-breaking resource that had never been used before in a deciding World Cup match – the team landed in Recife, the north-eastern coastal town where the Seleção had finally clicked after a poor start in the qualifiers, and whose local supporters had given the team such a roaring welcome that CBF president Ricardo Teixeira had promised to pay them back with a victory parade.

The team then headed to Brasilia for the inevitable presidential handshake and photo opportunity. It was already late in the evening when the DC10 touched down in Rio de Janeiro, where another parade awaited. But the crowd of supporters waiting outside and across some of the main roads in the city did not know the world champions were threatening a massive walkout: news that the Brazilian Inland Revenue would not provide a customs amnesty for the huge number of products purchased in the United States by players and technical staff had led the players to decide not to hop on the fire engines waiting for them – there are no such things as open-top buses in Brazil, by the way.

It would later transpire that the Seleção had left Brazil with 3.4 tons of equipment and luggage only to come back with 14.4 tons on 19 July (left-back Branco, for example, had brought back kitchen appliances and fittings worth US$18,000). After some tense negotiations, a phone call from Teixeira to a government minister settled the matter and the players were excused from paying the import duties. Only the youngest member of that squad, Ronaldo, hadn't broken the $500 import limit, having apparently only treated himself to some CDs. And while he enjoyed the marathon of victory parades, it was fair to say the striker felt like something of an outsider in the group. But just four years later, his world had been turned on its head in a way that he couldn't even have dreamed of when he became Brazilian football's biggest superstar since Pelé – but with expectations and responsibilities far in excess of those faced by the King.

Ronaldo had been a last-minute addition to the 1994 squad – an experienced group that contained many members from Brazil's catastrophic World Cup 1990 campaign, where a round of 16 exit against Argentina had resulted in a horrendous backlash both in Brazil and abroad. Aged just 17, he would travel to the USA but fail to play a single minute of football in the Seleção's seven games. He had been a professional footballer for only a season, but had already caused a stir. In 14 games for Cruzeiro, Ronaldo had netted 12 goals and finished the 1993 Campeonato Brasileiro as the third most prolific scorer – only three goals off the top. His performance in a 6-0 mauling of EC Bahia grabbed the headlines as he put five goals past legendary Uruguayan goalkeeper Rodolfo Rodriguez and set a single game tally that had never previously been reached by a Brazilian player.

Ronaldo just couldn't stop scoring for Cruzeiro. During the 1993 and 1994 seasons, he scored 44 goals in 46 matches and became an unwelcome headache for the Seleção manager, Carlos Alberto Parreira. Criticised by the public and the media for his rigid brand of tactical football, Parreira had been forced to publicly backtrack on his decision to drop Romário from the national team after the Barcelona striker had publicly spat the dummy when Parreira started him on the bench for a 1992 friendly against Germany. Romário was duly dropped from the team for almost a year before an injury to São Paulo FC striker Müller forced Parreira to recall him for a match against Uruguay at the Maracanã that would decide Brazil's fate in the qualifiers – Rio boy Romário, whose presence had been demanded even by supporters and journalists from São Paulo, scored both goals in the 2-0 victory and became a national hero. The last thing Parreira wanted was another controversy at a time when he felt Romário was causing unwelcome distractions for his pragmatic team.

But Ronaldo's form could not be ignored, so Parreira called up the shy boy for a tour of Europe and North America for two friendlies against Germany and Mexico. Ronaldo did nothing more than watch the action from the bench, but the call-up was already making an immense difference to the boy's life.

Ronaldo Luis Nazário de Lima was born in Rio de Janeiro on 18 September 1976, in conditions quite familiar to many other Brazilian footballers: in a poor family that was struggling to escape the vicious cycle of destitution. Until his teenage years, Ronaldo would share a sofa bed with brother Nelio in the living room of the modest one-bedroom house his parents, Nelio Sr and Sonia, had built in the grounds of Ronaldo's grandfather's house in Bento Ribeiro, a working-class neighbourhood on the outskirts of Rio. Football was part of the lifeblood in the house. Both Ronaldo's father and his uncles (who were both former footballers) would religiously attend the neighbourhood's Sunday league games and his brother Nelio loved nothing more than having a kickabout in the street. It wasn't long before Ronaldo was joining him. But Nelio was more than a sporting companion, he was a safety net for Ronaldo. The latter had only started speaking at four and his sparse use of words had worried his parents. But his quiet demeanour stemmed from an acute shyness and a cripplingly low self-esteem, which manifested itself in sleepwalking, fear of the dark and him often wetting the bed. In the presence of other kids, Nelio became his minder – until Ronaldo started being picked ahead of him in football games.

They would develop a fierce rivalry that would often lead to physical punishment from their mother. If picked by different teams, the Nazário brothers would fight private battles that were more and more regularly won by Ronaldo, on pitches that would sometimes be nothing more than concrete paths.

Ronaldo fell so deeply in love with football that the game became a serious obstacle to Sonia's plans to have all her kids properly attend school. She pretty much had to drag her son to classes and stand guard at the gates to ensure he didn't just turn around and run out of the school. Ronaldo was a terrible student and it was only thanks to his mother's efforts that he negotiated passage through primary school.

At ten, Ronaldo was already earning a name for himself in footballing circles and he earned a place in the futsal youth squad of neighbouring club Valqueire Tennis. His impressive skills were not only a source of great pride to the family, but also earned them a much-needed leisure option – for playing for the team allowed Ronaldo and his family the right to use the social club for free. Ronaldo was drafted during desperate times for Valqueire, who were then the linchpins in the Rio League. Incredibly, he started as the goalie in order to get into the first team, but after a couple of practice sessions was moved into the outfield and repaid the coach's faith with four goals and an assist in Valqueire's massive upset of league leaders Vasco da Gama.

In the stands was scout and futsal coach Fernando Carvalho, who after lengthy negotiations with Ronaldo's mother that included guarantees that her son would not fail at school, took the boy to Social Ramos, a bigger club in the Rio futsal scene. In his first season, Ronaldo scored 166 goals and finally started to entertain the idea that he could play football for a living. Having grown up supporting CR Flamengo and worshipping their most famous player ever, Seleção legend Zico, Ronaldo wanted to get into Flamengo's renowned youth academy.

That, however, was easier said than done: Brazilian football clubs are still famous for a selection process nicknamed *peneira* (sifter), where hundreds of players are observed during a series of short games played over a single day. It is hardly a scientific process and Brazilian football folklore is full of cases of great players who slipped through the net. Former Seleção captain and double World Cup winner Cafu, for example, was reportedly rejected by 12 clubs before being picked up by São Paulo feeder club Nacional. Clubs have an immense network of informal contacts and they are often alerted in advance if a special kid is coming their way. Ronaldo did not know anybody who could have put a word in for him, but he still managed to be selected: at just 13 and after taking part in sessions involving over 400 kids, Ronaldo cleared the first hurdle and was told he needed to come the following day for further evaluations. Skint, he asked if the club could pay for the bus fares. He was denied this and then matters were made even worse when he was mugged on the way home by a gang of street kids, so he did not go back the next day. Flamengo would forever kick themselves for missing out on him and Ronaldo would pay them back with interest almost 20 years later by snubbing them on his return to Brazilian football in order to join Corinthians instead.

For now, however, the boy was heartbroken and had to find another opportunity. It came from one of the most unlikely places. In the late '80s, São Cristóvão FR was a zombie club: founded in 1909, the club had its peak in the 1920s, winning the 1926 state championship, but since the late 1970s had fallen into a spiral of decline that was symbolised by the decision of the Rio authorities to open a new expressway that hid the club's tiny Figueira de Mello stadium from view.

São Cristóvão was still attractive enough, just, for Social Ramos to accept a partnership where they would borrow futsal players to reinforce their youth team. Ronaldo was among the first to be shipped to São Cristóvão, as he realised that dropping down a division could at least provide an entry point into professional football. It would be more difficult than he thought: while Ronaldo's skills were already impressive, his tactical sense was non-existent and the São Cristóvão youth academy manager, Alfredo Sampaio, soon discovered that Ronaldo also hated training drills and physical work. Sampaio had immediately noticed Ronaldo didn't like heading the ball and marking. The striker also seemed to enjoy listening to instructions only to immediately forget them as soon as he stepped foot on the pitch. But for all these failings, it would invariably be Ronaldo who scored São Cristóvão's goals, and the boy would soon be noticed by the man who coached the first team, 1970 World Cup winner Jairzinho.

Famous for his explosive brand of football, especially the way he outmuscled the opposition, earning the nickname 'Hurricane', Jairzinho immediately noticed a similarity of styles with the boy. The Seleção legend would be a useful ally for Ronaldo, but not only on the pitch: he had developed a partnership with agents Reinaldo Pitta and Alexandre Martins, whereby Jairzinho would introduce talented youngsters to the agents in exchange for transfer profits. Introducing Ronaldo to the agents was a way to avoid him being poached. An extremely draconian contract was put in front of Ronaldo: in exchange for basically only the promise of future earnings, he would sign away numerous rights that included his freedom to decide which club he wanted to play for. In essence, he would belong to Martins and Pitta and then be loaned to São Cristóvão. The contract also gave the agents carte blanche to exploit the player's image. As noted by writer Jorge Caldeira, an expert in Brazilian colonial history and a football fanatic who ended up writing a Ronaldo biography, the document drafted by Martins and Pitta was eerily similar to some servitude deals from the slavery era. On 7 June 1992, Ronaldo, via father Nelio, signed the deal. He was 15.

While Martins and Pitta could easily be accused of exploitation, they also provided for him: Ronaldo, his mother and siblings (their parents had separated a few years before) were moved to a bigger and more comfortable house in São Cristóvão, with rent paid by the agents. Things on the pitch started moving when Jairzinho convinced CBF scout Jairo dos Santos to attend a São Cristóvão game. Santos was looking for players that could join Brazil's under-17 side that would play the South American Championship a few months later.

He attended a game that saw São Cristóvão steamrollered 4-0 by Vasco da Gama, but was impressed enough to inform the U17 Seleção manager Humberto Redes about the player.

Redes himself went to see Ronaldo at another match: he left in the middle of the game, after seeing Ronaldo finish a slalom run through the opposition defence by hitting the post. Despite the miss, he had impressed enough to be called up for the South American Championship in Colombia. The Seleção failed for the first time in years to win the tournament, which also deprived them of a shot at the U17 World Cup, but Ronaldo was the tournament's top scorer with eight goals. When he returned home, it was already time to pack up. Martins and Pitta had sold his services to Cruzeiro for just over US$20,000, which represented a 55 per cent stake in the player's rights – a deal that was unheard of in the amateur environment of Brazilian football at the time. Ronaldo left São Cristóvão with the impressive tally of 44 goals in 73 games.

At Cruzeiro, he blossomed. It is crucial to note that Ronaldo was a breath of fresh air at a time when most of Brazil's best players were plying their trade abroad. In 1993, the same year Ronaldo really began to make his name, Romário was playing for Barcelona under Johan Cruyff, Bebeto played for Deportivo La Coruña, and Seleção captain, Rai, who had taken São Paulo to back-to-back Copa Libertadores and Intercontinental Cup titles, wore Paris Saint-Germain's colours. Out of the Seleção first XI, only three players that would start Brazil's 1994 World Cup campaign were playing domestic football. In 1992, the CBF began to compile statistics of international transfers and found that a total of 235 Brazilian players had been signed by foreign clubs – a number that 10 years later would surpass more than a thousand in a single year. Ronaldo, fresh-faced and smiley, was a sweet reminder that Brazilian football could still have some outstanding talent based at home. In their naivety, fans thought Ronaldo's youth would spare him from following the well-trodden path to Europe.

In early 1994, the striker scored a wonder goal for Cruzeiro in a Copa Libertadores match against the mighty Boca Juniors at La Bombonera, the intimidating Buenos Aires ground that is one of the spiritual homes of club legend Diego Maradona, and the public clamour for his call-up to the Seleção went into overdrive. On 23 March, with ten minutes left in Brazil's 2-0 friendly victory over Argentina, Ronaldo won his first cap for the Seleção, replacing Bebeto. It was hardly enough time to showcase his skills but Parreira, even after voicing his concerns about taking such a young player to a World Cup, had no other option than to recall the boy for Brazil's last official friendly before the World Cup: the European clubs had refused to release their players for the match against Iceland and the manager was forced to field only domestic-based players. In the absence of Romário and Bebeto and with São Paulo's Müller injured, Ronaldo was picked to start alongside Corinthians striker Viola. The game was played on 4 May 1994, just three days after Brazil's greatest sporting idol at the time, triple Formula One world champion Ayrton Senna, had died horrifically in an accident at the San Marino Grand Prix. At Ressacada, a modest 17,000-seat stadium in the state of Santa Catarina in the south of Brazil, Ronaldo gave the country something to cheer by scoring his first goal for the Seleção as Brazil ran out 3-0 victors.

Five days later, Parreira announced Ronaldo's name among the 22 that would travel to the United States. Immediately, the whole 'Pelé was 17 in 1958' came to the fore, the excitement spiked by the fact that there had been 28 years since the last teenager – winger Edú, in England 1966 – had been part of a Seleção squad. Enthusiasm soared further when newspaper *Folha de São Paulo*, famous for its number-crunching articles, came up with this staggering statistic: Ronaldo's goal average in his first 50 professional games (49 goals, or 0.98 per match) was superior to Pelé's (41 goals, or 0.82 per match). That Pelé's games in his first years as a professional (1956) had been in Paulista League games, at a time when there was not a Brazilian championship, made Ronaldo's average even more impressive. Which did not go unnoticed by club suitors. Martins and Pitta then made what looked like a foolish decision: they sold Cruzeiro their 45 per cent stake in Ronaldo's economic rights for US$1 million. Instead of killing the golden goose, though, they had pawned it: with the money, they bought Jairzinho out and became the sole controllers of Ronaldo's career.

By the time Ronaldo joined his Seleção team-mates on the plane to Los Angeles, he had already starred in a controversial commercial for Brazilian brewery Brahma and appeared in a TV commercial to encourage young Brazilians to vote. But his promotion to the Seleção's World Cup squad was an inevitable catalyst for a move away from both Cruzeiro and from Brazil. Martins, Pitta and the Belo Horizonte club had been regularly approached by European teams in the months leading up to the World Cup. Porto, Milan and Bayern Munich reportedly all made enquiries. Cruzeiro were understandably looking to get as much as they could but the US$10 million price tag they had attached to Ronaldo looked unreasonable in the 1990s, when no player had left Brazil for anything near that amount. Then the club announced that Dutch side PSV had tabled a US$6 million bid for Ronaldo. As much as they looked like outsiders in a race against bigger European counterparts, the Eindhoven club had a pedigree with Brazilian players, having been the first European destination for Romário, whose prolific five years at PSV catapulted him to Barcelona and Johan Cruyff's mentoring in 1993.

Ronaldo immediately sought out Romário to discuss the pros and cons of life in Holland. One of Ronaldo's idols, the striker told him that PSV could be the same stepping stone for Ronaldo as it had been for him. A well-structured club, PSV played in a much less competitive league than those in Italy or Spain and Romário felt that would give Ronaldo a good basis to adapt to European football. So PSV found themselves the surprise winners of the race. Ronaldo met with Frank Arnesen, then a director at the Dutch club, at the Brazilian headquarters in California.

Another interesting appointment at the hotel involved Cees van Nieuwenhuizen, a Nike director. Ronaldo was sponsored at the time by Japanese rivals Mizuno, but Nike were keen to take over the deal. Diadora reportedly offered more than the US$150,000 per year that

Nike were willing to pay, but Pitta and Martins, often vilified in Brazil as money-grabbing opportunists, acted in what they believed were Ronaldo's best interests in this instance and shook hands with the Americans. While Nike had definitely started to move into football by 1994, it was still relatively virgin territory for them and they had initially set their sights on more established players, like Romário, who actually featured in one of the company's TV ads for the 1994 World Cup. Furthermore, they had their sights fixed on securing the sponsorship of the entire national team.

1994 was the fifth year of Ricardo Teixeira's reign as president of the CBF. Without any football background, the businessman had taken Brazilian football by storm in 1989, wrestling control from incumbent president Octávio Pinto Guimarães. Hardly a likeable character, Octávio had won the 1985 elections simply because he was older than his competitor, Medrado Dias (they drew in the votes cast by the presidents of the state federations and the CBF statute to this day still uses seniority as the tie-breaker). His tenure was marked by the shambolic 1986 Campeonato Brasileiro, where a confused dispute pairing first and second-division teams together meant 80 clubs contested the title and led to an average of little more than 13,000 spectators per match, at that time the fifth lowest of all time.

The next year, Guimarães had to deal with the threat of civil war in Brazilian football: spurred by TV Globo, Brazil's most powerful free-to-air TV channel, the top 16 clubs in the country formed a breakaway league – five years before a similar move in England led to the creation of the Premier League. In the end, the CBF won the arm-wrestling competition and punished the revolting pack by making an example of the two finalists: Flamengo, who had won the title in a season of redemption for Zico – a year before he had missed the penalty that cost Brazil a place in the 1986 World Cup semi-finals – and Internacional were excluded from the 1988 Copa Libertadores and replaced by the de facto second division champions – Sport and Guarani, who the ruling body declared national champions. The revolt ensured some concessions for the clubs: the 1988 Campeonato Brasileiro would be contested by a much smaller number of clubs than before (24) and for the first time in the history of the competition relegation and promotion were implemented. But the Guimarães administration had been irremeamably wounded.

It was no secret that Ricardo Teixeira was João Havelange's son-in-law. Married to the FIFA president's only child, daughter Lucia, Havelange treated him like the son he never had – his wife had miscarried two baby boys before Lucia was born. Since 1971, Teixeira had given Havelange three grandchildren. His son-in-law was also a chance for Havelange to regain influence over Brazilian football, which he had lost a decade before. Relishing his puppet-master role, Havelange started gathering support for Teixeira's candidacy as early as 1986, when he used FIFA's funds to invite state federation presidents to watch the Mexico World Cup and listen to a series of talks in which Teixeira presented his modernising agenda for Brazilian football. Three years later, his son-in-law did more than defeat Guimarães in the elections: overwhelmed by the support amassed by his opponent, the incumbent president withdrew and Teixeira was elected with the support of 26 state federations. The result was seen as an endorsement of Havelange more than anything else. Teixeira, though, was more than just a front man – and he needed to be, for he took over a governing body in financial tatters.

Barely surviving on the money provided by the federal government, the CBF had resorted to all sorts of palliative care, including a ludicrous endorsement from the Brazilian Coffee Institute in which the Brazilian crest was 'desecrated' with a coffee plant as an advertisement. So in the red were they that Brazil had to search for donations from businessmen to avoid the Seleção missing the 1987 Pan-American Games due to absolute lack of funds.

On his first day in the job, Teixeira noticed there wasn't enough cash to pay the CBF employees' wages. Four years later, Brazil signed a deal with English apparel company Umbro that guaranteed a US$1.5 million yearly income to the ruling body until 1998. The CBF wouldn't see out that deal, though. After the commercial success of USA 1994, Nike started to pay more attention to football and over the following four years would invest over half a billion dollars in the sport, which the company saw as the key for business diversification and global sales growth. A significant chunk of that money was allocated to a groundbreaking sponsorship contract with the CBF in 1996: a ten-year deal through which the ruling body would receive a total US$200 million. It was the biggest deal ever involving a national team and the cash injection transformed the CBF's fortunes as well as giving Nike an amazing merchandising vehicle for the 1998 World Cup, which would be played in Europe, a continent where the American company were dwarfed by German competitor Adidas. But there were controversial points that made the deal unique: Teixeira agreed to give the sponsor the right to organise and profit from 50 Seleção games, where the American company would choose the opposition team. The CBF also committed to fielding at least eight players that were individually sponsored by Nike in those games.

The Nike deal also accentuated the financial gulf between the ruling body and the clubs. It gave the CBF a huge budget to work with at a time when Brazilian clubs, constrained by the peculiar structure of the football industry in their country, were each day struggling more and more to get by. Lacking substantial TV money, widespread stadium ownership and appropriate arenas (which inhibited commercial turnover at times of dwindling attendances) and with European clubs invariably poaching their talent, they were the opposite of the CBF's *bons vivants*. The weakening of the Campeonato Brasileiro didn't really matter to the CBF when its coffers were full, the Seleção were doing well and some of the best European clubs were taking care of their star players.

The very special terms of the Nike contract would not be leaked until 1999. Still, the revelation would deepen the crisis the Seleção and Ronaldo would go through after the 1998 World Cup.

After their triumph in 1994, the Seleção started to plan for another title defence. Once again there was some rebuilding to be done. A significant number of representatives from the class of 1994 would not be available for the next campaign. But the CBF sent a strong continuity message with their choice of replacement for manager Carlos Alberto Parreira, who had chosen to leave the Seleção at the top and accept an offer to manage Spanish side Valencia.

The chosen one was Mário Zagallo, who worked as Parreira's assistant in the USA in 1994 and became famous during TV interviews by performing a countdown of how many games were left for the Seleção to win the title. Teixeira had instigated the partnership after a mixture of suggestion and imposition from his famous father-in-law in Zurich, in 1991. The job had become vacant after Seleção legend Falcão resigned in protest that same year over an alleged attempt by the CBF president to influence call-ups. After Parreira and Zagallo delivered the 1994 World Cup, Teixeira saw no reason not to promote Zagallo. For a record third time the 'Old Wolf' would be managing Brazil in a World Cup.

The appointment, however, did not have the universal support the CBF was hoping for. At 63, Zagallo had last managed a club in 1991 – Vasco, for whom he failed to win any silverware – and while his presence in the Seleção as Parreira's deputy wasn't a major problem, the promotion to the main job raised some concern. Zagallo had hardly endeared himself to the nation in 1974 and few people believed that he could cope with how much the game had evolved in two decades. At the time, Brazil had a crop of young managers who had done well, most notably Vanderlei Luxemburgo, who in 1994 won his second Brazilian title in a row with Palmeiras.

Zagallo, ironically, was a perfect poster boy for the biggest achievement of the Teixeira administration so far – since Havelange, no other CBF president could boast a World Cup win on his watch. Reservations aside, the Old Wolf was hardly without a winning history. As the CBF and Zagallo himself would remind people constantly, he was the only person to have actually been present during four World

Cup wins and only Franz Beckenbauer had matched his incredible feat of winning the trophy as both a player and a manager. In Teixeira's view, Zagallo's experience could prove priceless in overseeing the changes in Seleção personnel, especially at a time when the CBF had turned their attentions to another Brazilian hoodoo – the Olympic Games – which became even more important as Brazil would again be excused from the South American World Cup qualifiers as world champions.

After winning silver in 1984 and 1988, the Seleção had failed to qualify for Barcelona '92 and the 1996 Atlanta Games provided another shot at the elusive gold medal and a good test for the youngsters before France 1998. Age restrictions determined that only three players over the age of 23 could take part in the Olympic squad, which immediately should have been great news for Ronaldo – especially as both Bebeto and Romário were unlikely to be picked at the same time as wild cards.

In the last game the Seleção played in 1994, a friendly against Yugoslavia in Porto Alegre, Ronaldo was part of the first XI. He also featured on other occasions, including in the Umbro Cup, a friendly international tournament in England featuring the hosts, Brazil, Sweden and Japan. Ronaldo played in all three games and scored the second in Brazil's 3-1 win over England at Wembley, which gave the Seleção the title. But a couple of weeks later, during the 1995 Copa America, he had been benched by Zagallo. Brazil still made it to the final, but were defeated by hosts Uruguay in a penalty shoot-out. In 1995 alone, Zagallo used seven different strikers. The fact that Ronaldo would finish his two seasons at PSV with 54 goals in 58 games did not seem to impress the manager, although one should point out that the player spending a good part of the 1995/96 season sidelined with an injury might have played a big part in Zagallo's reasoning.

Brazil started 1996 by taking part as guests in the Golden Cup, the most important tournament for national teams in North America, Central America and the Caribbean. With a team consisting exclusively of under-23 players, the Seleção started well, thrashing Canada 4-1 and Honduras 5-0. They then defeated a more experienced USA side 1-0 but Mexico, who also fielded their main stars, overcame Zagallo's team 2-0.

Zagallo then started testing veterans in Brazil's next match, a friendly against Ghana in São José do Rio Preto, near São Paulo. Midfielder Rivaldo, who had missed the cut for USA 1994, and veteran defender Aldair, a World Cup winner, helped settle the youngsters in an 8-2 drubbing of the Africans.

A month later, the Seleção travelled to Johannesburg to face South Africa, fresh from their historic African Cup of Nations title, won only four years after the country, now free of its apartheid regime, had its FIFA membership reinstated. Striker Bebeto was present, but there was no Romário, much to the annoyance of both fans and media. The 1994 World Cup hero had returned to Brazil in 1995 after seven years abroad, signed by Flamengo in a massive coup over local rivals Vasco, where Romário had blossomed. He was hardly setting the world alight, but the memories of 1994 were still strong in Brazil and calls for his return for the Olympics were ringing in Zagallo's ears. The pair couldn't have more diverse personalities: the disciplinarian manager and the striker who defied authority. While Parreira had served as a buffer between the two at the World Cup, Zagallo was in charge and the relationship was fraught.

Brazil, however, almost made a mess of the friendly in South Africa. Masinga and Khumalo put the hosts 2-0 ahead in the first half and Zagallo's irritation was enhanced by the effusive celebrations by Bafana Bafana manager Clive Barker, who ran on to the pitch to do an 'airplane' dance. Flávio Conceição and Rivaldo levelled the match in the second half before Bebeto won the game in the dying minutes with a gorgeous volley, celebrated by Zagallo with a mocking impersonation of Barker's 'flight'. The result, nonetheless, would still be used as evidence by the pro-Romário camp that he was the missing ingredient in the team.

Zagallo, however, continued to ignore the lobby and tested more strikers, although he did admit that he was struggling to find an attacking midfielder that could fulfil his tactical vision for the

Seleção. In an attempt to distance himself from criticism of the stiff 4-4-2 formation the team had used in the 1994 World Cup, Zagallo had decided to switch the system to a 4-3-1-2 and hyped up the role of the link player. But none of the ten different names deployed in the role were succeeding in giving a tactical balance to the team, and some of Zagallo's allies began to publicly criticise the manager for his insistence on persevering with the system.

This was a small problem, however, in comparison to what awaited the Seleção in the Olympics. They travelled to Atlanta with Aldair, Rivaldo and Bebeto as the over-23 choices and although Ronaldo made the squad, he was unceremoniously benched for the opener against Japan. The decision was largely seen as retaliation for the commotion he had caused in the Brazil camp when the announcement was made that Barcelona had paid over £13 million to sign him from PSV, in one of the most expensive deals in the game at the time. Barcelona's directors wanted to meet him at the Seleção headquarters and to give him a quick medical, a demand that was fervently denied by Zagallo, who accused the Catalans of disrespecting the Seleção and Ronaldo for 'thinking too much about money' – the irony would not be lost on those old enough to remember that Zagallo had become the first Brazilian player to buy himself out of a contract in 1960 in order to sign for higher wages elsewhere, and whose career as a manager had relied upon several lucrative posts in Arabian football. The manager not only forbade the visit from the Barça entourage but reportedly assigned two security personnel to watch Ronaldo to ensure that there were no sneaky meetings.

Ronaldo's absence in the Olympic opener ended up being a blessing in disguise: after an abysmal performance, Brazil were defeated by the Japanese for the first time in their history, courtesy of a innocuous long ball that both goalkeeper Nélson Dida and Aldair tried to intercept, only to clatter into each other. Ronaldo was drafted in to start against the Hungarians and scored the opener in a 3-1 victory in which he also drew attention when he was caught urinating on the pitch.

Two days later, he secured qualification for the next round for Brazil by scoring the only goal in a victory over Nigeria. Two more came in the 4-2 win against Ghana in the quarter-finals. Then came the Nigerians again: the Seleção seemed to have everything under control and led the Africans 3-2 with only five minutes remaining. Zagallo then withdrew Ronaldo, who hadn't been on the scoresheet, replacing him with winger Sávio – only for Nwanko Kanu to equalise in the 90th minute and complete a remarkable comeback with a golden goal four minutes into extra-time. Once again Brazil had fallen short in their Olympic quest, and the fact that they had been leading 3-1 against the Nigerians until the 77th minute worsened the criticism levelled at Zagallo.

But the manager held on to his job and began 1997 by calling up Romário to face Poland in a friendly. The World Cup hero was deployed alongside Ronaldo up front and the partnership clicked brilliantly, with the pair netting 13 of the Seleção's 18 goals in the next six games. In one of them, the Ro-Ro partnership bailed Brazil out against Italy in the Tournoi de France – the World Cup warm-up competition hosted by the French and also attended by the English.

The amazing firepower up front helped divert attention from Zagallo's tinkering elsewhere. A year before the World Cup the manager had not made his mind up about his first XI and had resorted to luring previously banished players back in from the cold. The first was Cláudio Taffarel, the iconic goalkeeper who had stopped Daniele Massaro's kick in the 1994 final shoot-out before Roberto Baggio skied the last penalty. Criticism over his performance against Uruguay in the 1995 Copa America led to Taffarel's retirement from the Seleção; he changed his mind a couple of months later, but initially received the cold shoulder from Zagallo on a recall. After the Atlanta debacle, however, the manager thought that more experience was needed in the number 1 shirt.

The second return, however, caused surprise everywhere – even to the man who received the call. In 1997, Dunga had been in Japan for two seasons, attracted by that country's increased interest in football during the 1990s and the hefty wages that could be earned even by veteran players. The J-League became a driver for an increase in Brazilian player exports in the 1990s thanks largely to the pioneering work done by Zico with his move to Kashima Antlers in 1991. At 33, however, former captain Dunga had fallen off the radar and was deemed surplus to requirements. But not only was he recalled for a friendly against Mexico in April 1997, he also found himself wearing the captain's armband once more.

With these old heads back in place, the team at last seemed to be gelling: spearheaded by Ronaldo and Romário, Brazil reached the 1997 Copa America final after beating Costa Rica, Mexico, Colombia and Paraguay, with 12 goals scored and only two conceded. Bolivia remained the only obstacle between the Seleção and their first ever South American title won away from home. The hosts tried to make things as hard as they could: the final was played at the Hernando Siles Stadium in La Paz, 3,600 metres above sea level – the same ground where, four years earlier, Brazil had been beaten in the World Cup qualifiers while gasping for air.

After drawing first blood with an Edmundo goal in the 40th minute, the Seleção conceded a soft equaliser soon afterwards in which Taffarel misread an innocuous Erwin Sánchez shot. Bolivia launched everything they had at the Brazilians and hit the post three times. Taffarel redeemed himself with a miraculous close-range save from Sánchez but the Seleção were running out of steam pretty quickly in the thin high-altitude air. Then Denilson set up Ronaldo for a run that ended with a shot hitting the roof of the Bolivian net. Zé Roberto squeezed an injury-time winner but Ronaldo was the one who left the pitch as the hero. The only sour note of the day was an astonishing outburst from Zagallo on live TV in which he almost spat at the camera before screaming that his critics would have to 'swallow my success'.

Ronaldo's heroics in the altitude of La Paz had mirrored his incredible recent club form. His first season at Barcelona had gone at such a blistering pace that his victory in the 1996 FIFA World

Player of the Year vote was hardly a surprise. He would finish his sole season at the Camp Nou with 47 goals in 51 matches in Spain and abroad. Ronaldo was on fire and his impact also resonated heavily off the pitch. Not since Pelé had Brazil boasted a player with such star power and, unlike the King, his heir apparent was living in the right era to fully exploit his commercial potential. Ronaldo's contract with Barcelona, for example, established that a reasonable chunk of his wages would come from image rights partnerships with the club – the Brazilian had a share, for example, in the sale of Barcelona shirts with his name. The downside was that his agents had also tied him into a series of commercial and sponsorship deals that frequently required a lot of travel and countless hours of studio shoots and PR appearances. After what, in retrospect, had been a tiny initial investment (by their standards), Nike were now gleefully convinced that they had bet on the right horse. They had both the best Brazilian player and his national team under contract – although that US$150,000 per year deal signed in 1994 needed to be updated and Ronaldo's agents this time held nothing back: they negotiated a new contract that guaranteed Ronaldo a windfall that would outlast his playing career – over US$200 million in total, according to estimates. In the meantime, the boy, who had now turned 20, fell in love with Brazilian actress and model Susana Werner, who lived in Rio de Janeiro – and for months this relationship saw Ronaldo clock up even more air miles.

By the time the Seleção reconvened after the Copa America, Ronaldo had gone through further intense off-field distractions: after difficult negotiations between Barcelona and his agents, the striker had been sold to Inter Milan for a then world record US$27 million fee during the European summer. His wages climbed to US$5 million per year, the highest of any footballer at the time, and his earnings would be boosted by private endorsements that were sanctioned by the Italians, who even guaranteed him days off specifically to handle commercial interests. With those privileges, however, came the challenge to justify all the investment. At Barcelona, he left with three trophies in one season, but the Catalans still lost the La Liga title to Real Madrid. Demands would be tougher at Inter who, at the time, had not won the Scudetto since 1989 and whose last European Cup win had taken place in the '60s.

Still, Ronaldo duly attended the Seleção friendly against South Korea in Seoul (one of the games organised by Nike) and scored in Brazil's 2-1 win on 10 August. Three days later he was again on the pitch for the 3-0 victory over Japan. Despite the team's success, when the Seleção arrived in Saudi Arabia in December for the 1997 Confederations Cup, Zagallo announced that the two striker spots were still up for grabs, with Bebeto back in the running for a starting place. Ronaldo and Romário started in the 3-0 victory over the Saudis, but the Inter man didn't score and again fired blanks when he was paired with Bebeto in a disappointing 0-0 draw against Australia.

Zagallo freely explained to the Brazilian media that Ronaldo's performances were being affected by 'all the pressure he is facing at the club'. In the 3-0 win over Mexico, Ronaldo failed to score for the third game in a row and was replaced by Bebeto in the second half. The manager constantly referred to 'father to son' conversations he had with Ronaldo and when Zagallo selected him to start against the Czechs in the semi-final he described it as a gesture of confidence in the player – who at last repaid the faith by scoring in the 2-0 triumph before claiming a hat-trick in Brazil's 6-0 thrashing of Australia in the final; Romário scored the other three.

The Ro-Ro partnership seemed to be key to the Seleção's success and that became even more evident a couple of months later when Ronaldo was not released by Inter for Brazil's participation in the Gold Cup in February 1998. Brazil were knocked out by the USA in the quarter-finals and barely scraped through a third-place play-off against Jamaica where not even a 77th-minute Romário goal was enough to avoid boos from the 91,000 crowd at Los Angeles' Memorial Coliseum. Despite the notable absence of Ronaldo and other European-based regulars such as Rivaldo and Roberto Carlos, Brazil's substandard display led to a massive outcry back home, with suggestions that Zagallo had run out of ideas. A common argument was that the absence of an assistant in the same role that he played alongside Parreira at USA 1994 was hampering his work, but the manager rubbished the idea. Three days later, however, Ricardo Teixeira intervened: legend Zico was unveiled as Zagallo's assistant for the World Cup in a move that seemed to be much more of a charisma injection than a technical solution. And the move created tensions, for while Zagallo said the hierarchy had not been affected, Zico didn't shy away from expressing his opinions about the team in public.

On 23 March, however, the Seleção beat Germany 2-1 in Stuttgart, with Ronaldo scoring the winner – his 25th goal in 37 games for Brazil – a result that brought some breathing space for the team. One month later a friendly with Argentina at the Maracaná would be the last home game before the campaign in France. It was all set to be a celebratory farewell in front of a crowd of 95,000 people, but instead, the Seleção would take a massive bruising on the night of 29 April. With another return from the 1994 squad, Rai, the Seleção failed miserably to inspire the fans. Worse, they were beaten by a Claudio López goal that incensed the crowd to the point where some players would be the target of fierce abuse – including Cafu, for whom the situation was all the more traumatic because his family was present at the time. 'My father could barely hold back the tears when we met after the game,' the right-back recalls. 'It was definitely one of the worst nights of my life.'

But as bad as losing to Argentina always is for Brazilian pride, the most worrying problem was that, with less than two months to the start of their title defence in France, the Seleção still didn't seem to have an established first team. To make matters worse, the Maracaná defeat removed the autonomy the manager seemed to have in picking his squad. On 5 May, when the list of players for the World Cup was released, Teixeira said he had 'suggested' players to Zagallo, who in turn insisted it was not a big deal. 'To allow the president to make suggestions is part of the routine in any company,' he argued.

It was also announced that Brazil would return to the 4-4-2 formation that worked so well in 1994. The list of players was in itself a series of contradictions: Barcelona's Giovanni, then absent from call-ups for over a year, not only made the World Cup squad but was immediately promoted to the starting XI by Zagallo during his press conference on that May afternoon. Meanwhile, Juninho – the former Middlesbrough player then at Atlético Madrid, who had played regularly in 1997 before being sidelined with a leg break – was absent, despite the Seleção's physio Lidio Toledo declaring him fit to play. Toledo's opinion, however, was respected in the case of defender Márcio Santos, a 1994 World Cup winner, who suffered a thigh injury a week after his call-up playing for São Paulo: he was dropped and replaced by AC Milan's André Cruz, who at the time had not played for months after back surgery. The strangest case, however, involved Deportivo's Flávio Conceição: he was also dropped following the announcement of the list after Toledo claimed the club doctors had warned him about fitness problems. Deportivo officially disputed the physio's version of events and then Toledo backtracked. Still, Conceição stayed out and his place was given to São Paulo right-back Zé Carlos, who had yet to play a game for the Brazilian national team.

But the biggest personnel problem was still to explode: a few days after the Seleção had set up in Paris, Romário was diagnosed with a thigh injury. A scan showed a 12cm oedema that immediately sent waves of panic through the camp. Not only had Romário been fundamental to Brazil's success four years earlier, but he was also the Seleção's leading scorer in the current World Cup cycle. At 32, the striker was a key leader in a group who would need as much unity as they could muster in their challenge to retain the trophy. Those were reasons enough for the technical staff to tread carefully while analysing what to do with the player.

Brazil had previously taken players to World Cups that were not in peak condition at the beginning of training camps. Pelé travelled injured in 1958 and healed in time to help Brazil win the trophy for the first time. Tostão had been sidelined for a couple of months before Mexico 1970 as he recovered from eye surgery. Zagallo's own assistant, Zico, made it to the 1986 tournament after a battle to shake off knee problems – he missed the first two games before he was declared fit to play. Branco, who had scored the winning goal in the quarter-final against Holland in 1994, had also struggled with fitness for most of the preparation. On 2 June, however, just eight days before Brazil would open the 1998 World Cup in Paris, it was announced that Romário would be sent back home. A teary striker appeared on his own in an improvised press conference during which he publicly disagreed with the verdict and vowed to be back in training for his club, Flamengo, while the Seleção were still in France. To a few journalists that he was close to, Romário went further and accused Zico directly for his dismissal. The two had clashed on numerous occasions before over comments regarding the 'ugly' style of the 1994 team, but that would look like playful banter in comparison to what was to come. 'Zico screwed me over because he's a born loser,' fired Romário.

The striker's departure was felt all the more deeply within the squad because the players had been divided about the decision. Dunga and Ronaldo, for example, were particularly in favour of Romário staying even if only to help motivate the group. The players were also puzzled by the choice of replacement: defensive midfielder Emerson, who had been absent from most of the Seleção's previous games. Ronaldo could also be excused for defending his attacking partner: without Romário, the burden of expectation had been placed squarely on his young shoulders.

A few days later, when a training session was interrupted so that the Seleção could attend a reception organised by Nike in Paris, all hell broke loose. The players were visibly uncomfortable with the event and captain Dunga went further by going on record to criticise the sponsor: 'Bringing the team here was not the best decision at this moment. We are pretty close to the first game and need to spend more time on the pitch.' Even Ronaldo, Nike's biggest star among the squad – the American company had, by now, personal sponsorship deals with more than half of the players – agreed that the distraction was hardly welcome, albeit in more diplomatic terms. 'The event will not harm the team, but we should have been practising,' he said.

There was also bickering among the players. Forward Edmundo, who had finished the 1997 Brazilian season by winning the title with Vasco and breaking a three-decade-old scoring record in league games, was frustrated by his lack of first-team opportunities. He immediately started lobbying the press, saying that he should be Romário's replacement. Leonardo, who was back at a World Cup after his inglorious red card in USA 1994, this time reinvented as a midfielder, also spoke to whoever he could about how he could help the team. 'Whatever unity they had seemed to be gone,' said Cees van Nieuwenhuizen, the Nike director who in 1998 had already been sent by the company to look after their offices in Rio and was a regular attendee at the training camp in France.

Zagallo also still had doubts about the best make-up of the team. Taffarel had earned back his place in goal, while Cafu, Jorginho's deputy in 1994, took over the right-back slot. After Márcio Santos' departure, Aldair would operate in central defence with Júnior Baiano, whose volatile temper had previously made managers wary of bringing him to the Seleção. Absent in 1994, Roberto Carlos now owned the left side, fresh from a Real Madrid season in which the club had won their first Champions League title since 1966. Already one of the most recognisable Brazilian players alongside Ronaldo, he starred in TV ads, including one that referenced his fearsome left-foot shot, made famous by a viciously curving free kick scored against France in the Tournoi a year before – in the ad, he manages to cause damage to the façade of a Madrid building with a loose flip-flop. Carlos, however, had also created controversy with undiplomatic remarks about the financial position he was enjoying after moving to Europe. In a famously reproduced piece of banter, he gloated about his expensive Rolex watch. 'I carry a whole flat on my wrist,' he said.

The midfield was Zagallo's greatest source of frustration. Dunga was back in his enforcer role, this time without the injured Mauro Silva. César Sampaio, another player based in Japan, had slotted in, but the creative roles were still open. Zagallo's previous attempts to pair up Rivaldo and São Paulo FC's Denilson had resulted in problems because both players simply played as forwards for their clubs and struggled to adapt to their roles for the Seleção, which had resulted in Giovanni's surprising recall for the World Cup. Up front, the manager never hid his preference for Bebeto to partner Ronaldo.

Brazil had been drawn in Group A alongside opponents who would not normally cause supporters to sweat. Scotland were back at the World Cup after failing to qualify for the 1994 tournament, manager Craig Brown hardly believing that they would have to play the Seleção for the fourth time in six tournaments; and Morocco hadn't impressed the Brazilians in a friendly played the year before. Norway, however, were a different case: their 4-2 win over Brazil in Oslo the year before had caused Zagallo a fair amount of grief in the press and the manager was even more incensed by some taunts thrown in his direction by flamboyant Norwegian manager Egil 'Drilo' Olsen.

On 10 June, Brazil entered the Stade de France to face the Scots, repeating the 'human chain' walk they had famously used in every game since the qualifiers for USA 1994 to show the unity of the squad. But in 1998 it was an action that looked forced given the signs of disarray in the previous week.

When Sampaio appeared in the middle of the Scottish defence to head Brazil in front after only four minutes, it looked as though they would negotiate easy passage through the opening game. However, it soon became clear the team simply had not had enough time to gel and it would be in individual runs rather than constructed play that Brazil would give Scotland the biggest scares. Ronaldo was being watched by a little crowd of players and was constantly frustrated in his attempts to break free. The Seleção leaked an equaliser when Sampaio pushed Kevin Gallacher in the box and John Collins buried the penalty to Taffarel's right. In the second half, with the left-footed Leonardo playing on the right side of midfield, replacing Giovanni, Brazil tried to exert more pressure but would only go ahead on the 73rd minute thanks to a clumsy own goal by Tom Boyd. It didn't look good, but the Seleção had scraped through.

Two days later, the vision of Ronaldo climbing on the team bus with an ice pack strapped to his left knee sent waves of panic through a nation. Player and technical staff dismissed the problem as a light discomfort and seemed to prove the point on 16 June: with only nine minutes gone against Morocco, Ronaldo scored his first ever World Cup goal with a blistering run to connect with a long Rivaldo pass, thumping the ball past the keeper. Almost immediately he would receive a horrendous studs-up challenge from midfielder Youssef Chippo, who aimed for his left leg.

Despite the early goal, the Seleção still appeared unsettled and in the 36th minute tensions escalated: while trying to organise the wall for a Moroccan free kick, Dunga got annoyed by Bebeto not coming in fast enough to help. The captain berated his team-mate and they had to be pulled apart by other players. An injury-time goal by Rivaldo helped cool the tensions before half-time and in the second half Brazil added a third through Bebeto.

The infighting, however, was the hottest topic of conversation afterwards and the fact Bebeto didn't turn up in the mixed zone after the match fuelled mounting speculation that all was not right behind the scenes. The incident would soon be forgotten, however, thanks to escalating rumours about Ronaldo's knee and stories about a painkilling injection helping him to play against the Moroccans circulated in the Brazilian press.

Zagallo decided to shift the focus and began to engage in mind games with Egil Olsen, promising that the Seleção would avenge the 1997 defeat by 'stuffing' Norway. The game in Marseille, however, would become another source of worry for the Seleção. With Ronaldo quiet and after a pedestrian first half, the Seleção only managed to break the deadlock in the 78th minute with a Bebeto header. Five minutes later, the Norwegians equalised when Tore André Flo skinned Júnior Baiano before burying his shot in the net. Then with three minutes remaining, the Norwegians were awarded a penalty after Baiano pulled Flo's shirt in the box. The chance was converted and Brazil suffered their first group stage defeat since 1966. The result opened the floodgates for a cascade of moaning, with players publicly complaining about each other – apart from Dunga, who had vowed not to speak to his team-mates after the criticism received over the 'Bebeto incident'. To increase the tension, images of Romário training normally with Flamengo heaped pressure on the Seleção technical staff for making an error with the diagnosis of his injury.

Despite the defeat, the Seleção still qualified in first place because Norway had drawn their first two games. Chile would be Brazil's first opponents in the knockout stages and the South Americans boasted a respectable forward partnership in the form of Iván Zamorano and Marcelo Salas. They had escaped from a group which also included Italy, Austria and Cameroon and after Brazil's poor display against Norway there remained some tension in the camp. The match would throw up an interesting clash between Internazionale team-mates Ronaldo and Zamorano, with the Chilean on a mission to regain some pride after being replaced by the Brazilian as the Italian club's main striker, also losing his coveted number 9 shirt (Zamorano then used the 18 with a small '+' between the numbers to make a point).

Although traditionally the underdog in encounters with Brazil, Chile had begun to buck the trend in recent years. It all started with a 4-0 win over the Brazilians in the 1987 Copa America – with Zamorano on the scoresheet – that set the tone for a tense dispute for a place in the 1990 World Cup. In a group with Venezuela, the two teams basically had a play-off. A poor match in Santiago finished 1-1 and the return game at the Maracaná was stopped with Brazil 1-0 up after a flare fell on the pitch and seemed to hit goalkeeper Roberto Rojas. Photographs from the attending press, however, would later expose a cunning plan by the Chileans to try to disturb procedures (Rojas had hidden a razor blade in his glove in order to cut himself at a certain point in the game, so he could barely believe his luck when the flare came from the crowd). FIFA punished Chile harshly: they would be suspended for two World Cups and Rojas, who at the time played for São Paulo, was banned forever from the game, while manager Orlando Aravena received a permanent international ban and a five-year national one.

So France '98, the first World Cup contested by Chile since 1982, put the two South American countries head to head again. Images from the national anthems at the Parc des Princes showed the Chileans singing as if they were going to battle – only the French renditions of 'La Marseillaise' looked more impressive. But after only 27 minutes Brazil were already 2-0 up with an unlikely brace from Sampaio, which at that point turned the midfield enforcer into Brazil's top scorer at the tournament. Tensions still burned through the team despite their comfortable lead, as Dunga and Ronaldo argued heatedly during the first half over the striker's positioning, but Ronaldo responded with a great run that resulted in a penalty in the 46th minute which he took himself to score his second goal of the tournament. Salas scored in the 68th minute to give the Chileans some pride, but Ronaldo quickly hit back with a fourth for Brazil. The striker would hit the post twice in the second half and the 4-1 result flattered Chile; the Seleção looked to be finally playing the brand of football expected of them by the fans. So it seemed that on 27 June, Brazil had finally arrived at the World Cup.

Two days later, Lidio Toledo decided, inexplicably, to stir up more trouble for the squad just when they seemed to have turned a corner, by revealing to the press that he thought Ronaldo was fat. The comment came as the answer to a question about how a possible knee problem could be affecting the striker. 'Ronaldo's problem is that he is slower because of an excess of weight. He looks a bit tubby. It might even be psychological because of all the expectations people are putting on him,' said Toledo, who would later say Ronaldo was 7kg above his ideal weight. The interview understandably caused a huge commotion, which only increased when the Seleção fitness trainer, Paulo Paixão, publicly disagreed with the physio. Later, the technical staff would claim there had been a mistake and Toledo had accidently used measurements from the 1994 World Cup before Ronaldo went through an intense training regime with PSV to 'beef up' for European leagues. The explanation only served to make things look even more shambolic, especially because in that same week before the quarter-final match against Denmark, it was officially announced that the knee was indeed troubling Ronaldo to the point that he could not train properly.

The striker also had to deal with gossip about his personal life: Susana, his girlfriend, had been hired by host broadcasters TV Globo to work as a reporter during the World Cup alongside a male colleague; when Ronaldo was one day seen without the ring he had worn since he and Susana moved in together, it immediately became a sign of difficulty in their relationship. It is a miracle that he could then focus properly for the match against the Danes in Nantes.

Denmark had raised a few eyebrows with their clinical 4-1 disposal of Nigeria in the round of 16 after coming second to France in the group stages. It is unlikely that no one in the Seleção set-up watched that game to study their opponents, but it certainly looked that way when the Danes went ahead after just two minutes through Martin Jorgensen after Brian Laudrup quickly took a free kick without waiting for the whistle – a trick they had used against the Nigerians. Brazil came back in the 11th minute thanks to a Ronaldo assist that put Bebeto away with only Peter Schmeichel to beat – the fact that Ronaldo was then buried under a pile of team-mates suggested that the adversity he was suffering was building bridges in the group. Clearly trying to protect his knee, Ronaldo had become an advanced midfielder, and he would play another crucial pass 16 minutes later for Rivaldo to put Brazil ahead, cheekily flicking the ball over the falling Manchester United goalkeeper. The second half started with Carlos failing to hit an overhead kick clearance that instead fell into the path of Brian Laudrup's right foot, and he buried it sweetly into the net. Rivaldo produced a moment of individual magic on the hour to score Brazil's third with a swerving low shot to Schmeichel's left but the Danes didn't give up and missed a few very good chances. Cafu then received his second booking for time-wasting, which meant he was out of the semi-finals. Brazil survived, and for the second World Cup in a row they would have to meet Holland. There could not be a more dramatic opponent for Zagallo.

One could expect that questions about 1974 would inevitably be fired at both camps ahead of the semi-final in Marseille. But for the Brazilian manager it had a special meaning. The defeat in the last-four match in Germany 24 years before (it was the last match of a round-robin group where both Brazil and Holland were tied on points) had defined Zagallo's Seleção legacy. And quite unfairly, it could be argued, for his tactical work with the 1970 World Cup squad had allowed the team to field a raft of attacking players without suffering a defensive meltdown. However, Zagallo's dismissive comments on Rinus Michels' 'carousel' four years later ended up echoing louder than his triumphs. He was present in 1994, when the Seleção overcame the Dutch in a dramatic quarter-final in Dallas in which the Dutch cancelled out Brazil's two-goal advantage before being downed by a Branco free kick.

In France 1998, however, the Dutch had put together arguably their best side since they had won the European Championship in Germany ten years previously, with the likes of Gullit and van Basten. The 1998 squad boasted the likes of Dennis Bergkamp, Patrick Kluivert, Edgar Davids, the de Boer twins, Clarence Seedorf, Jaap Stam (then the world's most expensive defender), and Jimmy Floyd Hasselbaink. The first round had not seen them at their rampaging best in a group with Mexico, Belgium and South Korea. But in the play-offs they had started to click beautifully and had seen off Yugoslavia and the mighty Argentina, who had defeated England on penalties in the previous round. Now they would play a Brazil team rattled by the game against the Danes and with their most important player struggling with injury. Surely the Dutch fancied themselves in Marseille, a place that gave the jitters to superstitious Brazilians.

At the same stadium, Brazil had lost the 1938 semi-final to Italy and more recently had been beaten there by the Norwegians.

Dutch manager Guus Hiddink, though, was more interested in the absence of Brazil's mercurial right-back, Cafu, who would be replaced be Zé Carlos, making his Seleção debut in a World Cup semi-final.

That the score was still 0-0 when the teams went to the dressing rooms at half-time must have infuriated Hiddink. Holland had wasted a number of good opportunities, including several created by Boudewijn Zenden's probing advances down the right side of the Brazilian defence. But with less than 30 seconds of the second half gone, Ronaldo outran Phillip Cocu in pursuit of a long Rivaldo pass and slipped the ball under Edwin van der Sar to score. The game opened up brilliantly as a spectacle after this and it was Brazil's turn to start to miss chances, one of them a free run from Ronaldo, whose shot drifted agonisingly wide of the right post.

Kluivert hit a perfect header in the 87th minute to force extra-time, during which Ronaldo was denied by a fine Van der Sar save and had an overhead kick cleared off the line by Frank de Boer.

On penalties, Brazil scored all four of their attempts, while Taffarel saved from Cocu and Ronald de Boer to repeat his heroics from 1994. The Seleção had managed to reach their sixth World Cup final with Ronaldo delivering just when they needed him most. From a squad that had seemed doomed after the departure of Romário, the team had defied expectation. Even Zagallo, thanks to an emotional pep talk given to the players on the Velodrome pitch that had been caught by cameras and microphones, had won back some affection. The last hurdle between the Seleção and their fifth title, however, was the host nation, France.

Far from playing anything close to the dominating and exciting football that they were capable of, the hosts had struggled through the knockout stages. First, they had required a Golden Goal to defeat former Seleção star Paulo César Carpegiani's Paraguay in the round of 16 (although the French had had to do so without influential playmaker Zinedine Zidane, who had been sent off in the 4-0 group stage win over Saudi Arabia for stamping on an opponent). Against Italy in the quarter-finals, both teams battled for 120 minutes without scoring (Italy's villain from 1994, Roberto Baggio, went really close to scoring a winner in the dying minutes of extra-time) before France won 4-3 on penalties. In the semi-final, the French had to work hard against a valiant Croatian team, who went 1-0 up in the 46th minute but were then undone by two Liliam Thuram wonder goals; until that July night in Paris, the right-back had never scored for his country. But they had made it to a dream home final against Brazil, a nation whose footballing style had enchanted the French as early as the 1938 World Cup.

But admiration did not mean that the French were not fired up. After two painful semi-final defeats to Germany, in 1982 and 1986, France missed out on qualification for Italy 1990 and USA 1994 and they wanted to make up for it. This was their final. This was Paris. It was going to be a hell of a battle.

Statistically, World Cup hosts have tended to win the tournament if they reached the final game. There were two exceptions: Brazil in 1950, with the Maracanazo and all that; and 1958, where hosts Sweden were overrun by Brazil.

French manager Aimé Jacquet started the World Cup knowing that he had to shelter his players from the frenzy that would envelop the nation, and he had literally confined his players to a chateau on the outskirts of Paris during the tournament. After the Croatia game, Jacquet increased the isolation even more in the hope that he could avoid the overwhelming euphoria of their countrymen distracting his players. There was a job to be done and he needed to devise a strategy to neutralise the Brazilians. A point of order would be dealing with the constant advance of full-backs Cafu and Roberto Carlos. Another was stopping the young bald striker who for the last two seasons had been voted the best player in the world. With four goals in six matches, Ronaldo was behind Croatia's Davor Šuker in the chase for the Golden Boot but led the assists ranking, which made him even more dangerous. During the build-up to the final, French captain Didier Deschamps gave interviews expressing how important it was for Les Bleus to close Ronaldo down as much as possible. Little did Messrs Jacquet and Deschamps know that France were in for a massive helping hand.

Calm, Ronaldo wasn't. In 1994, he had been a fringe player for the Seleção; now he was regarded as their saviour. Romário had been in the same position four years earlier, but Ronaldo had reached that same exalted status at 21 and, unlike Romário, was struggling with niggling pain on his knee.

He took some comfort from his stats: up to that point, Ronaldo had played in four finals for club and country, winning and scoring in all of them. While gossip-hunters were still probing for relationship crisis stories, the player had hardly demonstrated any annoyance with the press intrusions and, in fact, publicly expressed a lot of confidence that the Seleção could do the job in Paris on 12 July.

So, on the night before his date with destiny, the striker had a physio session on his troubled left knee with Joaquim da Mata and then went to bed. He woke normally the following morning and at lunchtime ate a plate of steak, salad, mashed potato, rice and beans before going for a nap at around 1pm. When he woke up, around three hours later, the world had been turned upside down – he just didn't know it yet.

Ronaldo must have felt something was amiss when he saw Mata at the end of his bed. Still, according to what the doctor would later state in front of a parliamentary inquiry, the striker went to take a shower and complained about feeling a bit stiff, but chatted normally with the doctor and room-mate Roberto Carlos. Ronaldo then proceeded to the players' restaurant, where the rest of the group were already sitting down for supper before leaving for Paris. It was then that team-mate Leonardo and Mata broke the news: Ronaldo had suffered a convulsion while sleeping and that would rule him out of the game against France. 'I remember Leonardo talking to me about life having more important things than a football match and I found it very strange, but when the doctor told me about what happened, I was shocked,' said Ronaldo. 'I was prepared to play the game of my life and it's not every day that you have the chance to take part in a World Cup final. So the first thing I did was ask the doctor if there was anything I could do to be deemed fit to play.'

The doctors suggested that Ronaldo should undergo a series of examinations and the striker was then smuggled to a Paris clinic via the hotel's service entrance at around the same time as the team bus left through the front gate. Zagallo, who confirmed Ronaldo's place would be taken by Edmundo, had tried to rally the troops with anecdotes from the 1962 World Cup, when the Seleção lost Pelé through injury only for Amarildo to replace him and help the team to the title, but it became clear that the players were shell-shocked. The drums and tambourines that had previously provided the soundtrack on the team bus were left untouched on the way to the Stade de France. Apart from the deflating news about Ronaldo's absence from that crucial match, the players were confused by the events of the afternoon – because they weren't sure what exactly had happened. What seems striking about Ronaldo's episode is the amount of conflicting information. It all started with what Roberto Carlos, who was watching TV while Ronaldo slept, described as the terrifying scene of the striker pulling faces and looking distressed. The left-back ran next door and called Edmundo, who would describe the scene of Ronaldo 'shaking violently on his bed, foam coming from his mouth'. It was Edmundo who then alerted doctors Toledo and Mata. Before they arrived, César Sampaio dropped in and intervened; his father was epileptic and the midfielder was particularly worried about Ronaldo swallowing his tongue. Sampaio remembered seeing his team-mate 'huffing and puffing, and apparently not breathing properly'.

Toledo arrived first, followed by Mata. Both observed that Ronaldo was still sleeping and without the player waking up had to rely on what his team-mates had told them. So they both believed there could have been a convulsion. The problem was that the tests done on Ronaldo at the Paris clinic, which included CT scans, showed nothing. According to Mata, three French doctors analysed the results and concluded Ronaldo's neurological condition was normal and so discarded the hypothesis of a convulsion. What didn't seem to be taken into account was the fact that the patient had a history of somnambulism, something his relatives had talked about in the press. According to brother Nelio – the one with whom Ronaldo shared a sofa bed in the early Bento Ribeiro days – the player would wake him up at night with football match commentary, dreamy conversations and assorted speeches, to which the brother would retaliate by hitting Ronaldo with pillows until he quietened down. Somnambulism is a sleep disorder from the same family as night terrors, and although night terrors are much more common in children, the condition also affects adults and has been knowingly triggered by situations of anxiety and stress. Neither the Brazilian nor French doctors seemed to know about Ronaldo's history. And the player left the clinic with a document stating he was fit to play. Mata then called Toledo to inform him that he was taking Ronaldo to the stadium.

Regardless of the source of the problem, it did expose once again how unprepared the Seleção were to manage a crisis. Internally, like in the Romário case, the players were kept in the dark about what exactly had happened. Externally, the management had been able to keep things under wraps for several hours, but this would all change dramatically when the team sheets were released to the media an hour before the game: Brazil listed Edmundo as the starting striker and offered no explanation whatsoever for Ronaldo's absence.

The news caused pandemonium and the clamour for information was raised several levels when Brazil did not show up for the warm-up routine on the pitch – the first sight of the team would be their official entrance, Ronaldo included.

The chaos in the news rooms and media suites was not much different to the atmosphere in the Brazilian dressing room. The players were about to start their exercises before taking to the pitch when Ronaldo turned up in full kit, silver boots on and everything. At that point, kick-off was only 40 minutes away and nobody in the technical staff, not even Zagallo, dared take the decision to omit him from the team or not.

Journalists who were paying attention to the VIP area saw CBF president Ricardo Teixeira stand up and disappear from view. He had been summoned to the dressing room. There, he saw Ronaldo sitting down as if nothing had happened. After asking the player how he was feeling ('I'm fine and ready to play, Mr President,' Ronaldo answered), Teixeira addressed the doctors, who informed him the exams showed nothing. Zagallo then informed Teixeira he wanted Ronaldo to play. The president agreed and quickly went to meet the FIFA delegate to try to include the player in the starting line-up without the need for using one of the three substitutions allowed. Thus, after a hellish afternoon, the Seleção were about to kick off a World Cup final traumatised and with some players still worried about their team-mate. 'I was terrified he could suffer something on the pitch. Some of us thought he was risking his life,' says one of the players who started the game, to this day still wishing to talk off the record. Even if Ronaldo felt ready to set the game on fire, as he had promised Zagallo, it was highly unlikely the team could focus quickly enough for the game.

At 9pm local time and in front of a 75,000 crowd, France kicked off and within 15 minutes had twice come close to drawing first blood. Just as Deschamps had promised, France cut the supply lines to Ronaldo by keeping Rivaldo and Leonardo quiet. The game stats would show that Ronaldo received only 15 balls in the final, half the average of the other six games in the tournament.

Brazil, on the other hand, were then caught out in the 27th minute. Emmanuel Petit whipped in a corner from the right and Zidane, never a renowned header of the ball, rose above Leonardo to put France in front.

Then, on one of the few occasions that he managed to escape French attentions, Ronaldo found himself running towards a long ball from Dunga, only to be clattered by Fabien Barthez outside the box, scaring his team-mates even more.

Right on the stroke of half-time Zidane scored his second goal with another header, which he didn't even have to jump for. Brazil were all but defeated and all that France had to do was sit tight for the 45 remaining minutes. Match stats would show Brazil overall had the ball for almost 35 minutes, nearly 10 minutes more than the French. They also exchanged 512 passes against 342 for the French, but it was Les Bleus who scored once again – in injury time – to seal Brazil's heaviest ever defeat in a World Cup match.

The Seleção would now have to deal with the aftermath of the drubbing. Especially their biggest star, who had become the scapegoat for the events at the Stade de France. It started with captain Dunga berating the technical staff for allowing the striker on to the pitch. 'They didn't respect Ronaldo's health and should have thought of his human side,' he said right after the game. 'When we knew Ronaldo was going to play we all became tense. But even if I had screamed at everybody not to play him, it wouldn't have made a difference.'

Zagallo to this day claims there was little he could do. 'I could not let 160 million Brazilians down by telling the best player in the world he couldn't play a World Cup final, especially as the exams had shown nothing wrong. How could I explain it to the Brazilian people if we lost the World Cup with Ronaldo out of the team?'

The morning after a game to forget, Ronaldo had to explain himself publicly and he duly did, apologising for letting the people down and at the same time endorsing the version of events presented by the Seleção staff. 'I suffered a great scare and it obviously affected my team-mates,' he said. 'I hope I will never suffer a convulsion again. But I was not nervous and I did not panic with the responsibility of playing a high-profile game. I felt hesitant out there and that could have happened to anyone.' Without realising it, the striker had given his blessing to his transformation from hero to scapegoat. For the rest of his career he would be singled out as the man who helped Brazil lose that World Cup. It was understandable that Ronaldo pretty much went into hiding as soon as the Seleção arrived back in Brazil from Paris a few days later. In the middle of chaotic scenes at the airport, he probably didn't have time to notice a fan holding a placard in which a Brazilian flag had been altered to include a Nike symbol. But somebody else did.

Senator Aldo Rebelo, one of the last high-profile communist politicians in Brazil at the time, saw the images of the arrival on TV and felt vindicated in his argument that the Brazilians had sacrificed their sovereignty over the hugely lucrative Nike deal. He filed a petition in parliament for an inquiry into the contract, using the national interest card to trump what was meant to be a contract between two private entities. But he could not get enough signatures – even after the details of the controversial deal were leaked in January 1999, and the concessions made to Nike, especially their influence on the organisation of games and the picking of opponents, were exposed.

The straw that eventually broke the camel's back and granted Rebelo his investigation was a scandal that broke in 2000 when a former mistress of Seleção manager Vanderlei Luxemburgo accused him of evading taxes and taking bungs from agents. Shortly afterwards, Luxemburgo's Olympic team was sent packing early from the Sydney Games by nine-man Cameroon and in September that year, the manager was fired. Within days, parliament started procedures for an all-out investigation into the state of the national game. Rebelo had carte blanche to summon witnesses and he duly called up Zagallo and the former team doctors. Ronaldo was also 'invited' to attend. At the time, his career was in tatters after a series of injuries, including a horrific dismantling of his left knee broadcast live during an Internazionale match against Lazio, and there was genuine fear that he would never play at the top level again.

In December 2000, more than two years after the events at the Stade de France, the striker sat in the witness box in one of the many auditoriums in Brazil's futuristic Houses of Parliament to face a grilling from politicians. In a surreal scene that would make the British Prime Minister's Questions look like a Zen monastery, Ronaldo had to answer queries from MPs interested, for example, in the tactics used by Brazil against France and in the precise timing of when he had talked about his fit with Zagallo. But he also had to defend himself against claims that Nike had forced his presence in the World Cup final line-up. 'The only thing they [Nike] have ever asked me to do was to wear their boots during my games,' he angrily retorted when prompted to reveal details of his own endorsement deal.

In the end, the whole inquiry did not come to anything grandiose, especially when the CBF flexed their political muscle to have sympathetic MPs stall proceedings. Rebelo's outrage at the surrendering of national sovereignty gave way to his decision to become the Brazilian Sports Minister in 2011, a brief that included working on Brazil's controversial second hosting of the World Cup – at the time Rebelo took over, the organising committee still had as its president the same Ricardo Teixeira he had once tried to topple with the inquiry. But the parliamentary investigation forced both the CBF and Nike to revise their contract, ending some of the more controversial demands, including the quota on the number of star players to be in the line-up in friendlies and Nike's right to organise games for the Seleção. Nonetheless, the partnership between Nike and the CBF reached the 17-year mark in 2013 and the most recent deal, signed in 2008, provides Brazil with over £20m per year.

In the end, the pathetic crisis management skills shown in 1998 were to blame for Brazil's poor showing in the World Cup final, not the demands of the Seleção's biggest commercial partner – as tempting as it is to embrace the conspiracy theories. Assume that Nike had so much power over the CBF that they could force Ronaldo's presence in the starting line-up in order to protect their business interests; it is not only a wild accusation, it assumes both sides had total disregard for Ronaldo's health. Worse, however, were the elaborate theories insinuating that the Seleção threw the game against France. They are insulting not only because of the immediate reference to the 'dodgy corrupt Latino' stereotype but also for totally disregarding the importance of football for Brazilians.

So what happened to Ronaldo, then? The player himself has refused to discuss the events of 12 July 1998 in much more detail, but there has been no evidence of another convulsion. In 2002, the Brazilian press ran stories linking the reported convulsion to an allergic reaction to anti-inflammatory injections Ronaldo received on his knee in order to play through pain in France, but that scenario has been discredited by doctors. Besides, Ronaldo has always denied having received any injections, a practice that is not taboo in Brazil – Kaka, for example, openly talks about resorting to the injections in the 2010 World Cup.

'I am tired of talking about what happened, to be honest,' said Ronaldo on one of the last occasions he spoke about the incident, in 2011. 'There is really no use in continually revisiting that day. But I admit I was very young in 1998 and the pressure on me was immense. I don't remember what happened on that day and if the doctors haven't been able to find a definite explanation, what am I going to say? The fact is that I did all the tests and nobody found anything. People seem to want to forget that France played well, had the crowd behind them and scored two goals in the first half.'

By the time of that interview, Ronaldo had already completed one of the most remarkable personal and professional resurrections in any walk of life: recalled by Luiz Felipe Scolari for the Seleção only a few months before the 2002 World Cup, after having played only 15 games that season, the striker finally won the biggest tournament on earth, netting eight goals in the process. Finally the ghosts of 1998 were put to rest, at least in his mind. If in 1998 Ronaldo did not shed a tear on the Stade de France pitch, in 2002 he cried with pure joy and relief moments after scoring a brace against Germany in the World Cup final in Japan.

The boy had become the man he had always promised to be.

2010

SIX

2010
ENTER NEYMAR

T HALF-TIME AT the Nelson Mandela Bay Stadium, in Port Elizabeth, the search for the smallest queue for the bathrooms was a bigger priority to Brazilian fans who had travelled to the World Cup in South Africa than looking at the sponsor or institutional messages that flashed across the big screens in the ground. But for those who did look up when Beyoncé's 'Single Lady' began to boom loudly over a short film promoting Brazilian poultry giants Seara, there would have been a sense of mocking irony at the images on show. Seleção striker Robinho and two of his Santos FC team-mates were shown doing tricks with footballs. It was not necessarily a typical sports-related commercial, but what made it notable was the fact that both the young footballers playing second fiddle to Robinho had been the subject of a fierce debate in the national media in the build-up to the Seleção's South African campaign – one that had been focused particularly on the pint-sized and spikey-haired teenager who seemed so at ease in the presence of the camera, unlike his co-stars.

That teenager was Neymar Jr. Alongside Robinho and midfielder Paulo Henrique Ganso, he had set Brazilian football alight in 2010. The trio featured in a Santos XI that had won plaudits for a brand of attacking football that had enthused both fans and media. Thanks to a remarkable crop of players from the youth academy and the presence of more seasoned players like Robinho, himself a former teenage sensation at the club, Santos would finish the year with 180 goals scored and the São Paulo state championship and the Brazilian Cup double. Managed by Dorival Junior, who had won kudos after helping four-times Brazilian champions Vasco da Gama bounce back from a season in Second Division hell in 2009, he attracted a lot of attention for combining a disciplinarian style of player management with a surprisingly liberal way of playing the game. Santos played in a 4-3-3 formation that was made even more exciting because of the presence of Ganso as a playmaker whose deft touch and sharp reading of the game made commentators purr. A gangly 20-year-old, Ganso ('goose' in Portuguese) had caught the eye of the legendary Sócrates. 'The way he never seems to look at the ball amazes me,' said the Doctor. 'Ganso can pass like no other I have seen in the last 20 years. Why this kid has not been called up for the national team is something that I still don't understand.'

But while Ganso had become a player that both media and fans loudly demanded to see in a Seleção shirt, Neymarmania was already eclipsing him. Smiling and frequently attempting some outrageous dribble, the striker had quickly formed a substantial fan club, helped by a scoring tally that would automatically be compared with Pelé in his early days – Neymar would finish the 2010 season with 43 goals, but at the beginning of the year had already earned the status of 'next big thing'. Pelé himself decided to butt in and asked Seleção manager Dunga to consider recruiting the services of the then 17-year-old, claiming, rather unnecessarily, that he himself had been a risky bet in the 1958 World Cup team but ended up being crucial to that campaign.

The son of a former footballer who never really made it at the top level and had to hang up his boots to earn a living in low-paid jobs, Neymar was born on 5 February 1992 in Mogi das Cruzes, a working-class district in Greater São Paulo. Struggling to put food on the table for a family that included daughter Rafaella, Neymar Sr was forced to move his family to a room in his mother's house in São Vicente, near the seaside town of Santos. Despite their financial woes, one of the few luxuries that the family splashed out on was the fee to join Tumiaru, a local and humble social club where Neymar would spend hours kicking a futsal ball around. Soon another working-class club, Gremetal, a place where Santos steelworkers and their families would wind down, had spotted him and recruited the boy. Alcides Magri, who managed the youth department, was stunned by what he saw: at ten years old, Neymar was already playing against older kids and making them look like fools. 'We actually won a city tournament against Santos FC and Neymar destroyed them,' Magri recalls. 'I never taught him to do anything, my only job was not to inhibit all that talent.'

The year was 2002, when Brazil lifted the World Cup for a fifth time in a campaign that featured a reborn Ronaldo. Neymar was one of the kids who would idolise the striker and didn't hesitate in copying everything he did – including the horrendous haircut the Inter Milan player would parade in the final game against Germany in Japan. It was, however, one of the few flirts with footballers' perks that Neymar Sr would allow. A strict education, alongside the low family income, meant the father had to always keep his son on a tight leash. When word about Gremetal's futsal phenomenon started going round and Portuguesa Santista, a feeder club in Santos, came knocking, Neymar Sr demanded the club provide educational support for his son. One might be surprised to know it was quite a rare demand. In 1990, one in five Brazilians over the age of 15 was illiterate. Among football players, the most recent estimates by the Brazilian Football Confederation are that the vast majority only studied to primary school level, which is tricky when most jobs in the formal market demand many more years in formal education. Neymar Sr was also preparing himself for the eventuality that Neymar might not make it to the professional level at all or find himself playing at a low level like the majority of professional players in the country – a CBF study published in 2012 showed that 82 per cent of the 30,000 registered professionals in the country earn between £200 and £400 a month to ply their trade.

Neymar Sr dug his heels in and his son won a scholarship to Liceu São Paulo, one of Santos' finest schools, after Portuguesa Santista argued his case. Neymar was duly enrolled in classes and in the futsal team that would play the Interschool Championship, a traditional grassroots tournament that is shown on regional TV. In Neymar's first year, Liceu's team lost the final game to city rivals Anglo-American School. Neymar played well and immediately caused a diplomatic incident: rival schools lodged a formal complaint to the educational authorities, claiming that Neymar was merely being used by Liceu to play football and was not attending classes. Rather than a mere sporting matter, the accusation also reflected old prejudices – Neymar and sister Rafaella were poor kids now rubbing shoulders with privileged children. Headmaster Ermenegildo Costa had to attend a meeting to present attendance records in order to convince the authorities that the boy should be allowed to play. Thus, unlike many of his neighbours, Neymar spent very little time on the streets bunking off school. His kickabouts were actually training sessions and games for Portuguesa. His reputation quickly grew and game attendances followed suit. It would not take long for local top dogs to take notice.

After decades living in the shadow of Pelé's exploits, Santos FC experienced a radical turnaround in fortunes in the new millennium's first decade. In 2002, the club had finally broken their major honours drought by winning the Campeonato Brasileiro, beating Corinthians in the final – that was the last year the tournament was played in a play-off format. Under former goalkeeper Émerson Leão, a young team peppered with youth academy graduates shone brightly. But Robinho, Diego Ribas, Elano Blumer and Alex would soon be snatched up by European clubs and Santos needed replacements fast. The success of the Robinho generation led to a reshuffle of the youth system that placed ever more emphasis on the younger squads. Under-12s were a priority and securing the services of the most famous under-12 player in town became an obvious coup. 'We were looking for the best players and Neymar had to be part of our team,' said coach Alberto Vieira. 'His potential was already spoken of far and wide and if we didn't sign him somebody else would.'

Two-time world champion Zito, then working for his former club as youth academy coordinator, was brought in to take a look at Neymar and have the final word on the deal. On the same day,

Santos president Marcelo Teixeira got an exasperated phone call. 'I told him we need to close the deal at once,' said Zito. 'The little guy was just unbelievable with the ball at his feet.'

On 10 May 2004, Neymar Jr signed his first contract with Santos: a five-year deal worth a little over £100 a month. Not a fortune but a welcome top-up to the family. It would not stay like that for long, though: just a year later, the boy would be on the verge of becoming Real Madrid's answer to Lionel Messi. While negotiating selling Robinho to Real Madrid in 2005, agent Wagner Ribeiro spoke to the Spanish club about a much younger hot prospect back in Brazil. Real offered a trial and after assessing Neymar they got excited. Just like Barcelona did with Messi, they offered jobs for both the kid's parents in an attempt to make the transfer go through. 'We won't deny that the Real offer rattled us,' said Neymar Sr. But president Teixeira had other plans. In reality, just one plan: open up the coffers and treat Neymar like a professional player. The player was offered £250,000 to stay put and a monthly pay cheque of £5,000.

He hit the ground running, netting ten goals in the Brazilian championship, even though Santos finished in a less-than-flattering 12th place. It was enough, though, to get people raving about how he could help the Seleção in South Africa. Fast and intelligent, Neymar was also cheeky enough to try stunts such as nutmegs, keepie-uppies and even 'Panenkas' (softly chipping a penalty kick down the middle as the keeper dives to the side, named after Antonín Panenka who won the 1976 European Championship for Czechoslovakia with the move against West Germany) that incensed opponents but also excited whoever was watching his shenanigans. 'Neymar and Santos are the only reasons that prevent me from falling asleep in front of the TV whenever I try to watch Brazilian football these days,' raved Sócrates a few months before the 2010 World Cup. The Doctor, like many other people in Brazil, subscribed to the argument that the Seleção had diverted too far from its entertaining traditions – a debate that had become one of the hottest and touchiest topics in Brazilian football in 2010.

At home, however, Neymar Sr still ruled the roost. His son was given a hefty allowance (something around £2,500 a month) and a credit card with what his father described as 'a reasonable limit', but he would have to work hard to earn further indulgences. Things like earrings and fancy clothes would be subject to performance. In 2010, when he turned 18, Neymar wanted what every Brazilian at a legal age always does: a new car. He got one, but only after reaching the target established by his father of winning the Under-20 South American championships with Brazil and scoring at least a brace in the final game. 'Just because we can afford things now I will not simply allow him to burn his money,' said Neymar Sr in an interview he gave at the beginning of 2010. 'He needs to learn the value of things – so Neymar will get treats as long as he reaches targets.'

By then Neymar was already living in a grand apartment near the seafront in Santos. His monthly wages would amount to almost £40,000. Success had also attracted interest from companies keen to sponsor him and soon his earnings would rocket as a result. Unsurprisingly, the whole lobby for Neymar to join the Seleção grew louder. From the outside, it was puzzling to see so much ado about a player who had shown potential but who still remained relatively untested at a senior level; but at the twilight of the noughties Brazilians were desperate for new heroes to replace some of their most iconic figures who were either disappearing into the sunset or morphing into villains.

To understand why, it is necessary to go back in time four years.

In early March 2006, Moscow was not the place where one would expect a voluntary visit from Brazil. With temperatures constantly falling below minus 15°C, the Russian capital could not have been a more inappropriate place for the Seleção to play their last friendly before the World Cup in Germany – even the Russian league does not finish its winter break until the middle of the month. But there the defending champions were, ready to fulfil a contractual obligation with brewery Ambev, one of their biggest sponsors, who after lengthy efforts to secure an opponent for the last FIFA-approved international date, had managed to conveniently find a team whose rich financial backers had paid around £1 million for the privilege and where the company was actively looking for business opportunities.

Three months before the World Cup, the Seleção were in festive mood. After a wobbly start to another cycle as world champions, where they had been unceremoniously dumped from 2003's Confederations Cup in the group stages, the team had gelled during the South American qualifiers – after 2002, FIFA had decided that current world champions would lose the right to an automatic spot in the following World Cup. With only two defeats in 18 games, the Seleção had easily topped the ten-team mini-league, scoring 36 goals, and looked pretty confident that they were on course for a good show in Germany. To make matters sweeter, the team had won the 2005 Confederations Cup. After a jittery group stage, where they lost to Mexico and were held to a 2-2 draw by Japan, Brazil beat hosts Germany 3-2 in the semi-finals before thrashing Argentina 4-1 in the final.

However, by the time they reported back to duty a couple of months later in Moscow, the tables had turned. Both Ronaldo and Adriano, Brazil's formidable striking partnership, were struggling at their clubs (Real Madrid and Inter Milan) and looked worryingly out of shape – an accusation that could be particularly levelled at Ronaldo, who at the time still had the chants of 'fat boy' from Real's own fans ringing in his ears. It looked increasingly evident that the Brazilian would struggle to build upon his spectacular 2002 resurrection.

In 2006, Ronaldo was still young at 29, but with each passing day it seemed that he had lost the hunger for another tilt at the FIFA trophy. The fact that Brazil defeated the Russians with a single goal after a Roberto Carlos shot was deflected by Ronaldo's belly just made the whole thing even sadder.

As for Adriano, the problem was his thirst. Shy and homesick at an Inter side dominated by Argentine players, he had resorted to drowning his sorrows with alcohol. Knowing this, manager Carlos Alberto Parreira probably wasn't shocked by the sight of both strikers arriving at the World Cup training camp several kilos over their ideal weight. It would be revealed after Germany 2006 that Ronaldo showed up weighing almost 100kg, 13 more than his official 2002 weight. Chances of a focused recovery were spoiled by the CBF's decision to turn the training camp into a money-spinning opportunity. Following an agreement with Swiss-based company Kentaro, the Seleção set up camp in Weggis, near Lake Lucerne, and would stay there for two weeks. Training would be witnessed by a battalion of journalists and by an average crowd of 7,000 people who would pay for the privilege. 'For two weeks we trained with fans screaming in our ears and the press broadcasting training sessions live,' explains midfielder Gilberto Silva. 'We never had the chance to work in peace and that left everybody a bit edgy.' Compounding the difficulties, some of his colleagues decided to hit the Lucerne nightclubs and reportedly regularly arrived back at the team hotel at dawn, drunk and dishevelled, which didn't really contribute to a harmonious, professional atmosphere either.

With 11 players returning from the 2002 World Cup-winning team, the 2006 squad was dominated by stars such as Ronaldo, Cafu, Roberto Carlos and Ronaldinho – the latter on fire for Barcelona, winning that year's Champions League and at the time the back-to-back FIFA World Player of the Year. They were a pretty difficult bunch to handle and Parreira was struggling to get them under control. 'At the end of the day, there are limits to what a manager can tell players to do when they are not on national team duty. Different from a club, where there is a daily routine, in international football you spend months without actually seeing the players in person. So you just tell them to look after themselves, you can't really foresee that players might turn up overweight. That group, perhaps, wasn't as hungry to win as one that had never won a major tournament.'

Despite the problems, those were the players Parreira would take to his second World Cup as the Seleção manager. Alongside him as assistant coach was Mario Zagallo, who, during the 1994 World Cup, had become famous for his public displays of naïve optimism whenever he was asked a tricky question on live TV. Brazil had been drawn alongside Croatia, Australia and Japan. Without any great flamboyance, Brazil negotiated safe passage to the knockout stages with three victories, seven goals scored and only one conceded – to a Japan side managed by Zico, who for the second tournament in a row had the strange experience of trying to mastermind a defeat of the Seleção. Ghana were comfortably brushed aside in the round of 16 and then came a match-up against France. For all the talk of revenge for 1998, Brazil were a pale bunch against a revived Zidane. The 1-0 defeat stung badly and would provoke a generational cull. Above all, it would make CBF president Ricardo Teixeira decide that the new manager would have to be a disciplinarian. Teixeira, nonetheless, had also witnessed an interesting phenomenon that had taken place at Germany 2006: the Klinsmann effect.

Under the guidance of Jürgen Klinsmann, a Mannschaft legend who had never even managed a pub side before being catapulted to the main job, Germany had been one of the feelgood sporting stories of 2006. Amidst a wave of national euphoria in a country where patriotism still raises eyebrows within and without its borders, a discredited German team had endeared themselves to fans by making it to the semi-finals before a tearful capitulation against Italy. Klinsmann's enthusiasm had become a trademark of the team and the experience did not go unnoticed. But while the former Inter Milan and Tottenham striker had sought to bring more flair and inventiveness to his side, Brazilians were looking for someone who could tame inflated egos. Teixeira would not even need to go back to Brazil to talk to the man he wanted, for Dunga had been working in Germany as a TV pundit. The man who captained Brazil's 1994 World Cup-winning side would become the Brazilian answer to the Klinsmann effect. He would take no prisoners.

Like Klinsmann, Dunga had never worked as a coach before and in his own words he never expected to. Two years before being unveiled at the CBF headquarters in Rio de Janeiro, the former captain would be found killing time in sporadic tours with the Brazilian Masters team. He was part of the XI who faced Exeter City in a friendly to celebrate the 90th anniversary of the Seleção's first ever game and after the match he spoke freely about his reservations of the dugout experience. 'Our football directors are amateurs and I don't think I can stomach the lack of competence they show in running our teams,' he said, while sipping a pint of bitter in a nondescript Dorset pub. 'It is enough for me to be remembered as a guy who gave his heart for his country as a player.'

For all this, Dunga's change of heart was understandable: apart from an unbelievable professional opportunity, the call from the Seleção also meant the Seleção once again needed Dunga. And that always mattered to him. A member of the class that in 1983 won the U-23 Youth World Cup, at a time when Brazilians were still licking the wounds of the Seleção's painful exit from the 1982 World Cup, Dunga had been awarded a handful of caps since 1984, the year he represented Brazil in the Los Angeles Olympics, but failed to impress as vividly as team-mates Jorginho and Bebeto. After playing for Internacional, Corinthians, Santos and Vasco in the space of seven years, he left for Italy in 1987 to defend for minnows Pisa.

Away from the spotlight, he fell down the pecking order and hardly featured for the Seleção until 1989, when new manager Sebastião Lazaroni, who had worked with the midfielder at Vasco, brought him back for his ambitious experiment for the 1990 World Cup. A no-nonsense midfielder forged in the tough, physical environment of southern Brazilian football, Dunga rose through the ranks to help Lazaroni's 3-5-2 system, a formation which had raised a lot of controversy on the back of some poor results, such as a 4-0 routing by Denmark in June. A month later, he was lining up for the national anthems in Salvador, where Brazil would open their 1989 Copa America campaign. While strikers Bebeto and Romário became media darlings after the Seleção recovered from an inauspicious start to become South American champions for the first time in 40 years, it was Dunga who the media turned into a symbol, for better or worse. The 'Dunga Era' was the term created to explain the transition from Telê Santana's artistic style into a more tactically conscious ('Europeanised') way of playing football. Brazil went on to beat Italy and European champions Holland away in the final months of 1989 and Lazaroni seemed to have won the battle against his critics. But it all fell apart spectacularly in the 1990 World Cup – after negotiating hard-fought wins against Sweden, Costa Rica and Scotland, Brazil were sent packing by Argentina in the round of 16, after a great Diego Maradona move was finished by Claudio Cannigia. Ironically, Brazil had lost after their best game in the competition and were unlucky not to have won quite comfortably after hitting the post several times. The knives were out back home, however, after the Seleção's worst result since the 1966 shambles and the public and media were quick to condemn Lazaroni and to turn Dunga into the symbol of a failed generation.

The midfielder would not get a game for Brazil under new manager Falcão and even his successor, Carlos Alberto Parreira, took his time to bring Dunga back to the fold. Between June 1990 and June 1993 Dunga would only start one game under Parreira and it was only after Brazil's horrendous start to the 1994 World Cup qualifying campaign that he was drafted in to help. The press immediately cried foul and the midfielder spent the whole campaign under fire – his goal against Ecuador in São Paulo, a venomous shot with the outside of the right boot, was celebrated with a hug from team-mate Jorginho and some less than kind words for the crowd that had been booing the team's nervous performance. By the time Brazil went to the United States for the 1994 World Cup, Dunga was already a crucial cog in Parreira's machine on and off the pitch. Tactically, his midfield partnership with Mauro Silva would be an effective shield to the centre-backs and led to a formidable defensive record in that tournament, with only two goals conceded in seven matches. But Dunga was also a leader in a group eager to bounce back from the horrors of 1990, when players were pelted with coins at the airport in Rio, and Parreira did not hesitate in using him as a 'shadow' for the temperamental Romário, on whose goals Brazil depended in order to succeed. The two players were chalk and cheese – Romário a cheeky chap and Dunga the man with the eternal frown – but they formed an extraordinarily close bond.

Dunga wasn't Parreira's formal choice of captain. The armband had been given to Rai, the stylish midfielder and brother of the legendary Sócrates. But the player failed miserably to deliver in Brazil's group stage matches and was duly dropped, with Dunga stepping into what was his natural role. That meant the man so reviled by his fellow countrymen in 1990 would be the one to lift the FIFA trophy on 17 July 1994, when Brazil broke a 24-year duck in the World Cup. Liked or not, his detractors would have to acknowledge that Dunga was now a World Cup winner. But the fact that the player had used the occasion to address the press corps in less than flattering terms while still holding the trophy had left a sour taste.

Twelve years later, Dunga was a near universal choice to try to pick up the pieces after the disaster of 2006. Even sectors more opposed to his appointment agreed that the former captain was the right name to symbolise a new regime for the Seleção after the perception that the big stars had outstayed their welcome. In his first interview, the new manager repeated exhaustively that collectiveness would trump prestige in his team. 'The real star here is the Brazilian shirt, which represents the country that has won more World Cups than any other. No player is more important that this shirt.'

Dunga was swift to put his money where his mouth was: when the Seleção reconvened in August 2006 for their first game since the France defeat in Frankfurt, a friendly against Norway in Oslo, only eight of the 23 players who had gone to Germany made Dunga's new squad. Among the surviving members were defenders Lúcio, Juan and Luisão, midfielder Gilberto Silva, full-backs Cicinho and Gilberto and strikers Fred and Robinho. In the space of a month, the likes of Ronaldo, Roberto Carlos and Cafu had been retired by one of their former team-mates, while Ronaldinho and Kaká, both younger than the aforementioned trio, were used as an example of stars who would have to earn back their places in the squad. Dunga also made a point that not only players plying their trade in top Europeans leagues would get a shot: the first call-up was peppered with Eastern Europe-based players, including midfielder Elano, whose 2004 move from Santos to Shakhtar Donetsk had been publicly criticised by the then Seleção manager Carlos Alberto Parreira, who had frequently left out players based in clubs east of Berlin. One of them, CSKA Moscow's Daniel Carvalho, would score the first goal of the 'New Dunga Era' and spare Brazil some blushes in a 1-1 draw against the Norwegians.

Although they were bundled together in Dunga's push for a humble pie banquet, Kaká and Ronaldinho were experiencing very different outcomes from the debacle in Germany. Kaká was one of the few Seleção stars spared the vitriolic criticism directed at the team. A devout Christian, the AC Milan forward not only stood aside from the party animal lot led by Ronaldo, but he was also much younger than the veterans. He was only 20 when taking part in the 2002 World Cup as a sub (and only saw 20 minutes of action in a group stage game against Costa Rica). Four years later, however, he had become an influential player on the pitch, having won Serie A with Milan and reached a Champions League final in which he supplied two assists for Hernán Crespo to score a brace in the Italian club's dream first half against Liverpool, when they led 3-0. In Germany, he scored the winner for the Seleção in the opening game against Croatia but couldn't really fulfil his potential in a team that was so unbalanced with its heavy attacking duo and fading full-backs. Dunga's decision to have Kaká sit out the Norway friendly received mixed reactions in Brazil. The player himself was surprised, but chose not to antagonise the new manager. Especially as he agreed with Dunga's new humble approach. Kaká had witnessed up close how Ronaldo, Cafu and Roberto Carlos had lorded it up in 2006, to the point where manager Parreira was seen by many other players as having lost control of the group. 'I appreciate Dunga's proposal to make the group more important than the individuals,' Kaká said when questioned about his absence from the squad. 'That is the way teams win. But I would like this idea not to be restricted to speeches.'

Ronaldinho, however, was quite another story. After winning the FIFA World Player of the Year trophy in 2004 and 2005 and leading Barcelona to the 2006 Champions League title, he had become a messianic figure in the football world and Brazilians were certain that the 'Buck-Toothed One', as they tenderly referred to him, would lead the charge in Germany. Reality proved very different: Ronaldinho failed to ignite the World Cup and left the tournament with no goals, one assist and only four shots on target. Saying that he underperformed was an understatement, no matter how naïve it was to imagine Ronaldinho could carry the entire team on his shoulders, especially when Parreira did not use him on the left wing where he so powerfully dominated for his club. While at Barcelona the Brazilian could rely on sharper and faster team-mates such as Deco, Samuel Eto'o, Xavi, Iniesta and a blossoming Lionel Messi, and his team-mates at the Seleção weren't of the same calibre. And to compound matters, Ronaldinho's name is still associated with partying hard in Barcelona, which he did overtly in the build-up to the 2006 tournament; this, and his appearance in a number of TV commercials, became a source of criticism in Brazil after the France game. So it was that Ronaldinho's omission from Dunga's first squad earned the manager kudos in the media.

Despite this, the Barcelona man and Kaká were back in the fold in September for Brazil's London friendlies against Argentina and Wales. Struggling with back spasms, Ronaldinho limited himself to watching the displaced South American derby at the Emirates Stadium. Kaká had suffered the same fate during the first 45 minutes, having been benched by Dunga. It was another controversial decision fully exploited in the news ahead of the game, but the manager could barely hide his grin when Brazil went 1-0 up through Elano. If Dunga wanted to put Kaká on his mettle, the plan worked brilliantly: the Milan man set Elano up for his second before scoring the third in the 89th minute, after stealing possession from Messi in Brazil's own half and slaloming past the Argentine defence.

Two days later, at White Hart Lane, Ronaldinho finally made it on to the pitch under Dunga's watch, but the 2-0 win against Ryan

Giggs' Wales did not mask another underwhelming performance by the Barcelona forward, the 11th consecutive game in which he had failed to score for the Seleção.

One month later, Ronaldinho would start the Seleção's next friendly – a bizarre match against Al-Kuwait – but he sat on the bench for the following two games against Ecuador and Switzerland and Dunga did nothing to hide his lack of enthusiasm for the player's performances. 'Ronaldinho needs to adapt himself to the team,' ranted the manager, in what sounded like criticism towards Ronaldinho's celebrated set of skills. 'A great player is the one that can steal balls, give assists and score goals. The rest is just folklore.' Statements like that helped to reignite old controversies involving the former captain. Dunga had always been specifically sensitive to criticism about the tactical rigidity that marked Brazil's displays in the 1994 World Cup. He wouldn't hold back even if comments came from 'sacred cows' such as Zico and Sócrates. 'The 1982 generation was a losing one but people still love to hail the beautiful way they played football,' said Dunga scathingly. 'But what is the point of playing artistically if the results don't come? My generation was one of the most accomplished in the history of Brazilian football. We won the U-23 world title, reached two Olympic finals and lifted a World Cup for Brazil after 24 years. We taught Brazil how to win again. People said we played ugly, but the fact is that we brought the trophies home and some people, including former players, still can't cope with that.'

Zico, then coaching Turkish side Fenerbahçe, responded by blasting what he saw as a lack of recognition for coaches who had been working in Brazil. 'I am not questioning what Dunga represents for Brazilian football, but I do think his appointment sent the wrong message. Experience in the job should count at the time when somebody picks the manager of a national team. What about the guys who have invested time in careers and courses? A good CV should be crucial for a job like managing Brazil.' It should be noted that Zico had ruled himself out of contention for the job, so his words were not the result of any bitterness at having lost out.

Dunga, however, could point to results like the drubbing of Argentina as evidence that the rebuilding of the Seleção was not going as badly as some people were making out. But by the time Brazil returned to London, in February 2007, the atmosphere had changed. Rumours were rife that Ronaldinho and Kaká had approached Dunga to ask to be relieved from playing in that year's Copa America so that they could focus on their club form, but the manager had vehemently denied that anyone would get time off like that. The week got more tense after Portugal dealt Dunga his first defeat in the job, a result that knocked Brazil off the top of the FIFA rankings for the first time in 55 months; the result was especially bitter as Portugal were being managed by Luiz Felipe Scolari, a fact that the Brazilian media couldn't seem to mention enough.

Criticism intensified after Brazil needed a 92nd-minute equaliser to avoid defeat to England at Wembley, although the team had bounced back from the Portugal defeat with wins over Chile and Ghana. A goalless draw against Turkey in Dortmund didn't help Dunga's case and when it was officially announced that he and the Brazilian FA had granted the wishes of Kaká and Ronaldinho and excused them from playing in the Copa America in Venezuela, expectations for Brazil's first official tournament since the 2006 World Cup could hardly have been more deflated.

Brazil opened their campaign with a 2-0 defeat to Mexico but recovered by beating Chile and Ecuador. A 6-1 drubbing of the Chileans put the Seleção in the semi-finals, where a penalty shoot-out triumph against Uruguay sent them to another final against Argentina. Against the odds, since Argentina were unbeaten in the tournament, Brazil triumphed with a 3-0 scoreline. Amid enthusiastic celebrations, players and manager complained about a perceived lack of respect for the team, and Dunga spouted some extraordinary quasi-philosophical quips. 'I dedicate our title to every child in the world who suffers with war and hunger. These are people who are pure, they don't have envy or evil.'

A month later, Ronaldinho and Kaká were back in the team and helped the Seleção beat Algeria, the USA and Mexico comfortably. But then came the South American qualifiers for South Africa 2010 and Brazil stumbled: the Seleção drew two of the first five games and lost so convincingly to Paraguay that panic set in. A 2-0 defeat to Venezuela in a friendly in Boston, the first ever loss suffered by Brazil against their northern neighbours, sparked a public taunt by General Hugo Chávez in a meeting with president Lula da Silva; public outrage, meanwhile, was exemplified by the crowd's behaviour during Brazil's goalless draw against Argentina in Belo Horizonte: Brazilian fans booed the Seleção while applauding Messi whenever he touched the ball. It was at this time that sources close to the CBF started briefing Brazilian journalists that the manager would be put to the sword if Brazil didn't come back from the Beijing Olympics with anything less than gold. Thus, when Brazil were sent packing after Argentina repaid the past drubbings with a 3-0 win of their own in the semi-finals, the cover of influential newspaper *O Globo* was designed like the funeral classifieds and communicated the 'demise' of the manager. The scene was all set for the mercy shot from CBF president Ricardo Teixeira.

Only it didn't come. Dunga was kept in the job and was obviously less than amused by *O Globo*'s announcement. The episode resulted in a siege mentality among the management which was very quickly transmitted to the players. Brazil stumbled again in the qualifiers, drawing against Bolivia and Colombia, but were still in one of the four qualifying spots. A 6-2 win against Portugal in the last friendly of 2008 bought Dunga some breathing space over the holidays. It seemed to be just what he and his squad needed. Refreshed and refocused, 2009 started with a win against Italy in London in February and qualification for the World Cup a month later – with three rounds to spare – after a 3-1 win in Argentina, the first triumph in their most famous rivals' territory in 14 years. There were barely 1,000 Brazilian fans at the Arroyito, but their singing in praise of the manager must have felt good for the man who just a couple of months before had been hounded by donkey chants. At the press conference, however, he showed that forgiveness would take time. Asked if he thought Argentina had played badly, the manager addressed the local hacks with a scowl. 'I don't know if you understood the question. It's because in Brazil we never think we have merited our victories; instead we have to think our opponents didn't do enough.'

Dunga seemed, at last, to have galvanised the players. Brazil went to the Confederations Cup in South Africa and after a nervous 4-3 win over Egypt they went on to win the tournament for the second time in a row with a remarkable comeback against the USA in the final – the Seleção went 2-0 down but won the game with a last-gasp header by defender and captain Lúcio. Since Dunga had taken over, Brazil had finished at the top in every competition they took part in – including the qualifying tournament, which they eventually topped despite the stumbles. While it could be argued that they often didn't win pretty, the results were undeniably remarkable and the players took notice. 'We knew Dunga had arrived at the Seleção without any management experience but that didn't mean that he did not know football,' said Gilberto Silva. 'Above all, he seemed to be getting the best out of the players during a changing of the guard. The players respected him as a leader, a world champion, but above all he never tried to hide behind excuses or to blame us when things went wrong. That appeals to a lot of footballers, let me tell you.'

The manager had control of the dressing room and could finally look forward to a fourth World Cup. The year ended with lukewarm friendlies in the Middle East – a 1-0 win over an injury-ridden England in Doha and a 2-0 triumph against Oman in Muscat. Between June 2008 and October 2009 the Seleção had been unbeaten for 19 games, a sequence only broken by a 2-1 away defeat to Bolivia in the last qualifier.

They had also parted company with Ronaldinho, whose last appearance under Dunga came as a substitute in Brazil's 3-0 win over Peru in April 2009. Sent packing from Barcelona at the end of the 2007/08 season as part of Pep Guardiola's attempts to rejuvenate the squad and avoid having Messi dragged down by the Brazilian's hell-raising lifestyle, Ronaldinho had signed for AC Milan and had once again begun to show some glimpses of his phenomenal ability. It was enough to convince Dunga to give him another chance. Attentions then immediately turned to Neymar as a means of giving the Seleção a touch of unpredictability. Thanks to FIFA's changes in the calendar during the '90s, the number of friendlies played before the World Cup during the European club season had been reduced to a single match. When the Santos youngster's name didn't show up in the squad for Brazil's visit to Ireland in Dublin in March 2010, it had become clear that only an injury to another squad member would see Neymar make it to South Africa. To make sure everybody understood the message, Dunga gave his own take on the player's development. 'In the history of the Brazilian national team you can see that the players that worked out the best were the ones that were tested over time. In Brazil we are always saying that this or that player is special, but many never live up to expectations. If a new Pelé comes through you can be sure I will call him up.'

So in May 2010, the manager announced his 23-man squad. No place for Robinho, Ganso and Ronaldinho. Brazil would be challenging for a sixth crown with a squad that contained a combination of physicality, tactical discipline and counter-attacking speed, mixed with individual attributes such as Kaká's skills and Luis Fabiano's poaching instincts. It was seldom pleasant to watch this Brazil in action, but they were also a team that had put five goals past Italy and six past Argentina with no response. Goalkeeper Júlio César, right-back Maicon and centre-back Lúcio were fresh from winning a Serie A, Coppa Italia and Champions League treble with José Mourinho's Inter. Lucio, as a matter of fact, formed with Roma's Juan a centre-back partnership that only lost three out of 37 games for Brazil, with an impressive average of less than one goal per game. Gilberto was indeed eight years older than in 2002, but was still a rare case of a Brazilian defensive midfielder who didn't have to resort to heavy tackling to disarm opponents, a task more appropriate to Felipe

Melo of Juventus, whose fiery temper often diverted attention from his work with the ball. Elano had already departed Manchester City after an unhappy time under Mark Hughes, who had also lost the respect of fellow Seleção player Robinho. After City broke the then British transfer record in 2008 to buy Robinho from Real Madrid for £32.5 million, the player had a promising first season at Eastlands but failed to establish himself in the Premiership and had to resort to forcing a loan move back to Santos in order to get first-team football. For the Seleção, though, Robinho had been instrumental, scoring 19 goals since the beginning of the new World Cup cycle.

On paper, Dunga had put together a team that had to be considered as a contender for the title in South Africa. The only visible chink in the armour was the absence of a convincing option for left-back. The decision to retire Roberto Carlos exposed a curious quality gap in a position where Brazil had traditionally churned out talent after talent. The Seleção had boasted the legendary Nilton Santos, the player who broke the mould that restricted full-backs to defensive duties and who became one of the symbols of the 1958–62 double-winning generation. Leovegildo Gama Júnior was immortalised in the 1982 side and later reinvented his career as a resourceful midfielder and even featured under Parreira in the rebuilding work for USA 1994. In that tournament, the heroics of left-back Branco, who scored the winning goal in a tricky quarter-final against Holland, stood out. Since Carlos' departure, however, nobody had owned that left side of the pitch. Under Dunga, a string of players had been tested in the position, including a promising mercurial Fluminense FC player named Marcelo, later a Real Madrid household name. The drought had forced Dunga to use right-back Dani Alves as improvised cover during the World Cup qualifiers but at the end of 2009 Dunga decided to give a maiden cap to Lyon's Michel Bastos, to the surprise of fans, public and even the player. Especially the player, since Bastos had, for at least three seasons, played in midfield for Lille and Lyon, information that didn't go unnoticed in Brazil. In fairness, the then Lyon winger had been initially brought in as cover for Liverpool's

Fábio Aurélio, who Dunga had hoped would resolve the positional problem. But injuries hampered the plan and Bastos was catapulted into the spotlight. The manager's choice for a second left-back also raised eyebrows: in came veteran Gilberto, Carlos' deputy in 2006, and remembered in Europe for a difficult time at Tottenham Hotspur, where over two season he played a mere ten games before returning to Brazil to play for Cruzeiro. At 34, he had also abandoned the left-back role to earn his living in midfield.

Brazil had been dealt an interesting draw in South Africa. Alongside Cristiano Ronaldo's Portugal and Didier Drogba's Ivory Coast, the Seleção were pooled with North Korea, back in the World Cup for the first time since their 1966 exploits – they had knocked out Italy before capitulating against Portugal, after going 3-0 up against Eusébio and co. The team from the reclusive rogue state would be Brazil's first opponents, followed by the Africans and the Portuguese. While qualifying was not supposed to be a major concern for Dunga's team, the fact that European champions Spain could be waiting in the round of 16 put extra pressure on the campaign. But it also offered the manager a perfect excuse to score points in his tussles with the media: the Seleção would prepare for South Africa in what could be called an isolation regime, where players would have restricted contact with fans and journalists ahead of the already restricted FIFA guidelines for activities during the tournament. While Dunga's approach was attacked as being draconian, it was not a top down resolution. The players had made it clear to the former captain that they wanted to distance themselves from any festive mood. 'Even the guys who had not been part of the 2006 squad knew about the problems created by the preparations in Weggis,' explains Gilberto. 'Nobody wanted to be exposed to that atmosphere because we knew it wouldn't do us any good and in the end the players could get a lot of flak if things went wrong at the World Cup. After we qualified, Dunga approached the players and asked what we wanted to do in terms of preparations. We were the ones saying we needed exactly the opposite from what had happened in 2006.'

The former Arsenal player insists the manager was more messenger than enforcer, but the fact is that Dunga himself had the chance to witness the Swiss circus in 2006 when he worked as a TV pundit. In his conversations with the CBF to take over the Seleção he had reinforced the need to avoid a similar situation, just like he had protested against the infamous cancellation of a training session for a Seleção promotional appearance in France 1998. 'I am here to address the Seleção's needs, not wishes,' he had informed president Teixeira. Dunga, however, had made powerful enemies with his style of command. If moans from the press seem to come with any national team manager's job description, the former captain looked particularly pleased to frustrate Globo TV, for decades the powerful holder of the rights for every game played by the Seleção. They had enjoyed special access to players for as long as people could remember and did not expect the situation to change under the new command. But relations had begun to sour in 2008, right at the time where the manager's position had been particularly under threat, and Dunga retaliated by turning down interview requests and creating what he called a 'discomfort zone' for the channel. To have an idea of how much power Globo TV holds in Brazil, one has just to point to the 1989 presidential election, the first time in almost 30 years that the country could vote freely. The winner was Fernando Collor de Mello, who before Globo's patronage had been the governor of minnow state Alagoas in the north of the country. Collor ended up beating some major Brazilian political heavyweights, but not without the help of massively skewed coverage from a channel that to this day still commands the highest audiences in Brazil and is still the main reason why cable TV didn't manage to upset the apple cart in sport broadcasting in the country.

But Dunga did not feel intimidated and bickered openly with Globo TV, issuing a ban on exclusive interviews and any media activities outside the daily 30-minute press conferences – a scenario that was in complete contrast to Germany 2006, when players were made available for the channel even after midnight. The ban contributed to an understandable increase in the already tense relationship between manager and media, which also spiralled into the playing ranks. Robinho was forced to apologise in front of the other players for daring to speak to an 'enemy' camera crew while walking around a Johannesburg shopping mall.

Other players were also far from buffered from controversy. Since Brazil had been firmly cautioned by FIFA in 2009, when the players had prayed in the centre of the pitch and wore shirts with religious messages during celebrations for the Confederations Cup title, the issue of religious behaviour within the Seleção had been rekindled. During a press conference, Kaká, who openly professed his Christian devotion by having 'I Belong to Jesus' sewn on his boots, would lash out against reports that he had a serious groin injury and was playing through pain by playing the religious card. 'I am being attacked because of my faith in Jesus Christ,' vented the 2007 World Player of the Year. 'In the same way as I respect non-believers, I'd like to be respected for my religious beliefs.'

As well as Kaká, Lúcio was a vocal evangelist whose public displays of faith had openly bothered FIFA, the governing body clearly uncomfortable with the involvement of religion in football. But in Brazil the warning to calm the religious fervour of the players touched deeper issues. Although it still has the biggest Catholic population in the world (123 million out of a population of 190 million people), the country has witnessed a substantial growth in Protestantism over the last 40 years and Catholicism has decreased in that time from 92 per cent of the population to 57 per cent. If the bulk of this swing can be seen in the political sphere, where the so-called 'Evangelical Block' became a force to be reckoned with in the Brazilian Congress, football became a much more visible arena for religious militancy. In 1984, a group of footballers led by Baltazar, a cult hero centre-forward nicknamed 'God's Striker' given his professed faith, founded Christ's Athletes, an association of Protestant sportsmen that would prove to be one of the most influential power groups in Brazilian football over the next decade. Their influence within the Seleção was specifically felt during the 1990 World Cup, during which they would meet regularly for prayer, invariably led by right-back Jorginho, who 20 years later would be working alongside Dunga in South Africa.

Jorginho never shied away from giving faith testimonials and even in informal conversations with journalists he liked to bring the subject to the fore – during a 2009 trip to Qatar, he even spoke openly about Jesus and the Holy Spirit while sitting down for lunch, oblivious to the heretical nature of that kind of conversation in a Muslim country. In a more heated press conference before the World Cup, the assistant coach and 1994 World Cup winner actually said that people wishing bad things to the Seleção would be 'excommunicated by Jesus'.

Religious fervour was hardly a monopoly of the evangelical lot. As previously mentioned, references to the supposed colour of Mother Mary's shroud (blue) were dropped to reassure a superstitious Brazilian squad ahead of the 1958 final after the Swedes won the right to play in yellow. In 1994, the whole Brazilian squad prayed together in the centre of the Rose Bowl pitch in Pasadena after the penalty shoot-out victory against Italy – and the Buddhist beliefs of Roberto Baggio, who skied the deciding penalty, were often mentioned in the aftermath of that World Cup by the Brazilian media. And while Luiz Felipe Scolari may hardly come across as a religious figure, the manager walked 18km between the cities of Goiania and Trindade ('trinity' in Portuguese) in 2003 to visit a Catholic sanctuary as a thanksgiving exercise after the World Cup win he masterminded in the previous year. But the preaching of the evangelicals had never been comfortably received by large swathes of the public or the CBF.

No pun intended, but spirits were far from jovial when Brazil stepped on to the Ellis Park pitch for their opener against North Korea. On a cold night, the Seleção looked frozen and struggled to impose themselves against a team ranked far below the FIFA leaders. After a goalless first half, Brazil opened their World Cup account in the 55th minute courtesy of a Maicon strike that exploited the naivety of keeper Guk, who had expected a cross to the right-back. On the 71st minute, Elano put the result beyond doubt after latching on to a Robinho low pass from almost the halfway line. It wasn't the routing predicted by many and the mood turned sour when Maicon was caught out of position which allowed Yun Nam to rove into the Brazilian box and hit a howitzer of a shot past César two minutes from time.

The Seleção had failed to impress and had failed to build a comfortable goal cushion, but at least a goalless draw between Portugal and Ivory Coast made the result in Johannesburg a bit less grim. Still, during his press conference, Dunga lashed out at a Brazilian journalist who had asked about Robinho's good game. 'I have the memory of an elephant and I remember you were one of the experts demanding for Robinho to be dropped from the national team last year because he wasn't doing well at Manchester City,' he scowled.

Five days later, this time at Soccer City, the Seleção lined up to face the Ivory Coast with a point to prove. Drogba, who had picked up an elbow injury a few days before the tournament, had recovered in time to face the Brazilians. The Africans needed a win to keep their chances of qualifying for the second round (without depending on Portugal's results) alive, but their game plan under Sven-Göran Eriksson revolved around physical intimidation, which Dunga's team responded to accordingly: a total of 40 fouls would be registered by FIFA's statisticians and French referee Stéphane Lannoy would hand out five yellow cards and one red. But Brazil took control of the match in footballing terms in the 25th minute: a Kaká pass put Luis Fabiano into space with only goalkeeper Boubacar to beat and the Sevilla forward whacked the ball past him to put an end to a six-match goal drought. Fabiano would controversially increase Brazil's advantage five minutes into the second half when the striker escaped the attentions of two markers with the help of what appeared to be a handball. After 62 minutes, a great run by Kaká on the left ended up with a low cross for an Elano tap-in. Brazil couldn't be playing better after the underwhelming performance against the North Koreans. The feelgood factor, though, was dented seconds after the third goal: Elano was hit by a reckless challenge by Tioté and left the pitch in tears. Kaká, who had spent a good part of the second half complaining to the referee about the rough treatment from the Ivorians, was sent off after a clash with Keïta that incensed the Brazilians, particularly Dunga. It was Kaká's first career red card and it gave a worrying sign of tensions within the team and in Kaká's mind.

Three years before, Kaká could hardly put a foot wrong. He led Milan to their fifth Champions League title in 2007, when the Italians avenged their shocking 2005 defeat to Liverpool by overcoming the Merseysiders in Athens. He finished the tournament as top scorer with ten goals, the first time a Brazilian player had managed the feat and even though Milan finished their domestic season 36 points adrift of local rivals and title winners Internazionale it did not diminish the impact of his season. The Brazilian won the FIFA World Player of the Year vote by a landslide, with 1,047 points against 504 for Lionel Messi and 426 for Cristiano Ronaldo. His place as Brazilian football's focal point was duly ratified. Two years later, he would become the second-most expensive signing of all time when Real Madrid paid Milan £56 million for his services. By that time, though, Kaká was beginning to struggle with his fitness. Groin problems were plaguing him; his left knee was also feeling the stress of so many games for club and country. In his last three seasons in Italy he had played 148 games, including his Seleção commitments, and his body was showing signs of fatigue. In his first Real season, leading up to the World Cup, he still managed 33 outings for Real but missed over ten matches through injury and by the time he joined his Seleção team-mates he was in far from his best condition. It would later be revealed by Brazilian physician Turibio Leite that Kaká had played through pain since 2008 and by the time South Africa kicked off the strength in the player's left leg was significantly compromised. So it was understandable that Kaká wasn't feeling particularly happy at the tournament and that the special attention received from Drogba's companions had worn his patience thin. Unlike biblical figure Job, Kaká's threshold was approaching its limit.

Between Elano's injury and Kaká's red card there was still time for Didier Drogba to poach a goal back for the Ivorians, but it didn't change the course of the game. Brazil won 3-1 with a convincing display that should have steadied the nerves of the Seleção. Instead, Dunga managed to attract more controversy: during his press conference, the manager swore at a TV Globo presenter who was talking on the phone during one of his answers – he whispered the words, but they were captured by the microphones. The channel promptly latched on to the episode in their post-game coverage and a complaint was lodged with FIFA. It was another chapter in a battle that once again looked to be taking up a precious chunk of the manager's time. It would later transpire that some of the media company's bosses had negotiated with CBF president Ricardo Teixeira a series of exclusive interviews that would be broadcast live during Fantástico, TV Globo's flagship Sunday night news magazine programme, only for Dunga to veto them.

Still, Brazil only needed a draw against Portugal to secure first place in Group G and theoretically avoid the early clash with Spain. At least theoretically: the European champions had made a mess of things by losing their opener against Switzerland, a weird game where La Roja had almost 40 shots on goal but were still unable to respond to a bundled goal by Gelson Fernandes after some comical and pathetic defending. Spain bounced back with a 2-0 win against Honduras and would play Chile on 25 June knowing that even a win might not be enough to guarantee passage to the knockout stages. They lay third after two games, a point behind Switzerland and three behind the valiant Chileans. Their encounter with the South American side would take place on the same day and at the same time as the Brazilians and Portuguese locked horns, so nobody could try to cherry-pick opponents.

Dunga, as expected, refused to be drawn into discussions about relying on Brazil's advantage, but it was clearly a tricky match for the Seleção. After drawing with the Ivory Coast in their opening game in South Africa, Portugal had gone on to dismantle the North Koreans 7-0. If they won the game against their former colony in Durban, they would nail the first-place spot on goal difference. Moreover, Cristiano

Ronaldo and co had several points to prove. First, they were desperate to avenge the 6-2 defeat to the Seleção in a 2008 friendly. Second, the squad hadn't taken kindly to Dunga's taunts at the time of the Final Draw, in December 2009, when the manager sarcastically alluded to the presence of Brazilian-born Deco, Liédson and Pepe in Carlos Queiroz' side. 'We will be playing against Brazil B in the World Cup,' he said after the ceremony. Queiroz responded with the argument that more letters of the alphabet should be used, since a significant number of Brazilians could trace their origins to Portugal.

Since 1966, encounters between the two sides had understandably become more charged, but geopolitics also played a big part in the banter. After almost 400 years of an often-oppressive Portuguese colonising experience, Brazil had declared independence in 1822 and although relations with the former power had normalised since, an element of resentment persisted on both sides. Jokes about a perceived lack of intelligence from the Portuguese are a common feature in Brazilian comedy while back in Lisbon the image of the inhabitants of their former colony as lazy and cunning persists to this day. As previously described, the Brazilian presence in Portuguese football had been influential for the development of the game in the 1960s. Cultural affinities also meant the Portuguese league would become the most popular destination for Brazilian football expatriates. Rivalries were heated even at youth level – Brazil and Portugal played a highly charged FIFA Youth Championship final in 1991 in Lisbon, where the European side featuring Luis Figo, Rui Costa and Nuno Gomes overcame the South Americans in a penalty shoot-out in front of a fanatical 127,000 crowd at Estadio da Luz, in Lisbon, two years after they had beaten Brazil in the semi-finals of the same competition in Saudi Arabia.

In South Africa, Portuguese fans had reasons to feel they could once again celebrate: Portugal had gone further than Brazil in Germany 2006 (they lost to France in the semi-final) and they also boasted Cristiano Ronaldo, the world's most expensive player. Brazil would have to do it without the suspended Kaká and were also deprived of Elano: the midfielder was out of the World Cup with a shin injury. Durban, the venue for the match, was also a place where Brazilian fans would find themselves in the minority: the city had been a major centre for Portuguese immigration to South Africa and also a refuge to whites of Portuguese origin fleeing the civil wars in Angola and Mozambique during the '70s and '80s. That meant that the Portuguese supporters went in numbers to the match. Both sets of fans, however, were in for a disappointment.

Much as he wanted to avoid playing Spain, Carlos Queiroz still preferred to go through to the knockout stage rather than risk Portugal being overtaken by the Ivorians – mathematically, the Ivory Coast could steamroll the North Koreans and then qualify if Portugal were defeated. Thus, both Brazil and Portugal entered the Moses Mabhida Stadium determined to play counter-attacking football instead of going for the kill.

Dunga was forced to make changes because of Kaká's red card and Elano's injury, so in came Júlio Baptista and Dani Alves – improvised as a midfielder – while striker Nilmar gave Robinho a breather. Portugal's intentions were clearly stated by a 4-5-1 formation, with Ronaldo as the sole striker.

Despite the reticent formations and approach from both sides, the Portuguese could have opened the scoring with a Tiago volley in the 18th minute. Brazil, meanwhile, went close twice: Nilmar hit the bar after 30 minutes and Fabiano could have done better with a free header in the 39th. Both teams were determined to win the battle for midfield and some flying tackles went in. Mexican referee Benito Téllez waved seven yellow cards in the first 45 minutes. Two of them were for Pepe and Felipe Melo, who were squaring up to each other frequently. This situation forced Dunga to substitute the Juventus man for Wolfsburg's Josué before half-time, fearing a sending off – in hindsight, a move that could have helped the Seleção immensely a couple of days later.

Portugal started the second half looking for an opener that almost came in the 55th minute after Raul Meireles managed to hit wide from inside the six-yard box. Two minutes into injury time, Portuguese goalie Eduardo did well to turn a deflected Ramires shot over the bar. In the end, Brazil had 61 per cent of possession, which motivated a frustrated comment from Dunga: 'Portugal turned up to defend today and only Brazil actually bothered trying to win this game,' he said. Nevertheless, Brazil at least managed to secure the first qualifying spot and Portugal earned a precious point that rendered the Ivory Coast's 3-0 win over North Korea worthless. Meanwhile, Spain's hard-fought 2-1 win over the Chileans meant the round of 16 pairings would be all-European and all-South American.

Under Dunga, Brazil had beaten Chile in five consecutive matches so the Seleção didn't fear another encounter with them, even though they had been outstanding in the continental qualifiers, finishing only a point behind the Brazilians in the round-robin tournament. Under Argentine manager Marcelo Bielsa, the Chileans had qualified for the World Cup for the first time since 1998 playing an unusual 3-3-1-3 formation with a lot of player reshuffling going on. They had pushed Spain to the limit and were confident they could do the same against their much more successful neighbours – Brazil had won 44 out of 64 previous meetings. It would have been a major upset if Chile had left Ellis Park on 28 June with a victory.

In the 34th minute, defender Juan rose above the Chilean defence to head in Brazil's first. Chile barely had time to compose themselves before, four minutes later, Kaká played in Luis Fabiano, who rounded goalkeeper Claudio Bravo and increased Brazil's advantage. Chilean hopes were all but extinguished 14 minutes into the second half: Ramires set off on a rampaging run and found Robinho for a first-time shot to Bravo's left. For the fifth World Cup in a row the Seleção had reached the quarter-finals. But they suffered another loss thanks to a silly yellow card picked up by Ramires. The midfielder had pounced on the opportunity to fill the gap left by Elano's departure and after Dani Alves' improvisation in the role hadn't particularly impressed Dunga. But Ramires picked up a second yellow card by fouling Alexis Sánchez in the 72nd minute and that meant the Seleção had a selection jigsaw to solve for the quarter-final.

Felipe Melo had missed both the Portugal and Chile games with an ankle injury and Baptista also had to sit out the round of 16 match against Chile. Brazil's opponents in the quarter-finals would once again be Holland, who had reached the last eight with four victories in four matches. After emerging from a group with Denmark, Japan and Cameroon, the Dutch overcame Slovakia 2-1 and for the first time since France '98 had managed to reach that stage in a World Cup. Led by playmaker Wesley Sneijder and winger Arjen Robben, Holland didn't particularly make their always-demanding public and media jump with joy. Like Brazil, they were criticised for a perceived compromise of style in favour of efficiency.

On 2 July, both Brazil and Holland were facing their strongest challenge yet in South Africa. Melo had recovered in time to re-join the Seleção's midfield, but Dunga once again resorted to deploying Alves on the right to make up for the absences of Elano and Ramires. Holland had lost defender Joris Mathijsen during the warm-up, drafting in former Ajax and Blackburn Rovers man André Ooijer, who had so far not featured at all in the competition.

Brazil were quick off the blocks and after eight minutes had already given the Dutch a scare – a Robinho goal disallowed thanks to a marginal offside call on Dani Alves. Two minutes later, Melo split the Dutch defence with a pass that Robinho diverted past Maarten Stekelenburg's reach with the softest of touches. Brazil followed this up with wave after wave of attacks that could have killed the game. Maicon side-netted and Stekelenburg produced an outstanding save from a Kaká curling shot. When Japanese referee Yuichi Nishimura blew for half-time, the Dutch players were visibly relieved. It would take something quite special to change the run of play. In this case, a single moment of madness from one of Dunga's most trusted lieutenants: Júlio César.

Although his first Seleção caps dated from 2003 and the then Inter Milan goalie had been the hero in Brazil's 2004 Copa America victory – he saved a penalty in the final against Argentina – César had failed to establish himself as Brazil's first-choice goalkeeper. Even after Dunga's arrival he still found himself behind choices such as Heurelho Gomes, Doni and Helton. César finally got the gig in late 2007 and after his exploits with Inter few people in Brazil contested his status. That the Rio-born player picked a World Cup quarter-final to make a mess of an innocuous ball was cruel. But César completely misjudged the trajectory of a Sneijder cross in the 53rd minute and almost punched Melo's head away instead of the ball, which bounced on the midfielder's scalp and went into the net. Just like that, Holland were level and the incident clearly rattled Dunga's team. Their psychological advantage from the first half seemed to have vanished. Holland smelled blood and concentrated their actions on the left side of the Brazilian defence, where Robben's pace had already created problems. Bastos had been booked for upending the Bayern player and Dunga, fearing a sending-off, replaced the young improvised left-back with the veteran improvised one, Gilberto. But Brazil were still shell-shocked and in the 68th minute would find themselves with a mountain to climb: Robben swung in a corner from the left and Dirk Kuyt had no trouble in flicking the ball for Sneijder, just 5ft 7in tall, to head in. The player celebrated the goal by repeatedly tapping his head, a part of Sneijder's body that until that game in Port Elizabeth had never been used to score. The climb for Brazil turned almost vertical soon after: having lost his temper after another of Robben's daunting runs, Melo got a red card for stamping on the winger.

With ten men, the Seleção would need something miraculous to get back into the game and a look at their bench made it clear that they didn't have that ace up their sleeve. Alongside goalies Gomes and Doni, Brazil had defenders Luisão and Thiago, midfielders Josué and Júlio Baptista and strikers Nilmar and Grafite. None of the attacking men were known for their prowess in operating far away from the box, which was what Brazil needed badly to try to get level. Nilmar was mobile enough to help create problems if he was deployed as a second man up front, but Dunga instead decided to send him into the game as a replacement for Luis Fabiano.

Brazil launched themselves forward desperately and had a good chance through Kaká in the dying minutes but Holland could and should have scored more goals. The final whistle brought a flow of tears to many Brazilian players, some heartbroken enough to sit sobbing on the pitch. Dunga, after punching the dugout cover, made his way straight to the dressing room without waiting for his players or trying to console them. For the second time in a row, Brazil were leaving a World Cup in the last eight. Players who had been in both campaigns were hurting. 'We were a group of experienced players who stuck together during some really tough times and we were certain we could have done something special in South Africa,' said Gilberto Silva. 'That first half against Holland was the best we had played in the competition, but all of a sudden we were going home. It just seemed unfair.' Our talk takes place more than three years after that game but the former Arsenal player's eyes well up with the memories of Port Elizabeth.

In the press conference, Dunga looked so defeated that his explanation about why he had elected not to use his third substitution sounded like gibberish. He used his time to announce he was leaving the job and before the squad departed South Africa the following morning speculation about his replacement was rife. Former Seleção player Leonardo, who had recently cut his managerial teeth at AC Milan, became the odds-on favourite to replace him.

Having dreamt of a triumphant closure to his Seleção story, Dunga once again left as public enemy number one. He was criticised for everything from his methods to his fashion sense (he had used his Seleção outings to promote the work of his daughter, a fashion designer). Dunga would disappear from public view, only returning to management in January 2013, taking over Internacional, his first club – he lasted nine months there. Meanwhile, a lot of soul-searching was going on in Brazil and the debate about a possible foreign replacement for the Seleção job for the first time became more than a wild proposition by media columnists.

Technically, the Seleção had already had a foreign manager, but the Argentinian Filipo Nuñes was in charge for only one game, a friendly against Uruguay in 1965, when his Palmeiras side was invited by the Brazilian FA to represent the country. Practically, hiring an Eriksson or a Capello had never been seriously considered. But after two World Cup quarter-final exits in a row, some Brazilians had to be excused if they thought the country was running out of ideas.

As previously discussed, the Hungarians Béla Guttmann and Dori Kürschner were a major influence in the 4-2-4 system which helped Pelé, Garrincha and co pick up Brazil's first World Cup trophy in 1958. Furthermore, Brazilian footballers had become the pinnacle of football globalisation, with top players already spending most of their careers working with foreign managers, languages and ideas. So the idea was not as preposterous as many in Brazil felt.

Three weeks after the Seleção's capitulation in Port Elizabeth, the CBF thought they were moving on by announcing Muricy Ramalho as the new national team coach. They had to backtrack the same day, though, after Fluminense, the club that had Ramalho under contract, refused to give them permission to talk to the manager. It would later transpire that president Ricardo Teixeira had also tried to entice 2002 World Cup winner Luiz Felipe Scolari back to the job, only to be turned down. As a plan C, Mano Menezes was duly unveiled and in his first statement announced his intention to adopt a playing style more pleasant to the eye. On 26 July, Menezes released a list of players for the first Seleção game after the World Cup – a friendly against the USA in New Jersey two weeks later. The 24-name list contained only four players from the World Cup squad (Robinho, Ramires, Thiago Silva and Dani Alves), but the fundamental difference from the Dunga era was symbolised by the presence of Neymar. By the end of 2013, the striker was already the most prolific Brazilian player in the Seleção, having netted 27 goals in 46 games. He was already 12th in the list of all-time Seleção scorers, tied with the legendary 1950 World Cup runner-up Zizinho.

Nonetheless, South Africa 2010 exposed a problem of quality in this generation of Brazilian footballers. It would take more than three years for the Seleção to beat a top international side and in their first competition after the World Cup, the 2011 Copa America, Brazil crashed and burned spectacularly in the quarter-finals, missing four penalties in a shoot-out against Paraguay. Catapulted to the post of next best thing, Neymar struggled with the pressure and the attention. European clubs started knocking at the door, which led Santos to take incredible measures to try to keep the player in Brazil until the World Cup. They waived their participation in Neymar's image rights, sold part of his playing rights to a group of investors and encouraged the player to look for as many personal sponsors as he wanted. By 2012, Neymar was already showing up among the ten best-paid players in the world and that level of earning was proving enough to fend off suitors such as Chelsea, Bayern Munich, Real Madrid and Barcelona – although the Catalans would finally secure Neymar's services in May 2013. 'If you look around, however, Neymar is the only outstanding player Brazilian football has produced in the last few years,' said Roberto Rivelino. 'There is something fundamentally wrong with the way we are preparing players at youth level. Our strength has always been the type of player that could work tactically but at the same time should not be burdened by formations and always brings that level of unpredictability. We seem to be losing that.' For 1970 legend Tostão, Brazil seem to be struggling to catch up with the changes in the game: 'It's a much more level playing field now and you see countries that a few decades ago would not be noticed now producing top-level players. But Brazilians sometimes think they are the only country with talented players. Worse, our managers seem to still believe we are going to win tournaments just by being Brazil.'

More contemporary players agree. Gilberto Silva, who returned to Brazil in 2011 after almost ten years in European football, believes Brazil have to change from within. 'For many years we have become used to thinking of the Seleção as a separate unit from the domestic game in our country,' he said. 'There are organisational issues in the domestic game that need to be addressed for Brazilian football to remain strong in the future. It is unacceptable that in the 21st century we still have clubs run so poorly. From what I have seen in my career abroad, Brazil are hiding behind the five world titles instead of building upon them.'

How long this scenario will remain the case is the most important question Brazilian football has to address. Sooner or later.

SEVEN

EPILOGUE

IN 97 WORLD CUP games, Brazil have achieved 67 wins, 15 draws and only 15 defeats and still hold a record five world titles that only Italy, owners of four crowns, come closest to matching. The country still ranks as the largest exporter of talent in the world game and failure to win the last two World Cups has yet to dent the Seleção's allure in what concerns public interest and commercial value. So why should one worry about past shortcomings, even the emblematic six that are dissected in this book? This question kept creeping up in my head at every step of this work. Surely Brazil's defeats cannot be merely attributed simply to themselves? Some might say the analysis might have overlooked the merits of the opposition, but I have tried my best to give credit where it was due. Brazilians are very proud of their football but never to the point where they block the sunlight with a sifter, as one of the most popular sayings in the country goes. It can also be argued that Brazil have shown a phoenix-like capacity to pick themselves up after defeats, even if not immediately. When focusing on the specific misadventures chronicled in this book, the key was to zero in on the issues that not only impacted on the performance of the team on the pitch, but which had wider implications for the country and its people.

Cruel and unpredictable as football can be, defeats in a World Cup reveal more than the sporting outcome. In the case of Brazil, it is even more interesting because of the way the game is tangled up with the non-sporting sphere. In a way, it is almost possible to say Brazil have managed to exceed expectations throughout the Seleção's history given how chaotic the structure of Brazilian football is. In the past, those shortcomings could somehow be compensated by a combination of athletic excellence and some organisation, but the Seleção also benefited from what even Brazilians consider an uneven playing field: blessed with a population bigger than any of the other top-level footballing nations, Brazil have been able to churn out talent at a higher rate than their rivals. It needs to be noted that the social and economic importance of the game in the country also widened the talent pool. These conditions were fundamental in allowing Brazil to deliver an outstanding display between 1938 and 1978, a period where they won three titles, took one second-place finish and reached at least the semi-final stage in nine tournaments.

And the most impressive aspect of this record is how Brazil managed to do so well with so much disarray back home. As our journey through the past shows, Brazilian football has been historically flawed in its organisation and structure. The capacity for ruling bodies and clubs to serially kill their golden geese has seemed relentless and this thirst for blood has barely been stemmed. With an amateur and paternalistic structure that both indulges and smothers the game, Brazilian football is not only in danger of losing relevance, but is also in danger of losing sight of its self forever in never-ending soul-searching. As we speak, the Campeonato Brasileiro already sits behind China and the US in the list of national championship attendance figures – in 2013, Brazil averaged 14,950 spectators per game, fewer than the English and German second divisions. While there is more money in the game thanks to an increase in TV revenues, studies also show that clubs' debts grew higher than those receipts in the last few years. It is a vicious cycle: clubs still have to sell their best athletes to Europe in order to generate cash to survive, yet the departure of this talent means that fans are less inclined to fill the stadiums to see those who are left; there are, of course, other factors involved in the emptying of the stands, such as a poor transport infrastructure and a persistent threat of crowd trouble, but a relatively 'pedestrian' league also has to be factored in.

It would be a miracle if these troubles did not affect the game at a grassroots level. Once again I could be accused of alarmism here and quite recently a friend in Brazil pointed out how the UEFA Champions League seems to be peppered with Brazilian players. It is, but recent figures show a sharp decline in these numbers: from the most represented nation in the tournament in the last few years, Brazil started the 2013-14 season behind Spain and Germany in the number of participants, with a sharp drop from 84 to 63 representatives. That can only indicate that the supply is faltering, and although it can be argued that the production of players is hardly an exact science, the situation is worrying for many important voices in Brazil. Seleção legend Roberto Rivelino, for example, often interrupted our interview about the 1974 World Cup to express his dismay at the current crop of top-level players in the country. 'I look at the national team and see there is a struggle to find centre-forwards. It beggars belief that this can happen in a country as big and football-orientated as ours.'

The FIFA World Player of the Year award also suggests that there is something wrong: after producing eight winners between 1991 and 2007, no Brazilian player has even made it onto the three-man shortlist since then. Of course, the existence of phenomenal players like Cristiano Ronaldo and Lionel Messi plays an important part, but there is a general impression in Brazil that the rest of the world has caught up and the country doesn't know what to do to push ahead again. 'Globalisation happened and these days a lot of countries can produce top players, which also made the game much more difficult than in previous years,' said Tostão, another 1970 legend. 'The challenge for Brazil is how to respond by improving their youth system, but that won't be enough if the way football is organised in the country as a whole doesn't improve substantially as well.'

Since Brazil's last World Cup win, 12 years ago, mystique and admiration seem to have shifted to Spain thanks to the exploits of FC Barcelona at club level and their part in the astounding success experienced by the Spanish national team after decades of false hope. Winners of the Euro 2008, World Cup 2010 and Euro 2012, Spain have stolen Brazil's thunder as the benchmark. For the first time in their history since becoming World Cup winners, Brazil find themselves seriously challenged in the game of perceptions: they are not the unanimous and immediate choice of favourites anymore. Thanks to the internet and the spread of television coverage, the tales of mismanagement, corruption and chaos in Brazil now regularly reach an international public and the Seleção jersey no longer shines as brightly as it once did. Revolutionary as he was at FIFA, Joao Havelange will be forever marked in Brazil by the bribery scandal that ultimately scarred his international reputation.

A third consecutive failure in the World Cup could have serious consequences for Brazil, especially as the Seleção are playing at home in 2014 and face expectations that will inevitably include the ghosts of 1950 – in this sense, the Organizing Committee's decision not to schedule a single match for Brazil at the Maracaná before the final has done little to help. The CBF will certainly have less leverage when the time comes to renegotiating the current deal with Nike, which expires in 2018, and neither will a defeat do any favours to the country's image which has already been tarnished by the poor organisation of the tournament so far, with stadium construction delays and unfinished improvements in infrastructure. The waves of protests in the streets of Brazil since June 2013 have also shown that football is not immune from public outrage, a feeling endorsed by the polls which have shown a substantial reduction in the numbers of Brazilians who support the hosting of the World Cup.

Having said that, the Seleção could not have done things much better on the pitch in the build-up to the tournament, or at least in the most important part: after dragging themselves from 2010 to 2012 without a proper victory over one of their bigger rivals, instead resorting to money-spinning games in the Middle East and Gabon, the team found a new lease of life under Luiz Felipe Scolari – once again, a returning manager. Under the 2002 World Cup-winning manager, Neymar and co gelled enough to secure impressive wins against France and Italy, before dismantling Spain 3-0 in Rio in the Confederations Cup final. For a dress rehearsal, it was an encouraging moment.

On the pitch, at least.

BIBLIOGRAPHY AND
FURTHER READING

BELLOS, A. and DUARTE, O. (2007). *Pelé: The Autobiography*. London: Simon & Schuster.

CALDEIRA, J. (2002). *Ronaldo: Glory and Drama in Globalised Football* (in Portuguese). São Paulo: Editora 34

FALCÃO, P.R. (2012). *Brazil 82: The Team That Lost The Cup But Conquered the World* (in Portuguese). Porto Alegre: AGE Editora

GUTERMAN, M. (2009). *Football Explains Brazil* (in Portuguese). São Paulo: Contexto.

McCOLL, G. (2010). *How to Win the World Cup*. London: Bantam Press.

NETO, G.M. (2013). *Dossier 50*. Rio de Janeiro: Maquinaria

PERDIGAO, P. (2000). *Anatomy of a Defeat* (in Portuguese). Porto Alegre: L&PM Editores

RODRIGUES, E. (2007). *Tough Game: The João Havelange History* (in Portuguese). Rio de Janeiro: Record

SALDANHA, J. (2002). *A Football Trauma: the 1982 World Cup* (in Portuguese). São Paulo: Cosac & Naif

WILSON, J. (2008). *Inverting the Pyramid: The History of Football Tactics*. London: Orion